Harmon Zieske

Introduction to Natural Language Processing

Introduction to Natural Language Processing

Mary Dee Harris
Loyola University
New Orleans

Reston Publishing Company, Inc.
A Prentice-Hall Company
Reston, Virginia

Library of Congress Cataloging in Publication Data

Harris, Mary Dee.
  Introduction to natural language processing.

  Bibliography: p.
  Includes index.
  1. Interactive computer systems. 2. Programming
languages (Electronic computers)—Semantics. I. Title.
QA76.9.158H37 1985   001.64'2   84-18242
ISBN 0-8359-3254-0

© 1985 by Reston Publishing Company, Inc.
A Prentice-Hall Company
Reston, Virginia 22090

10 9 8 7 6 5 4 3 2

Printed in the United States of America

To my son, Scott Shorter

Contents

Acknowledgments

I would like to express my appreciation to the many people who encouraged me and assisted me during the composition of this book. For having read and commented on various stages of the manuscript, I want to thank Ben Fosberg, Donald Walker, Robert F. Simmons, Raoul Smith, Terrence Pratt, Larry Reeker, Robert Dewell, Nell Dale, and Roger Schank. I did not always follow their suggestions, but they always gave a new perspective from which to view the material. In addition, I appreciate the comments and corrections made by the students in my Natural Language Processing classes; the book has been considerably improved by their suggestions. In particular, I want to thank my student and friend, Kit Hung Lou, for his assistance in many ways during the years of development of the book. I also want to thank my son Scott for giving up a lot—in particular, the computer—while I wrote the book. All these people and others provided the support I needed to complete this book. It is better for their efforts. However, I take responsibility for any errors or weaknesses remaining.

Mary Dee Harris
New Orleans

To the Reader

Natural language is any language used for communication by humans. *Introduction to Natural Language Processing* is an attempt to provide enough information about natural language and the problems involved in dealing with it to allow rudimentary natural language processing by computers and to make apparent what kinds of processing can be done now. In addition, and perhaps more significantly, what is not yet possible will be discussed. This book consolidates information about language from the literature of several disciplines: linguistics, artificial intelligence, psychology, and cognitive science, and describes the computer science tools and techniques available to deal with natural language.

From an information processing viewpoint, the language information to be processed must be conveyed from the outside world to the processor and the resulting text or utterance conveyed back to the outside world. In other words, a system to process natural language must be capable of input and output of natural language. No matter what the original form of the language: speech, printed text, or whatever, the external form must be communicated to the processor and stored in some internal form. After the processing is completed the data must be communicated back to the user—whether the form is video screen, hard copy (e.g., paper), or speech. Once the language data has been input to the system, it must be stored in a form that preserves aspects of the original and allows manipulation for whatever purpose needed. The language data must be organized into appropriate data structures which are capable of recording information at various levels: morphological, grammatical, contextual, etc. Information about the structure of the discourse and about its meaning must be stored. All of the representations of data can be referred to generally as natural language structures to correspond to the memory of the general information processing system.

Between the input of language and the output of language various manipulations will occur, depending on the purpose for which the system was designed. Processing a sentence can include various operations on a specific kind of natural language element: analyzing a sentence by breaking it into its constituent parts, translating the sentence into another language, generating a sentence to be output from the system. Any natural language unit can be manipulated. The primitive operations consistent with units at any level are: synthesis (generating the unit from smaller components); analysis (breaking the unit up into its constituent components); transformation (used in a general sense, changing the unit into an equivalent unit); and inference (drawing conclusions from the knowledge already stored).

These aspects of rendering natural language—synthesis, analysis, transformation, and inference—are necessary in order to understand natural language, to be able to use language as humans use it—for requesting information, for stating knowledge, or for restating discourse without loss of information. Systems which can do all these things can be used as question answering systems. They can generate well-formed sentences, interpret requests for information, paraphrase statements, and store knowledge provided. The amount of understanding that can be said to occur is dependent upon the size of the vocabulary used, the difficulty of the questions which are answered correctly, and the degree of subtlety and complexity of language handled.

This book has been designed for two primary audiences: undergraduate Computer Science students and programmers interested in adding natural language interfaces to their software products. As a textbook for Computer Science majors with at least two programming courses, some of the material will be review, such as the later sections of the chapter on text processing and the explanations of elementary data structures, such as stacks, linked lists, and trees, throughout the book. This material has been included for those readers who have not learned these concepts rigorously enough to understand the subject in general without at least a brief explanation. In addition the book can be read by non-technical people with little or no background in programming, if they skip the more technical sections. This book has been used twice in prepublication form for an upper-level undergraduate Computer Science course at Loyola University in New Orleans. The course covered all the material in the book, except the sections on text processing and data structures mentioned above, since the students knew those concepts. In addition to the text, the students developed four major programs based on the exercises, read additional articles from the bibliography, and wrote a term paper on some aspect of natural language processing not covered in the book. At the end of the semester the students were able to read current literature in natural language processing and cognitive science with no difficulty and were prepared to begin graduate study of a specialized area of the field.

In this book we consider the design of a natural language system (NLS) using as a paradigm the psychologists' model of humans as information processing systems. Our NLS communicates with its environment in written text. The discourse is translated into internal structures for rendering. These structures are interpreted abstractly; in other words we are concerned with the logical aspects of language and the structures inherent in it rather than machine requirements for representing a character, array, or pointer. Similarly the algorithms for rendering natural language relate to the kinds of operations to be performed on language. Defining appropriate data types and the operations upon them allows us as system designers to be concerned only with the definition and manipulation of language data, rather than the details of implementation.

The focus of this book is an attempt to understand language and the means of processing language from as many perspectives as possible, with emphasis on both analysis and synthesis techniques. The book is practically oriented in the sense that the elements of the system developed are not theoretical, and could be implemented on a computer system. However, the system is not guaranteed to deal with all problems of processing natural language. In fact, it is guaranteed not to solve all the problems because not all the problems have even been identified yet. And the techniques presented are not adequate to handle all the difficulties of understanding natural language. But natural language systems are relatively new; many people have considered the advantages of having computers capable of dealing with language, but natural language processing has not had the emphasis of many other areas of computer science. The treatment of the subject in this book is to provide some *nuts and bolts* techniques for approaching some simple problems in dealing with natural language and to explain some of the terminology and methodology used by researchers in the field. Anyone who works through this book will have a good grasp of major problems of computer *understanding* of language and should be able to apply these ideas to a restricted version of the English language. He will be able to read and understand the current literature describing research in Natural Language Processing and Cognitive Science. And hopefully, some readers will find better solutions to old problems and also uncover new problems.

The method used to describe data structures and algorithms is an algorithmic language or pseudo-code based on Pascal with several fairly standard extensions. For example, since text manipulation is facilitated by string functions, the pseudo-code will include UCSD Pascal string functions with some SNOBOL-like pattern matching functions defined in the chapter on text processing. Some of the processing operations to be discussed in Unit IV will require concurrent processes and therefore we will assume concurrent processing to be a part of our algorithmic language. The algorithms will look much like Pascal, but will in fact allow several features not in "standard" Pascal. Although much of the work in processing natural language has been done in LISP, I have chosen not to use it for this book because it is not as widely available nor as widely understood as a Pascal-like language. However, through the extensions to standard Pascal and the liberties I have taken with it, some of the pseudo-code will not always look like Pascal.

Computer science is not a spectator sport, and natural language processing is no exception. With that in mind, I have included exercises in each chapter to help the reader understand the concepts covered. To quote Donald Knuth's **"Notes on the Exercises,"** from Volume 1 of *The Art of Computer Programming,*

> It is difficult, if not impossible, for anyone to learn a subject purely by reading about it, without applying the information to specific problems and thereby forcing himself to think about what has been read. Furthermore, we all learn best the things that we have discovered for ourselves. Therefore the exercises form a major part of this work; a definite attempt has been made to keep them as informative as possible and to select problems that are enjoyable to solve. [1]

The exercises vary in difficulty and in orientation; extending Knuth's ideas, the reader is encouraged to work as many exercises as he can stand. Many of the exercises involve writing programs (of course). All programming attempts should start with a design phase before coding begins and end with a testing phase. Not only will this procedure reinforce good programming practice, but it will help the programmer understand the limitations of the approach taken in the book. In other words, the reader can discover for himself, during the design phase, what aspects of language are being ignored, and, during the testing phase, what kinds of discourse will be interpreted incorrectly. Constantly considering the limitations may seem to be a strange approach to follow, but doing so will remind the reader that the study of natural language processing has only begun. Even the non-technical reader can benefit from attempting the exercises, by writing a design in logical and clearly stated English. Experience has shown that non-technical readers can produce designs, which look very much like pseudo-code, thus accruing all the benefits of the understanding produced by designing a piece of software.

This book is organized to emphasize three primary aspects of information processing—definition of the input and output functions, description and manipulation of the data, and design of the overall software system, including both data and program structure. Unit I presents background material on the study of language and an overview of linguistics, for the benefit of those readers who have no knowledge of the field. The chapter emphasizes an understanding of the terminology that is used in the areas of linguistics, artificial intelligence, and cognitive science.

Unit II of the book deals with input and output of natural language. Chapter 2 describes specific problems of text processing, and Chapter 3 considers the lexical phase, especially the organization and access of the dictionary to hold the vocabulary for the system. An overview of the primitive operations of manipulating text seems within the scope of this book, even though much of the coverage will be review for many readers. The lexical phase extends the discussion of text manipulation into the specific considerations of lexical analysis and generation.

Unit III, Natural Language Structures and Algorithms, covers the three general areas: linguistic structure, the definition of the relationships among linguistic elements; the correspondence between linguistic structures and the world, how to represent the meaning of language elements; and cognitive processes, involving the structure and manipulation of knowledge required for storing concepts acquired through language input. This unit can be considered the heart of the book in that it describes the structure of the natural language data, the actual operations to be performed on that data, and suggests methodologies for these operations. Moving along the spectrum from syntax to semantics to representation of knowledge and from simpler to more complex problems, this unit presents problems of synthesis, dealing specifically with generation of sentences; problems of analysis, or parsing and interpreting sentences; and problems of transformation of language elements, paraphrasing, translating, and linguistic transformation. In addition, the capability for inference and question answering is evaluated for some of the methodologies discussed.

Unit IV, Natural Language Systems, attempts to incorporate the ideas from the earlier parts of the book into a design scheme for a complete system for manipulating natural language. This system is capable of acquiring knowledge from the input, answering questions about the knowledge stored, and generating appropriate responses for output. This unit covers the problems of data storage design and the organization of processing, with emphasis on the lexicon. Traditional approaches to system design are considered as well as more workable, recent schemes. All the methods discussed are evaluated in terms of the constraints and limitations imposed. The result is an understanding of the conceptual and pragmatic problems involved in designing a system for understanding natural language.

Part I

An Introduction
to the Study
of Language

Introduction

What is natural language? Natural language is any language that humans learn from their environment and use to communicate with each other. Whatever the form of the communication, natural languages are used to express our knowledge and emotions and to convey our responses to other people and to our surroundings. Natural languages are usually learned in early childhood from those around us. Children seem to recognize at a surprisingly early age the value of structure and uniformity in their utterances. Words, phrases, and sentences replace grunts, whines, and cries and better serve to convince others to recognize the child's needs. Natural languages can be acquired later in life through school, travel, or change in culture, but with very few exceptions, all humans in all cultures learn to communicate verbally in the language natural to their immediate environment.

In contrast to natural languages, artificial languages are languages created by humans to communicate with their technology, for example, computer programming languages. The term *artificial language* implies a language consciously crafted by humans rather than a language learned naturally and includes languages such as Esperanto, a *constructed language* and designed to be universal, easily learned by speakers of any natural language. The definition of natural language should not make excessively rigid distinctions that eliminate relevant languages. I will appeal to the reader's intuitive notions of natural language rather than attempting a rigorous definition.

Humans process natural languages whenever they read Shakespeare, dictate a business letter, or tell a joke. Sign language is used by the hearing impaired to communicate thoughts and feelings with others and replaces the language they are unable to hear. Despite the different forms of language in each of these situations, aspects of the language used are similar. Whether language is spoken or written, every message has a structure and the elements of language relate to each other in recognizable ways. Verbal communication or speech is characterized by the sounds which almost every human is capable of producing. Whether each person learns to produce a particular sound is determined by the languages learned rather than the anatomical speech production mechanisms, which are approximately the same for all normal humans. Speech is produced by stringing together individual human sounds in recognized patterns. The study of these patterns of sounds is called *phonology*. The study of the structure of language units and their relationships is called *syntax*. Phonology and syntax are both important parts of the field of linguistics.

Linguists are also concerned with semantics, the study of the relationship between the linguistic structures used and the meanings intended; in other words, how does what we say or write relate to what we mean? It is not enough for a sentence to be correct in form; it must also make sense. For example, the sentence,

The tree sang the chair.

would not in ordinary discourse, be a meaningful sentence, even though it is grammatically reasonable. The noun phrase, *The tree*, can be the subject of a sentence; *sang* is obviously a verb; and *the chair* is a noun phrase which can serve as a direct object of a verb. But trees do not sing, and nothing that sings, sings chairs. So, how can this string of words be a sentence, even an unreasonable one? Many people, including linguists, would say it cannot be considered a sentence. Imagine, for a moment, a fantasy movie set some place like Middle Earth or another planet, where trees were the intelligent beings and had what we consider human characteristics. If trees could talk in this world, then they might also be able to sing. And if we use our imagination some more, we might find that speech and song in this strange world were made of physical objects such as chairs and cups, rather than phonemes. That may seem farfetched, but sound waves are also physical and produce recognizable effects in physical objects. If that is too extreme, consider that the phrase, *the chair*, is the title of a song, and the tree is made up of Christmas carolers standing on bleachers in the shape of a Christmas tree. Does the sentence still seem to lack meaning? Could we not say under some circumstances, however strange, that the sentence, *The tree sang the chair*, makes sense?

Obviously language is complex and trying to understand language is sometimes hard for humans. People do not know very much about what it means to *understand* language, partly because they do not often think about language; they just use it. Lots of people can ride bicycles without *understanding* what makes it possible for them to be able to do so. One need not learn the physiological explanations for pedaling, steering, and balancing to get around on a bike. Physiologists know a great deal about how a person can ride a bicycle, how the muscles and ligaments interact with the eyes, the nerves, and the bicycle to produce a system that can be referred to as *riding a bicycle*. The same is true of language. Humans use language without knowing how to use language, and linguists attempt to explain the system that we call *using language*.

However, most of us know more about language than we realize. Some language researchers believe that language is an innate capability in humans, that all humans learn a language because the structure of the language is a biological aspect of the species. Studies of language acquisition seem to indicate that motor development and language development are related; most babies learn to talk at about the same time they start to walk. When babies start babbling before they use the language of their parents, their utterances frequently sound like they *should* make sense. A baby *talking* on a toy telephone, uses intonations and phrasing similar to his parents', even though the particular sounds have no recognizable meanings. In other words, the child's sounds have the structure of his parents' language without any content being associated with the sounds. Similarly we recognize that the following sentences have the same structure.

The tree sang the chair.

The students finished the exam.

The new, young vice-president in charge of financial affairs in the company established extraordinary regulations concerning the procedures for reporting exceptional situations in the payroll department.

Thus, something in language makes us aware of similarities among sentences despite the variance in subject matter. The systems used by linguists to describe these similarities are called *grammars*. The term *grammar* is also used to refer to the methods taught in school such as diagramming sentences. These methods are designed to show the relationships among the various structures within sentences. Grammars consist of the elements allowed within sentences and the rules for putting these elements together. For example, the structure of some sentences can be described as a noun phrase followed by a verb phrase. In this case, the elements are the *sentence*, a *noun phrase*, and *verb phrase*. A rule to express their relationship could be written as:

SENTENCE → NOUN PHRASE + VERB PHRASE

Obviously further definition of these elements would be required to describe noun phrases, verb phrases, and their components, and each of the components would have to be defined. This process of redefinition of the grammatical constructs would be continued until the elements were defined as specific words. The words in a grammar are called the *vocabulary*. The grammar is made up of the rules and the vocabulary along with the meanings associated with the vocabulary. Various grammars will be considered in detail throughout this book.

Besides linguists' use of grammars for describing language, grammars are used by logicians and formal philosophers to study formal languages. A formal grammar is essentially a set of rules and a list of elements upon which the rules can be applied. In natural language, the elements would be words and phrases, and the rules would specify how the elements can be combined. Formal languages are composed of sentences generated by a formal grammar, and provide a means to study the features of the language. Attempts to create formal grammars of natural language have produced many, but not all, of the forms actually used in that natural language. The logician Richard Montague did not make a strong distinction between formal and natural languages, but rather claimed that a subset of English could be considered a formal language. He wrote that "the syntax, semantics, and pragmatics of natural language are branches of mathematics, not of psychology," and the syntax of English is as much a part of mathematics as number theory or geometry. This view is a corollary of Montague's strategy of studying natural languages by means of the same techniques used in metamathematics to study formal languages. "... Generalizing [metamathematics] to comprehend natural language does not render it any less a mathematical discipline." [1] Montague created several grammars to define fragments of English. One of his grammars first defined the lexicon which specifies the basic expressions in the language, words, phrases, etc. It then gave the rules to combine the expressions from the various categories to build new expressions. Montague considered the meaning in the language to be related to the structural aspects. To quote Montague, "MEANINGS are functions of two arguments—a possible world and a context of use.... Meanings are those entities that serve as interpretations of expressions...."

Other logicians have sought to represent natural language by means of propositional logic. All sentences in the language considered are written as propositions and can be manipulated according to the rules of formal logic. The statement, *All teenagers drive cars*, could be rewritten in logical notation as:

FOR-ALL (x)(EXISTS(y)(TEENAGER(x) → (CAR(y) AND DRIVE(x,y))))

When a sentence has been thus transcribed, the rules of logic can be applied to test the validity of any references to the information contained in the sentence. However, propositional logic can express only a subset of all sentences in any natural language. The method only applies to statements about which the truth or falsity can be known. Other types of logic, such as modal logic and clausal logic, can handle sentences such as the examples below dealing with fantasy or conjecture:

Hobbits can be recognized by the dark fur on the tops of their feet.

John believed he would discover the fountain of youth despite many years of failure.

John believed he would be promoted despite his boss' refusal to discuss the matter.

Logicians can handle many instances of natural language, but their methods often must rely on restricting the language to certain types of statements. Researchers are continuing to derive methods for representing various types of sentences.

Cognitive psychologists, concerned with how humans think, approach language from a different perspective than linguists and logicians. They view language as a representational medium for thought rather than viewing language as an independent phenomenon.

> Any form of learning or memory involves some form of internal representation of past events. A set of internal representations is undoubtedly a set of symbols. The calculus of operations used to relate and manipulate symbols both to each other and to the external world is a system of thought. Language is a shared community of externalised symbols, and intelligence a comparative term that we use to describe our attempts to relate the thinking power of one organism to that of another. [2]

This view of language is derived largely from the notion of humans as general information processing systems. Humans can receive signals through their senses, can discriminate between trivial and important information, can remember and categorize many pieces of information collected from many varied sources, and communicate this information back to the external world through speech or other means. Some terms used to describe the components of such systems include *receptors* to obtain signals from the world external to the system, a *processor* to manipulate the information received, a *memory* to store information, and *effectors* to convey signals to the external world. Some of the terminology reinforces the analogy between human general information processing systems and *digital general information processing systems*, more commonly called computers. Some researchers argue that human information processing systems are devices with only a single channel for input and output, with a processor of limited capacity, while others believe that the human system is a *multichannel multiprocessor device* like computer systems developed in more recent years. [3] Whichever opinion one accepts, the notion of human intelligence being explained as an information processing system provides new insights into the field of cognitive psychology and will serve as a useful model for our discussion of processing natural language.

Other psychologists consider language not so much in terms of what it reveals about our thought processes, but rather in light of how it represents social interaction. We learn language from the people we are close to as children, and we talk to each other for emotional support and cooperation as well as for intellectual communication. A large percentage of all verbal utterances communicate emotional and social needs more than intellectual content. Written language is less often socially oriented than spoken language because the purpose of writing is generally to record ideas, rather than feelings;

however, writing personal letters is a good example of social communication. Language used for social purposes follows the same rules as other language, but frequently is highly formulaic. The same phrases are used over and over in similar situations, often losing their meaning somewhat, yet still serving their basic function. For example,

I love you.

Hello, how are you? Fine, thank you, and you?

Thank you very much for the gift. I like it a lot.

Hey, bro. Wha's hap'nin'?

Dealing with language of this sort requires different analysis techniques from other language. The meaning behind the words seems to be of a different nature than the content of language used to convey information. Yet the notion of language as social interaction still fits the paradigm of the human information processing system.

Another approach to defining and studying natural language is in the area known as Cognitive Science, a relatively new field combining knowledge and research methods from a number of other fields: computer science, particularly artificial intelligence; mathematics; psychology; and linguistics. In the first issue of the journal *Cognitive Science*, one of the editors, Allan Collins, attempts to answer the question, "Why Cognitive Science?"

> Cognitive science is defined principally by the set of problems it addresses and the set of tools it uses. The most immediate problem areas are representation of knowledge, language understanding, image understanding, question answering, inference, learning, problem solving, and planning. . . . The tools of cognitive science consist of a set of analysis techniques and a set of theoretical formalisms. . . . Unlike psychology or linguistics which are analytical sciences and AI which is a synthetic science, cognitive science strives for a balance between analysis and synthesis. [4]

Cognitive scientists do not view language as their primary area of concern, but, like the cognitive psychologists, approach language as a representation of thought and memory which is shared among some group of people. This sharing allows for communication by means of the language. Thus, language is not a separate and distinct concept or entity, and it cannot be understood without information about the context of the specific instance of language use and the background of the person using the language. Terry Winograd, well-known for his work in artificial intelligence, presents four *phenomenic domains* for understanding language in the article, "What Does It Mean to Understand Language?"

> *The domain of linguistic structure* which is concerned with the structural elements of language.

The domain of correspondence between linguistic structures and the world; in other words, what do the structural elements of language refer to, or "mean".

The domain of cognitive processes which involves the structure of knowledge and the manipulation of the items in the structure by the processor of the language (either human or computer).

The domain of human action and interaction which views language within time, relative to past language use and future expectations.[5]

These four domains recall the various views of language by several of the disciplines considered so far. The domain of linguistic structure has traditionally been the purview of linguistics, and has more recently been approached by the logicians. Psychology, linguistics, and philosophy have studied the domain of correspondence between linguistic structure and the world. Cognitive psychologists and biologists have investigated the cognitive processes and mechanisms involved in using language. And psychologists have always been concerned with the domain of human action and interaction involving any form of communication. Winograd believes that the field of cognitive science should attempt to integrate all these approaches and to use any of the domains required to extend their capabilities of understanding language.

In another article in the first issue of *Cognitive Science*, "Artificial Intelligence, Language, and the Study of Knowledge," Ira Goldstein and Seymour Papert discuss "the relationship of Artificial Intelligence to the study of language and the representation of the underlying knowledge which supports the comprehension process." They argue that AI has shifted its perspective from a "power-based strategy for achieving intelligence to a knowledge-based approach." [6] Quoting Minsky and Papert, they point out that,

The *power* strategy seeks a generalized increase in computational power. It may look toward new kinds of computers ... or it may look toward extensions of deductive generality, or information retrieval, or search algorithms, ... In each case the improvement sought is intended to be "uniform"—independent of the particular data base.

The *knowledge* strategy sees progress as coming from better ways to express, recognize, and use diverse and particular forms of knowledge. This theory sees the problem as epistemological rather than as a matter of computational power or mathematical generality. It supposes, for example, that when a scientist solves a new problem, he engages a highly organized structure of especially appropriate facts, models, analogies, planning mechanisms, self-discipline procedures, etc. To be sure, he also engages "general" problem-solving schemata but it is by no means obvious that very smart people are that way directly because of the superior power of their general methods. [7]

These ideas of knowledge-based intelligence are closely related to the ideas of Piaget, a psychologist who called himself an epistemologist. The significant point of the knowledge-based approach in contrast to the power-based strategy is "the view that the process of intelligence is determined by the knowledge held by the subject. The deep and primary questions are to understand the operations and data structures involved." [8] As I see their argument, a piece of text in natural language must be considered, not only in terms of the structures and meaning of individual words or sentences, but also as a *packet* of knowledge about the world in which the text was produced. And the many *packets* accumulated must be integrated into a cohesive body of knowledge capable of access. "The fundamental difficulties facing researchers in the field today are not limitations due to hardware, but rather questions about how to represent large amounts of knowledge in ways that still allow the effective use of individual facts." [9] Several methods for representing knowledge will be considered in later sections of the book.

There are many approaches to the study of language: lexical, morphological, syntactical, semantic, to name a few. Richard Montague cited Charles Morris' distinctions when he said,

> the study of language was ... partitioned into three branches—
> syntax, semantics, and pragmatics—that may be characterized
> roughly as follows. Syntax is concerned solely with relations between
> linguistic expressions; semantics with relations between expressions
> and the objects to which they refer; and pragmatics with relations
> among expressions, the objects to which they refer, and the users
> or contexts of use of the expressions. [10]

Syntax, as the study of "relations between linguistic expressions," is concerned with the rules for the interaction between various natural language units: words, phrases, clauses, and so on. Some linguists would restrict the study of syntax to the individual sentence, as much as possible. However, in certain circumstances, the relations between the expressions within a sentence cannot be accurately determined without reference to the context in which the sentence occurred. Let us look at two examples. First,

John told Bob that he had lost his hat.

The two pronouns are ambiguous if only this one sentence is available for interpretation. Each of the two pronouns could refer to either John or Bob or to someone else.

John told Bob that he [John] had lost his [John's] hat.
John told Bob that he [John] had lost his [Bob's] hat.
John told Bob that he [Bob] had lost his [Bob's] hat.
John told Bob that he [Bob] had lost his [John's] hat.
John told Bob that he [Tom] had lost his [Fred's] hat.

Only by knowing more about the situation being discussed, which is really pragmatics according to our definition, can the sentence be interpreted correctly.

The other example brings up another dilemma.

Joe works on the Mary Ann.

At first, one might think that this sentence is ungrammatical in that proper nouns, such as names, do not take determiners, in this case, the article, *the*. But the problem is more involved. Most people know that boats and ships are frequently given human names, often feminine names, and that the sentence is probably referring to a boat or ship named Mary Ann. Thus, the determiner is not ungrammatical. But we still do not know what the sentence means until we know what Joe's job is. If Joe is a cook, then the location of Joe's work is apparently in the galley of the Mary Ann; if Joe is a mechanic, then possibly the object of Joe's work is the Mary Ann. These two meanings have two different syntactic structures. The relations between the words differ in the two interpretations. If Joe is a cook, then the sentence can be analyzed as follows:

Joe—subject of the verb

works—verb

on the Mary Ann—prepositional phrase describing the location of the action of the verb.

If Joe is a boat mechanic, then

Joe—subject of the verb

works on—verb

the Mary Ann—object of the verb.

In this case, the syntax cannot be determined without reference to the meaning of the words, but meaning deals with *the relations between expressions and the objects to which they refer*, and that's semantics.

The dividing line between syntax and semantics is often quite difficult to draw. Syntax, after all, provides some of the meaning of the sentence, even without considering the meaning of the individual words. For example, in the famous lines from Lewis Carroll,

'Twas brillig, and the slithy toves
Did gyre and gimble in the wabe [11]

we know that the things being talked about are *toves* and the action taking place is *gyring* and *gimbling*. Thus, despite some linguists' attempts to separate the two levels completely, most people realize that syntax and semantics overlap.

The point of these examples is that the lines between syntax, semantics, and pragmatics are not as clearly drawn as one might infer from the definitions, nor as clearly drawn as one might prefer when trying to write grammars, or programs to process natural language. The fact is that natural language is naturally ambiguous; even humans cannot always disambiguate language. And, it is difficult to process such a slippery kind of data. The purpose of this book is to consider some of the techniques used to process natural language data and to evaluate these methods in light of the extent of understanding achieved with each.

Chapter 1

Basic Linguistics

Linguistics can be defined most simply as the study of language, in particular, natural language. In general, linguistics is concerned with how languages work and how they are used. There have been numerous approaches to the study of language even within the field of linguistics. This chapter will consider modern linguistics with special emphasis on contributions in the last thirty years.

Since man began to use language to communicate, he has undoubtedly been conscious of this important tool and has used language to discuss language. Any time one asks, "What does *antidisestablishmentarianism* mean?" or "Can you state that a different way?", language is being used to discuss language. Such self-referencing complicates the study of language. We use our language, in this book, English, to describe itself. And our language, any natural language, has many inherent ambiguities that complicate general communication and especially discussion of that language and its ambiguities. If I use the word, *chair*, I can be referring to a specific chair, for example the one I am sitting in to write these words: an office chair with a metal pedestal, upholstered in a gold fabric which has worn off the corners of the arms, a chair which exists, one that I can see and feel and sit on. However, if I want to define the word, *chair*, I am referring to *chairs* in general with no one specific chair in mind, but a definite concept: the idea of a *chair*, a physical object with legs (or other support), a seat and a back arranged in a manner that will support a person in a sitting position. The word, *chair*, would apply to a comfortable armchair, a baby's highchair, or straight wooden desk chair as well as to my chair. Other problems of ambiguity will be discussed throughout the book.

Historically, the study of language has dealt more with prescription than description. Most people concerned with language dealt with language as it should be, rather than as it actually is, used. The French Academy, for example, has existed since 1635 to determine how the French language shall be used and when it may change. This approach has been called *prescriptive,* in that the rules are established to deal with future use of the language, instead of the rules being derived from the past use of language.

Classical rhetoric, one of the early methods for dealing with language, was a prescriptive method concerned with both spoken and written language. The study of rhetoric was designed to enable the speaker or writer to convince his audience to agree with his argument, to persuade, often as much by the form of his language as by the content. Thus a student of rhetoric learned logic to shape his ideas and *figures* and *tropes* to shape his words into sentences. These techniques for shaping language, some of which we know as *figures of speech*, included assonance, metaphor, allegory, repetition, puns, and many others. Thus the educated person was in control of his thoughts and his words by having a system of rules for writing and speaking.

In the seventeenth century, members of the Royal Society, including John Dryden and some other writers, decided that the English language was deteriorating, (sounds familiar, right?) and in order to retard the process, they recommended the establishment of a British Academy to standardize the English language as the French Academy had done for French. The functions of the British Academy would be to standardize spelling and vocabulary, supervise dictionary making, and establish rules for use of the English language. The British Academy was not formed at that time, primarily because of the disruption of life caused by the Great Plague. Interest in the proper use of the language grew, however. Rules were developed for the use of English which were often based on classical rhetoric or derived from other languages, especially the scholarly language of the time, Latin. The result of these developments could be called a prescriptive grammar, a set of rules for how to use the language, but more often, for how not to use the language. For example,

Never end a sentence with a preposition.

Never split an infinitive.

An interesting point can be made about these two rules. They are derived from Latin, a language in which infinitives are one word, *amare*, which in English would be two words, *to love*. Thus, in Latin, it is impossible to split an infinitive; in English one must split an infinitive into two words even if the two words are not separated from each other by intervening words. Considering the second rule, we note that Latin has fewer prepositions than English. In general some of the relations expressed in English by the use of prepositions (*of, from, by*) are expressed in Latin by changing the form of the noun. For example, *the roads of the island* would be *viae insulAE*, in Latin. Many prepositions in Latin are part of another word, and like the infinitive, cannot be separated at all, much less placed at the end of the sentence. The point about these two rules, which many English teachers have spent their careers defending, is that they do not really apply to the English language. They have become a part of the prescriptive grammar taught in schools without having a very strong foundation for their existence.

Not all that is taught by English teachers can be rejected, however, just because some of the rules are not appropriate. Much of the study of language in elementary and secondary schools gives us a vocabulary for describing language and presents one or more methods for analyzing its structure. Let us review some of these language concepts, dealing specifically with English. Much of our discussion, like the schools' approach, deals with written language as if that were the only kind of language. (Remember that this discussion is only one way of approaching these notions about language; we will consider several more later. This section is included to provide some background material, especially basic terminology, and should be review of concepts learned in secondary school.)

REVIEW OF LANGUAGE TERMINOLOGY

The sentence is a basic element of language. A sentence expresses a complete thought and is made up of words, which individually or in combination with other words, represent ideas. Different kinds of ideas, physical objects, actions, relationships among other ideas, require different representations. These different representations are called, collectively, *parts of speech*. In order to express a complete thought, a sentence must have a subject and a predicate. The subject is what the sentence is about, and the predicate says something about the subject. In the sentence, *The cat has fleas*, the subject is *the cat*, and the predicate is *has fleas*. The two words used together for the subject make up a *phrase*; a phrase can replace a specific part of speech. For example, in the sentence, *the quarterback has been passing well for the whole second quarter*, the words, *has been passing* make up a phrase to express an action. A group of words used together that contains a subject and a predicate is called a *clause*. The sentence,

The company went bankrupt when the treasurer went to South America.

has two clauses: *the company went bankrupt* and *when the treasurer went to South America*.

The parts of speech are *nouns, pronouns, verbs, adjectives, adverbs, prepositions, conjunctions*, and *interjections*. A noun is a name for something, *a person, place or thing*. Some examples are *ball, liberty, John*, and *Cincinnati*. Pronouns are used to replace nouns, when the noun is already known.

The boy had a ball, and *he* threw *it*.

He replaces *boy*, and *it* replaces *ball*. Pronouns vary according to *number* and *person*, and must agree with the noun they are replacing in these aspects. Number indicates whether the noun being replaced is singular or plural; person identifies the relationship of the noun to the person producing the language. First person is the speaker, the *I* of the sentence; second person is the person being addressed, *You*; third person is *he* or *they*, the others.

Verbs are used to express *action, being, or state of being*. In the preceding sentence, the two verbs are *had* and *threw*. Generally verbs establish a relationship between the main nouns in a sentence.

The woman *is* an executive.

The girl *held* the trophy.

The word, "symbol," *encompasses* many ideas.

When the predicate consists only of a verb which possibly has some modifiers, the verb is called an *intransitive* verb. If the action of the verb requires a noun phrase upon which the action is to be performed, the verb is referred to as *transitive*. Some verbs, called *copulative* or linking verbs, function much as an equal sign does, linking the subject with some other concept:

The woman is an executive.

The woman = an executive.

In verb phrases one word is the main verb and the rest are *auxiliary* verbs or helping verbs:

He would have been swimming.

Swimming is the main verb, and *would, have,* and *been* are all auxiliaries.

Adjectives are used to modify nouns and pronouns.

The *tall* tree grew on the *green* mountain.

The *complicated* algorithm confused the *young* student.

Adverbs modify verbs, adjectives, or other adverbs.

The boy drove the *bright* red car *very fast*.

A *preposition* establishes the relationship between a noun or noun phrase and some other part of the sentence. The preposition and the noun and its modifiers (or noun phrase) are called a *prepositional phrase. On the green mountain* is an example of a prepositional phrase. Other examples are *in the beginning, at the hop,* and *under the table.* Prepositions frequently identify spatial or temporal relationships: *near the river, before dawn,* etc.

Conjunctions join words or groups of words together. There are two major kinds of conjunctions; *coordinate* conjunctions, such as *and, or, nor*; and *subordinate* conjunctions, such as *before, because,* and *until*. Coordinate conjunctions connect words, phrases or clauses of equal rank: the girl *and* her brother, left *or* right. Subordinate conjunctions convey a relationship between two clauses of unequal rank:

I stayed *until* you came.

He cried *because* his program failed.

Interjections express strong feelings, and are sometimes considered to have no grammatical relationship to the sentence.

Help, help, there's a bee after me.

Oh, no, I left out the Read statement.

Because verbs are the major element of a sentence, in that they express the action or primary relationship within the sentence, they carry much of the significance of the sentence through their grammatical representation. Verbs have the following properties: voice, tense, person, and number. Verbs must agree with the subject in number and person. The tense indicates the time orientation of the sentence: past, present, future. Voice identifies the *actor* in the sentence, whether the noun phrase in the subject does the action expressed by the verb or is the recipient of the action. In *active* voice, the subject of the sentence is the *actor*. In *passive* voice, the subject of the sentence is the recipient of the action.

John broke the window.   ACTIVE

The window was broken by John. PASSIVE

Sentences are classified by structure and by use. To designate the structure of a sentence, one must identify the clauses and the conjunctions connecting them. A *simple* sentence consists of one independent clause: a subject and a predicate that together express a complete thought.

All zoos should have an elephant.

A *compound* sentence combines two or more independent clauses, either with coordinate conjunctions or with semicolons.

The girl ate her ice cream cone, but the boy spilled his on his shirt.

The committee deliberated for two hours; no decision was reached.

Complex sentences are made up of an independent clause and one or more dependent clauses.

After John had written his essay, he typed it on his word processor.

The teacher, who had left for lunch, returned to the classroom when she heard a loud crash.

When a sentence has more than one independent clause and one or more dependent clauses, it is referred to as *compound-complex.*

Bob and Ruth played tennis while the sun was out, and then they joined their friends for dinner.

Sentences are classified according to use as *declarative, interrogative, imperative,* or *exclamatory.* A declarative sentence makes a statement. An interrogative sentence asks a question. Imperative sentences express commands; the subject is generally understood to be the person to whom the sentence is directed. Exclamatory sentences express strong emotion; however since any type of sentence can be expressed as an exclamatory sentence, it is not a particularly useful category.

The bird is blue.	DECLARATIVE
Thomas Jefferson wrote the Constitution.	DECLARATIVE
Do you know the way to San Jose?	INTERROGATIVE
The moon is made of green cheese, isn't it?	INTERROGATIVE
Pick up your clothes.	IMPERATIVE
Don't fire till you see the whites of their eyes.	IMPERATIVE
The cat is stuck in the tree!	EXCLAMATORY
Pick up your clothes!	EXCLAMATORY
Who do you think you are!	EXCLAMATORY

The most common order for an English sentence is for the subject to be followed by the predicate, which is sometimes called natural order. However, many sentences change the order of some elements, for example, to change a statement into a question, the subject and part of the verb phrase are exchanged:

Steve has left the company.

Has Steve left the company?

The meaning of an English sentence is dependent to a large extent on word order. As the two sentences below illustrate, changing the order of the words in a sentence can alter the meaning significantly:

The dog bit the man.

The man bit the dog.

Some other languages, for example Latin, are not as dependent on word order as English because, as we noted earlier, some of the relationships among various elements of a sentence are expressed by changing the form of those elements. These changes are referred to as *inflections.* Some languages such as Latin are highly inflected whereas a language like English which is dependent on word order is not as highly inflected.

DESCRIPTIVE LINGUISTICS

Much of the study of linguistics of the last century has been *historical linguistics,* the study of how languages evolved and how they are related to each other, or *descriptive linguistics,* which as the term implies, is concerned with describing specific languages. In descriptive linguistics each language is considered a system of communication separate from any other language, and the significant feature of the language is its use. The descriptive linguist's primary questions about a language are what is the vocabulary of the language, and what are the rules inherent in the language? The rules here are the opposite of the prescriptive rules discussed earlier that state how the language *should* be used; instead, descriptive rules show how the language *is* used. A group of linguists known as the American structuralists concentrated on descriptive linguistics.

Franz Boas, a linguist with a background in anthropology, was highly influential in this area. He realized in the 1920's that many American Indian languages were being spoken by only small groups of elderly people, and knowledge of these languages would be lost forever if information was not gathered quickly from those who knew the languages. Another linguist, Leonard Bloomfield, developed methods for studying these languages, referred to as *discovery procedures*, which had a tremendous influence on the field of linguistics. Bloomfield was strongly influenced by the Positivists and the field of psychology known as Behaviorism, which argued that nothing could be known that was not directly observable. One of Bloomfield's major contributions to linguistics was a scientific approach which allowed for much more valuable information to be obtained than through the metaphysical speculations of previous generations of linguists. A textbook on linguistics cites two of Bloomfield's contributions:

> The object to be described is not the written language but the spoken one, and the relation of the linguist to the language must be that of a nonmanipulating observer.

> The set of structures that the linguist discovers in the language he is studying must be characterized in an absolutely explicit manner without any overt or covert appeal to the general cognitive or linguistic abilities of the individuals using the description. [1]

To quote Bloomfield himself on what he believed to be of proper concern to linguists,

> The student of literature observes the utterances of certain persons (say, of a Shakespeare) and concerns himself with the content and with the unusual features of form. The interest of the philologist is even broader, for he is concerned with the cultural significance and background of what he reads. The linguist, on the other hand, studies the language of all persons alike; the individual features in which the language of a great writer differs from the ordinary speech of his time and place interest the linguist no more than do the individual features of any other person's speech, and much less than do the features that are common to all speakers. ... The discrimination of elegant or "Correct" speech is a by-product of certain social conditions. [2]

Essentially, Bloomfield's methods recorded the phonological and morphological elements of a language with little concern for the semantics of the language: how the linguistic elements relate to the world, what they mean. Meaning is related to the context in which an utterance occurs and thus by Bloomfield's methods, falls outside the domain of the proper study of linguistics.

Briefly, let us consider the aspects of language with which Bloomfield was concerned: the sounds of spoken language. The smallest unit of sound is called a *phone*. Human anatomy allows the production of many different phones using the pharynx, the tongue, the lips, and the mouth cavity. The smallest unit of sound which can be distinguished from other sounds in a particular language is called a *phoneme*. The smallest unit of meaning in language is a *morpheme*. Sometimes a morpheme is a separate word, such as *horse*. However many words are made up of more than one morpheme, for example, *horses* is two morphemes, *horse* and -*s*. The study of combining morphemes to form words and deriving the morphemes from words is called morphology.

ZELLIG S. HARRIS

But what happened to the grammar rules that we discussed earlier in the chapter? Essentially the descriptive linguists who followed Bloomfield ignored the problems of syntax and semantics almost entirely. The discovery procedure that Bloomfield developed required that different levels of analysis be kept separate, that phonology must be independent of morphology, and both must be free of any syntactic or semantic considerations. However, some linguists found that after developing elaborate systems for explaining sound patterns, they were not adequately describing language and therefore tried to formalize the earlier attempts to find parts of speech by observing the language in use. Dividing words and phrases into *nouns, noun phrases, verbs, adjectives,* and so on, was called *immediate constituent analysis*. One of these linguists, Zellig S. Harris, developed a method of analysis called *repeated substitution* to categorize morphemes within an utterance. To quote Harris,

> The procedure ... consists essentially of repeated substitution: e.g., CHILD for YOUNG BOY in WHERE DID THE—GO? To generalize this, we take a form A in an environment C—D and then substitute another form B in the place of A. If, after such a substitution, we still have an expression which occurs in the language concerned, i.e., if not only CAD but also CBD occurs, we say that A and B are members of the same substitution class, or that both A and B fill the position C—D, or the like. [3]

This procedure could produce an analysis of a sentence such as the following:

The monkey has eaten the banana.
T   N1   v   V   T   N2

in which the traditional names provide most of the initials for the classes: N(oun), V(erb), A(djective), T(Article), (auxiliary) v(erb).

Harris also noted that some sentences could be *transformed* into other sentences by changing only the form or structure of the sentence. The relationship between *active* and *passive* sentences is one example:

The dog bit the man.

The man was bitten by the dog.

Another transformation that we have already noted is from a declarative to an interrogative sentence.

The man was bitten by the dog.

Was the man bitten by the dog?

NOAM CHOMSKY'S *Syntactic Structures*

Another linguist interested in many of the same problems of language as Harris was Noam Chomsky. In 1957 Chomsky published a book called *Syntactic Structures* that largely changed the direction of modern linguistics. Chomsky's work was grounded in the theories of Bloomfield and the American structuralists, but was at the same time a radical departure from their methods. Chomsky's theories depended on the rigorous approach to studying language developed by Bloomfield, but went beyond directly observable phenomena to derive rules about language. The distinction between *performance* and *competence* became significant. Thus, in addition to the language actually produced, and therefore directly observable, we must consider the language a person is capable of producing, whether it is ever actually produced or not. Chomsky noted that human language is infinite, that no matter how many sentences a person hears or says, there are always more sentences which are not yet a part of that person's experience, but which he is perfectly capable of producing or comprehending. When a person learns a language, it is not by hearing all possible sentences in that language and memorizing them, but rather by having some innate knowledge of the structure of language that all humans are born with. Chomsky attempted to delineate these inherent language structures by developing a series of generative grammars. The kind of grammar Chomsky described does not define what is correct or incorrect in language usage, but rather produces acceptable structural relations. As Chomsky explains in *Syntactic Structures*, a generative grammar is,

> a rules system formalized with mathematical precision that generates, without drawing upon any information that is not represented

explicitly in the system, the grammatical sentences of the language that it describes and assigns to each sentence a structural description, or grammatical analysis. [4]

The simplest type of generative grammar is called a *finite state grammar*, which Chomsky describes as follows:

> Suppose that we have a machine that can be in any one of a finite number of different internal states, and suppose that this machine switches from one state to another by producing a certain symbol (let us say, an English word.) One of these states is an *initial state*; another is a *final state*. Suppose that the machine begins in the initial state, runs through a sequence of states (producing a word with each transition) and ends in the final state. We call the sequence of words which has been produced a "sentence." Each such machine thus defines a certain language; namely, the set of sentences that can be produced in this way. Any language that can be produced by a machine of this sort we call a *finite state language*; and we call the machine itself a *finite state grammar*. [5]

However, natural languages are not finite and therefore cannot be adequately defined by finite state grammars. The next kind of grammar Chomsky defined is the *phrase structure grammar*. In these grammars the elements of the sentences are identified by the terms introduced earlier in the chapter as *parts of speech*, which later linguists called *constituents*, nouns, verbs, etc. A phrase structure (PS) grammar starts with a sentence and defines its parts, then defines each of the sub-parts, continuing the redefinitions until a sentence has been produced. A simple PS grammar might be:

$$S \rightarrow NP + VP$$
$$NP \rightarrow ART + N$$
$$VP \rightarrow V + NP$$
$$N \rightarrow birds, worms, boys, cars, rocks, \ldots$$
$$ART \rightarrow the$$
$$V \rightarrow eat, drive, learn, \ldots$$

(where S is sentence, NP is noun phrase, VP is verb phrase, ART is article, V is verb.) Thus, by applying one rule at a time, we have the sequence,

$$S \rightarrow NP + VP$$
$$ART + N + VP$$
$$The + N + VP$$
$$The\ birds + VP$$
$$The\ birds + V + NP$$

The birds eat + NP

The birds eat + ART + N

The birds eat the + N

The birds eat the worms.

(The structural representation, known as a *phrase marker*, for this sentence is shown in Figure 1.1.) From this grammar we can derive sentences such as,

The worms eat the birds.

The boys drive the cars.

The rocks learn the worms.

and with the proper vocabulary, our nonsense sentence from the Introduction,

The trees sing the chairs.

The PS grammar above has no recursive elements, in which elements are defined in terms of themselves. A more complete PS grammar would handle recursion, choice of multiple definitions for an element, and other more realistic

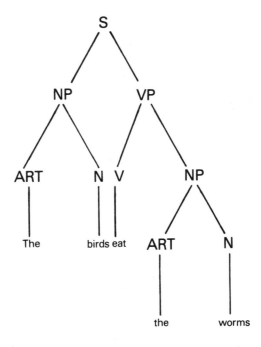

Figure 1.1   Phrase Marker for the Sentence, "The birds eat the worms."

complications of natural language. A more complex PS grammar of English might be as follows:

S → NP + VP
NP → Mod + N (PP)
Mod → (Art) (Adj)
VP → V (ADV)
VP → Aux + V
V → Vi
V → Vt + NP
V → Vc + Adj
V → Vc + NP
ADV → PP
ADV → Adv
PP → Prep + NP
N → bird, tree, boy, . . .
Art → a, the
Adj → dark, good, tall, . . .
Adv → fast, slowly, . . .
Prep → near, from, after, . . .
Vi → cry, swim, . . .
Vt → hit, break, eat, . . .
Vc → is, become, . . .
Aux → has, must, can, . . .

where the abbreviations are:

S	sentence
NP	noun phrase
VP	verb phrase
Mod	modifier
Art	article
Adj	adjective
ADV	adverbial phrase
Adv	adverb
V	verb
Aux	auxiliary
Vi	verb (intransitive)

Vt	verb (transitive)
Vc	verb (copulative)
PP	prepositional phrase
Prep	preposition

Elements in parentheses are optional. Note that NP can contain a PP which in turn contains a NP; therefore, NP is defined recursively. We must assume that the lowest level elements in this grammar would have to be defined with a larger vocabulary to include all the words that could occur in sentences of the language. Obviously, this grammar does not account for all aspects of the English language, by any means. For example, it does not contain any reference to conjunctions at all and therefore would not produce compound or complex sentences or compound sentence elements. This grammar also does not produce sentences that comply with the rules of subject verb agreement. In fact, Chomsky considered the PS grammar inadequate to describe actual language.

The most complex of the grammars that Chomsky developed in his early work was known as *transformational generative grammar*. In transformational generative grammar, the phrase structure component was only the beginning; two other components were required to produce acceptable English sentences: the transformational component and the morphophonemic component, which is also transformational, but in a different sense. Some aspects of the language are dealt with after the initial elements are generated by the phrase structure rules. Application of the transformational rules could change a sentence from its active voice form into passive voice or change a declarative sentence into a question. For example the sentence,

John will break the window.
NP1 – Aux – V   –   NP2

can be transformed into

The window will be –EN break by John.
NP2   –   Aux+BE +EN + V – by +NP1

Then the morphophonemic rules would apply to produce:

The window will be broken by John.

(See Figure 1.2.) The phrase structure rules can also produce a sentence such as,

The girl run after the dog.

in which the subject and verb do not agree. Thus, the morphophonemic rules must be applied to produce

The girl runs after the dog.

The sentence produced by the phrase structure rules was later called the *deep structure*, and the sentence as it would actually be used in speech or writing,

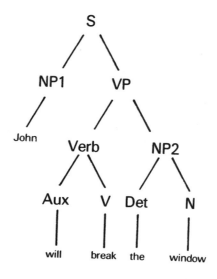

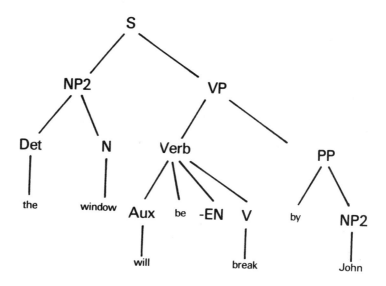

Figure 1.2   Phrase Marker for the Active Voice Sentence, "John will break the window," and the Passive Voice Sentence, "The window will be broken by John."

the *surface structure*. In some situations, the transformational rules are applied to the deep structure in order to produce a proper surface structure, such as forcing subject-verb number agreement. In other cases application of the rules is considered optional, such as negation of a sentence or formation of a question.

One mechanism for dealing with various aspects of more complicated sentences is what Chomsky called *generalized transformations*. If two sentences have a NP in common, i.e., *the girl*, then the two sentences can be combined by a series of transformations.

The girl is singing. The girl has a lovely voice.

[The girl [The girl is singing] has a lovely voice]

Because both instances of *the girl* refer to the same person, the transformations will produce the following sentences:

The girl who is singing has a lovely voice.

The singing girl has a lovely voice.

By combining the sentences the other way, we can produce,

[The girl [The girl has a lovely voice] is singing]

The girl with the lovely voice is singing.

This technique, called *embedding sentences*, has been claimed to be the source of all relative clauses, adjectives, and prepositional phrases.

Chomsky's theories were generally accepted and triggered a vast amount of linguistic research, which revealed some problems with the theories. For example, if the syntactic level is kept completely separate from the semantic level, then our phrase structure grammars are going to produce nonsense sentences as often, or maybe more often, than meaningful sentences. Also the notion of optional transformations was questioned; not that they could not be produced, but that a sentence and its transform do not necessarily carry the same meaning.

I am going on vacation.
I am not going on vacation.

signify very different ideas, in fact, directly opposing ideas. Another difficulty was that sometimes a single sentence, a surface structure, had more than one meaning, and thus could have been produced from more than one deep structure. A good example [6] is,

The chickens are ready to eat.

Here if we paraphrase, we have a sentence that means both,

The chickens have been prepared for us to eat them.

and

The chickens are hungry and ready to eat their feed.

Ambiguity rears its ugly head once more. Thus Chomsky's early theories do not seem quite adequate.

KATZ AND FODOR'S SEMANTIC THEORY

Jerrold J. Katz and Jerry A. Fodor developed some techniques for dealing with semantic problems within the framework of transformational grammar. In a well-known article published in 1964, *The Structure of a Semantic Theory*, [7] they presented the equation,

"linguistic description minus grammar equals semantics."

Part of the reasoning behind this equation was the continued desire to maintain the distinction between the levels of analysis, to keep syntax separate from semantics. The authors claimed that "Grammars seek to describe the structure of a sentence *in isolation from its possible settings in linguistic discourse (written or verbal) or in nonlinguistic contexts (social or physical).*" But grammars do not provide the ability to deal with the various meanings of ambiguous sentences. As Katz and Fodor express it,

> the construction of a grammar draws upon empirical data supplied by the exercise of the speaker's ability to distinguish well-formed sentences from ungrammatical strings, to recognize syntactic ambiguity, and to appreciate relations between sentence types.

However, *the ability to interpret sentences* is also needed.

> A semantic theory describes and explains the interpretative ability of speakers: by accounting for their performance in determining the number and content of the readings of a sentence, by detecting semantic anomalies, by deciding upon paraphrase relations between sentences, and by marking every other semantic property or relation that plays a role in this ability.

The authors proposed two components for a theory of semantics: a dictionary and a set of projection rules. The dictionary will provide, for every lexical item (or word) in the language, a phonological description, a syntactic or grammatical portion, "which provides the parts-of-speech classification for the lexical item, and a semantic portion which represents each of the distinct senses the lexical item [has] in its occurrences as a given part of speech." The projection rules are designed to produce all the valid interpretations of a sentence.

The lexical entries in the dictionary, or *lexicon* contain two primary parts: the grammatical portion and the semantic portion. (The authors ignored the phonological portion, and so shall we.) The grammatical portion provides *grammatical markers*, to identify the possible grammatical uses of the word. For example, the word, *stand,* can be a noun or a verb. The semantic portion includes *semantic markers* and *distinguishers*, which are used to distinguish the various senses of each grammatical use of the word. See Figure 1.3.

In the tree in Figure 1.3, the unenclosed descriptors are grammatical markers, in this case *noun*, the descriptors enclosed in parentheses are *semantic markers*, and the ones in square brackets are *distinguishers*.

The theory presented by Katz and Fodor is that there exist a finite set of semantic markers to describe items in a language, and these markers can be used to correlate the meanings between different words within a sentence. For example if a verb, such as *sing*, requires that its subject be animate, any word considered as the subject of that verb must have the corresponding marker. Since the word *tree* does not have that marker, to say *The tree sings* . . . does not make sense. It is not a meaningful statement in our language, unless, in a fantasy situation, trees acquire characteristics of animate entities. The distinguishers are used to select between the various senses of the word, to

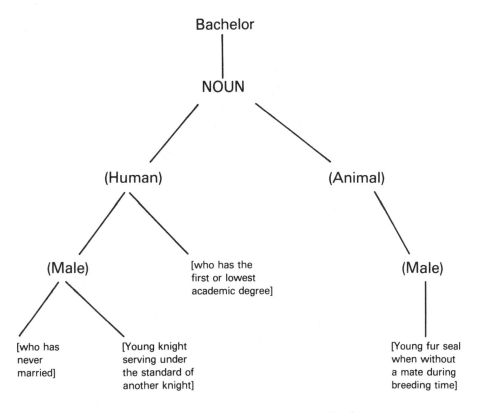

Figure 1.3   Tree Showing Grammatical Markers (From "The Structure of a Semantic Theory," p. 496.)

disambiguate the word. The projection rules match the various words in a sentence with the possible meanings of the sentence, by correlating the semantic markers and distinguishers of the various words in the sentence. Thus, in a sentence such as,

This suit is too light.

one must differentiate between the senses of the word, *light*. Does the sentence mean *light in color*, in the sense that a darker color would perhaps be more dignified, or *light in weight*, in the sense that the cool temperatures require a heavier fabric? The dictionary entry for the word, *light*, would undoubtedly include markers to allow for disambiguation. This process of applying the projection rules to the sentence and its semantic markers creates what Katz and Fodor called *amalgamated paths*, different interpretations of the meaning in the sentences based on all the possible combinations of semantic markers. The example Katz and Fodor used to explain the technique is the sentence,

The man hits the colorful ball. [8]

The NP, *the colorful ball*, has a number of meanings which can only be differentiated by the context in which the phrase occurs. The *paths* for the word, *colorful*, are

(1) COLORFUL → Adjective → (COLOR) → [ABOUNDING IN CONTRAST OR VARIETY OF BRIGHT COLORS] <(PHYSICAL OBJECT) v (SOCIAL ACTIVITY)>

(2) COLORFUL → Adjective → (EVALUATIVE) → [HAVING DISTINCTIVE CHARACTER, VIVIDNESS, OR PICTURESQUENESS] <(AESTHETIC OBJECT) v (SOCIAL ACTIVITY)>

The *paths* for the word, *ball*, are

(1) BALL → Noun concrete → (SOCIAL ACTIVITY) → (LARGE) → (ASSEMBLY) → [FOR THE PURPOSE OF SOCIAL DANCING]

(2) BALL → Noun concrete → (PHYSICAL OBJECT) → [HAVING A GLOBULAR SHAPE]

(3) BALL → Noun concrete → (PHYSICAL OBJECT) → [SOLID MISSILE FOR PROJECTION BY ENGINE OF WAR]

Thus, these two words, *colorful* and *ball*, give us six possible combinations of markers; however, Katz and Fodor note that the restriction in the second path for *colorful* that it be "<(AESTHETIC OBJECT) v (SOCIAL ACTIVITY)>" eliminates the third sense of the word, *ball*, since cannonballs are not aesthetic objects, usually. Thus there are four amalgamations for the phrase, *colorful ball*, in the following combinations:

(1) COLORFUL (1) + BALL (1)

(2) COLORFUL (1) + BALL (2)

(3) COLORFUL (2) + BALL (1)

(4) COLORFUL (2) + BALL (2)

By amalgamating these paths with the rest of the sentence, we can eliminate senses (1) and (3) because the verb, *hit*, would require an object with a semantic marker of (PHYSICAL OBJECT). Eventually we would probably be left with the sense of the phrase in (2), that of a brightly colored, spherical object. If the verb had been *threw*, as in the sentence,

> The man threw a colorful ball

the paths could not be restricted to one, since the verb, *threw*, could be that of giving a party, as well as propelling an object in the air. By matching the semantic markers within a sentence, the projection rules produced all the amalgamated paths, or readings, of a sentence and thus provided a mechanism for interpreting the *meaning* of the sentence.

CHOMSKY'S *Aspects of the Theory of Syntax*

By the early 1960's, many of Chomsky's early theories were being seriously questioned. Rather than defending a weak position, Chomsky moved beyond his early theories by incorporating the results of some of the other researchers, including Katz and Fodor, into a more complete and workable model. This later version of transformational grammar, sometimes referred to as the standard theory, was expounded in *Aspects of the Theory of Syntax*, published in 1965. Essentially the grammar consisted of the following parts:

```
A. Syntactic Component
   1. The Base
      Phrase Structure Rules
      Lexicon,
         with rules of lexical insertion
   2. The Transformational Component

B. Semantic Component

C. Phonological Component
```

The syntactic component was referred to as *generative*, in the sense that it produced the deep structures that were then input to the other two components. "The semantic and phonological components were called *interpretive*. That is, they were said to interpret the output of the syntactic component, with the semantic component giving as its output the meanings and the phonological component giving as its output the sound sequences." [9]

The phrase structure rules of the base in the syntactic component were much the same as in the earlier theory, but the addition of the lexicon changed the functioning of that component significantly. The lexicon was modeled after that of Katz and Fodor and included *features* to provide phonological, syntactic, and semantic information about each word in the lexicon. For example the word, *boy* would be marked with the features, [+Noun], [+Count], [+Common], [+Animate], [+Human], (and appropriate phonological features). A sentence generated by the PS rules would include the features required for the sentence to be interpreted as meaningful; see Figure 1.4, for example.

These nodes that terminate with a list of features are called *complex symbols*. The nouns carry the complex symbols, but the same features must be matched by the verb as well. Therefore in a sentence defined as,

S → NP + VP

VP → V + NP

the verb would get its features from the combination of the features of the noun phrases which surround it. See Figure 1.5.

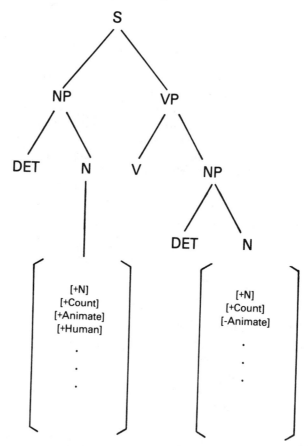

Figure 1.4   Phrase Marker Showing Features for Nouns (Reprinted with permission from Newmeyer, Linguistics in America, © 1980, Academic Press. All rights reserved.)

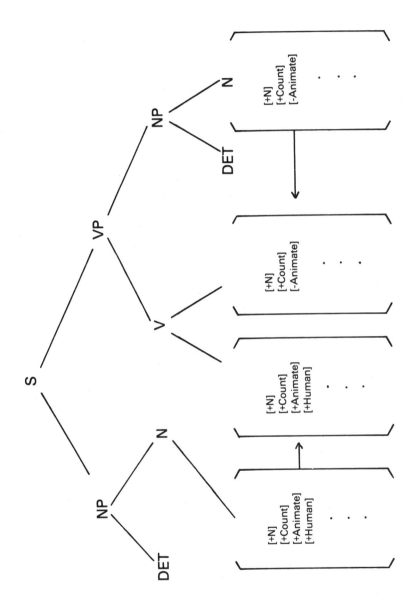

Figure 1.5 Phrase Marker Showing Features for Nouns and Verbs (Reprinted with permission from Newmeyer, *Linguistics in America*, © 1980, Academic Press. All rights reserved.)

The mechanism for establishing that the verb must be related to the noun phrases around it is a set of rules called *context sensitive* rules. (The PS rules that we have seen up to now are *context free* in the sense that there is no requirement at any point in the generative process that any other constituent be considered.) The rule to generate the verb in the sentence in the two preceding examples would be:

V → CS / a ---- (Det b)

which essentially means that a verb is generated sensitive to its context by taking the features for a subject from the NP preceding it and, if it has an object, taking the features for its object from the NP following it. Once the complex symbols are developed, the lexical insertion rules select specific words that fulfill the requirements of the features. Thus if the noun generated for the subject position had the features [+Count], [+Common], [+Animate], [+Human], as the word, *boy*, does, then the verb selected would be limited to only those which take an animate, human, countable subject, such as *sing* or *talk*. Adding the context sensitive rules contributes significantly to the amount of meaning in the sentences generated.

The output from the base component is the deep structure, which is then input to the other components to produce the surface structure. Another addition to Chomsky's theory at this point dealt with the problem of the optional transformations, such as negation and question formation which produced sentences with a different meaning from the original.

The tree is growing.

The tree is not growing.

Is the tree growing?

In the standard theory, these three sentences would not have the same deep structure; rather the latter two would have an *abstract marker* that identifies their negative and interrogative natures, respectively. Thus the deep structures for the three would be:

The tree grow—[+Progressive]

NEG The tree grow—[+Progressive]

Q The tree grow—[+Progressive]

The addition of the notion of including abstract markers was derived from the research of several linguists: Katz, Postal, Klima, and Lees, and allows for the proposition, "Transforms are meaning-preserving," which was to become the focus of a serious debate in linguistics. [10]

The semantic component of the Aspects theory depended heavily on ideas developed by Katz and Fodor. It uses projection rules and semantic markers to form amalgamated paths to identify the various senses of the sentence. The transformational component, which accepts the deep structure as input, operates much as the early transformational rules did to produce the surface structure. When the phonological component operates upon the surface structure, the appropriate sounds are produced to generate speech.

As you can see from Figure 1.6, the standard theory maintains the separation of the various components of the grammar. The syntactic component generates the deep structure and transforms it to produce the surface structure. The semantic component operates only on the deep structure, and the phonological component operates only on the surface structure. Therefore the semantic interpretation is totally distinct from the transformational and phonological stages. Essentially this split between the semantic and transfor-

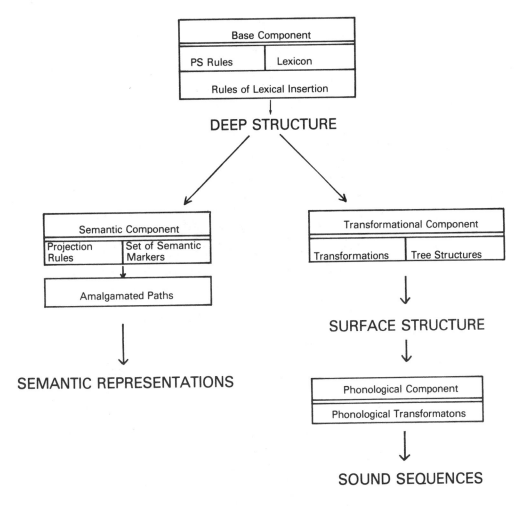

Figure 1.6   Chomsky's Standard Theory

mational components reinforces the claim that transformations do not change meaning.

However some transformations do change meaning, as several researchers pointed out. If the sentence,

John sprayed paint on the wall.

is transformed into,

The wall was sprayed with paint by John.

the meaning of the sentence changes. The first sentence can imply that John only sprayed paint on part of the wall, as well as meaning that he painted the entire wall. The second sentence seems to imply that the entire wall was painted. If the second sentence was produced by a transformation of the first, then both sentences are derived from the same deep structure. However, if they do not have the same meaning, they must be derived from different deep structures. Thus Chomsky's new theory seemed to be on shaky ground.

CASE GRAMMAR

In 1967, at a conference on the topic, *Universals in Linguistic Theory*, Charles J. Fillmore presented a paper called, *A Case for Case*. [11] In an attempt to deal with some of the problems evident in the standard theory, Fillmore revived the traditional notion of *case*, but presented it in a modified form. Traditionally, case forms, applied to nouns and pronouns, show the relationship of each word to the other words in the sentence. The English language has three cases, in the traditional sense: *nominative, possessive,* and *objective.* The nominative case is used for the subject of the verb or the *predicate nominative,* a noun linked to the subject by a copulative verb.

That bird is *a sparrow.*

The possessive case, also called *genitive*, shows ownership or possession:

The *boy's* book is heavy.

The objective case is used for nouns and pronouns which are the direct object of a verb.

The hammer hit *the nail.*

An indirect object is also in objective case in English,

The girl gave *him* her canary.

These two instances of objective case are sometimes given separate designations; the direct object can be called *accusative,* and the indirect object *dative* case. In a highly inflected language like Latin, these cases are always separate, and the words in the respective cases have separate forms.

One of the difficulties with case that Fillmore noted is that, assuming we have cases of this traditional sort, we also have cases of another sort. For example if a sentence is transformed into passive, such as,

The hammer hit the nail.

The nail was hit with the hammer.

the *cases* have changed. *The nail* is now nominative instead of objective, and *the hammer* is objective whereas it was nominative before. Also, there is another element of both these sentences which is missing: who caused the hammer to hit the nail, who was the agent of the action? If we stay away from Disney movies and fantasy situations, hammers are inanimate objects that tend to stay put unless wielded by someone. Thus, the sentence,

Someone hit the nail with the hammer.

expresses the same idea as the two previous examples, yet now the nominative subject is *Someone* and *the nail* is objective again. What's going on here? This confusion was Fillmore's basic concern.

Fillmore argued that the traditional concept of *case* dealt only with the surface structure of the sentence and was not significant in any meaningful way. The deep structure reveals the cases of importance to the meaning of the sentence. Thus, Fillmore postulated that

> The sentence in its basic structure consists of a verb and one or more noun phrases, each associated with the verb in a particular case relationship. The "explanatory" use of this framework resides in the necessary claim that, although there can be compound instances of a single case (through noun phrase conjunction), each case relationship occurs only once in a simple sentence. [12]

Thus in our example *someone*, the person performing the action, is referred to as the Agent, *the hammer*, used for the action, is called the Instrumental, and *the nail*, receiving the action, is the Object.

According to Fillmore, a sentence is made up of

> the *proposition*, a tenseless set of relationships involving verbs and nouns (and embedded sentences, if there are any), separated from what might be called the *modality* constituent. This latter will include such modalities on the sentence-as-a-whole as negation, tense, mood, and aspect. [13]

The rules for a sentence are as follows.

The first rule, then, is

$$\text{Sentence} \rightarrow \text{Modality} + \text{Proposition}$$

$$S \rightarrow M + P$$

where the proposition is the verb and the various cases related to it. The next rule is

$$P \rightarrow C1 + C2 + C3 \ldots Cn$$

where C stands for case, with the indices denoting that a particular case can only occur once in a given sentence. (See Figure 1.7.).

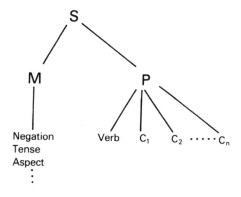

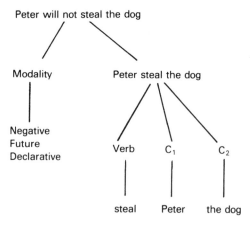

Figure 1.7   Case Grammar Representation for the Sentence, "Peter will not steal the dog."

The case notions comprise a set of universal, presumably, innate, concepts which identify certain types of judgments human beings are capable of making about the events that are going on around them, judgments about such matters as who did it, who it happened to, and what got changed. The cases that appear to be needed include:

AGENTIVE (A), the case of the typically animate perceived instigator of the action identified by the verb.

INSTRUMENTAL (I), the case of the inanimate force or object causally involved in the action or state identified by the verb.

DATIVE (D), the case of the animate being affected by the state or action identified by the verb.

FACTITIVE (F), the case of the object or being resulting from the action or state identified by the verb, or understood as a part of the meaning of the verb.

LOCATIVE (L), the case which identifies the location or spatial orientation of the state or action identified by the verb.

OBJECTIVE (O), the semantically most neutral case, the case of anything representable by a noun whose role in the action or state identified by the verb is identified by the semantic interpretation of the verb itself; conceivably the concept should be limited to things which are affected by the action or state identified by the verb. The term is not to be confused with the notion of direct object, nor with the name of the surface case synonymous with accusative. [14]

Following his initial list Fillmore repeats L:

LOCATIVE (L), The list of cases includes L, but nothing corresponding to what might be called directional. There is a certain amount of evidence that locational and directional elements do not contrast but are superficial differences determined either by the constituent structure or by the character of the associated verb. [15]

Fillmore added additional cases to this list, including *benefactive* (B), which he did not define explicitly. Other researchers modified the list of cases in various ways, as we shall see later.

Case frames are the mechanism for identifying the specific cases allowed for any particular verb. The case frame for each verb indicates the relationships which are required in any sentence in which the verb appears and those relationships which are optional. Let us look again at the sentences,

The hammer hit the nail.

The nail was hit by the hammer.

Someone hit the nail with the hammer.

(See Figure 1.8.) The verb, *hit*, allows three primary cases: agentive, instrumental, and objective. We have all three cases in the last sentence, but only two in the others. In fact, only one case is required with this verb,

The nail was hit.

Thus the case frame for the verb, *hit*, might be

HIT [--- O (A) (I)]

Or, to state the rule in words, the verb HIT occurs in sentences with a noun phrase in the objective case, and optionally noun phrases in agentive and instrumental cases. (The parentheses once again indicate optional elements.) Some examples of cases:

```
John opened the door.
The door was opened by John.
     A:   John
     0:   the door

The key opened the door.
     I:   the key
     0:   the door

John opened the door with the key.
John used the key to open the door.
     A:   John
     0:   the door
     I:   the key

John believed that he would win.
We persuaded John that he would win.
It was apparent to John that he would win.
     D:   John

Chicago is windy.
It is windy in Chicago.
     L:   Chicago

John had a dream about Mary.
John dreamed a dream about Mary.
     A:   John
     F:   a dream
     0:   Mary
```

When a sentence is being analyzed for cases, several aspects of the sentence must be considered. The relationship between the verb and the noun phrase may be expressed by a preposition.

Someone hit the nail with the hammer

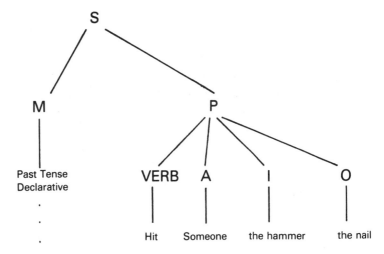

The girl gave him her canary

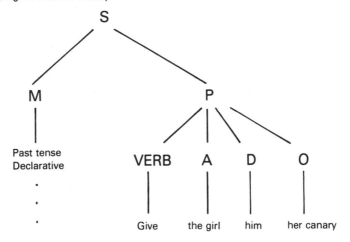

Figure 1.8   Case Grammar Representations for the Sentences, "Someone hit the nail with the hammer," and "The girl gave him her canary."

The rules for English prepositions may look something like this: the A preposition is BY; the I preposition is BY if there is no A, otherwise it is WITH; the O and F prepositions are typically ZERO; the B preposition is FOR; the D preposition is typically TO; the L and T (for time) prepositions are either semantically nonempty (in which case they are introduced as optional choices from the lexicon), or they are selected by the particular associated noun [ON THE STREET, AT THE CORNER (=intersection of two streets), IN THE CORNER (of a room); ON MONDAY, AT NOON, IN THE AFTERNOON]. Specific verbs may have associated with them certain requirements for preposition choice that are exceptions to the above generalizations. [16]

Obviously, not all noun phrases have prepositions to identify the case, but Fillmore suggests a notation that every noun phrase be written with a *Kasus* (K), to indicate the case and, to some extent, the particular means of identifying the case in that sentence. This gives us the rule,

C → K + NP

K is a preposition or zero (no element present). Figure 1.9 presents the revised version of the trees shown earlier. The *unmarked* cases must be determined by factors other than the preposition. Since all English sentences have a *surface subject*, even though it may be understood and not present in the sentence, as in imperative sentences (e.g., Shut the door.), the first rule for finding *unmarked* cases, concerns the subject: "If there is an A, it becomes the subject; otherwise, if there is an I, it becomes the subject; otherwise, the subject is the O." [17] For example, see Figure 1.10. The case frame for the verb OPEN is [-- O (A) (I)]. Since there is only one case, it must be O and must become the subject. In the sentence, "John opened the door with a key," John is the A, and also the surface subject. In the sentence, "The key opened the door," no A occurs; therefore, by our rule, the I becomes the subject.

The element NP can be further defined with an additional rule:

NP → N (S)

which states that, besides the noun in the noun phrase, there might be an embedded sentence, which, by means of transformations, could produce adjectives or relative clauses, a process mentioned earlier in the chapter.

GENERATIVE SEMANTICS

Fillmore's Case Grammar was similar in some respects to Generative Semantics, which also developed in response to Chomsky's Standard Theory. Fillmore's theory

Someone hit the nail with the hammer

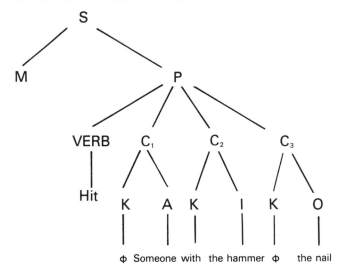

The nail was hit with the hammer by someone

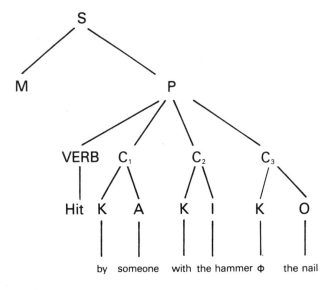

Figure 1.9 Active and Passive Voice Representations in Case Grammar Graphs

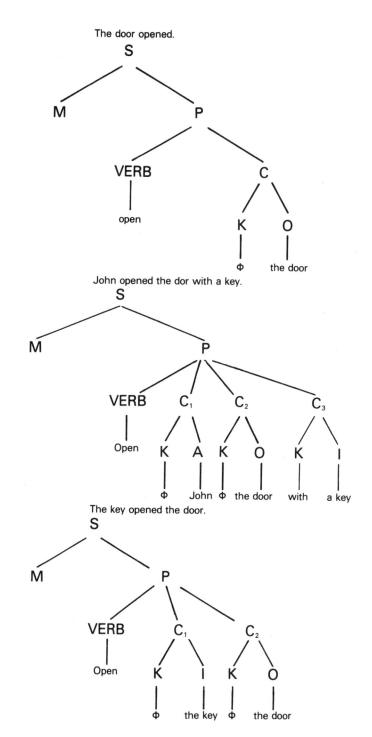

Figure 1.10   Active and Passive Voice Representations in Case Grammer Graphs

defines a level of deep structure more abstract and more "semantic" than the standard deep structure level, and correspondingly employs fewer interpretive semantic rules. Those who might be expected to be sympathetic to this position, i.e. generative semanticists, have in fact overtaken it. Generative Semantics has a deep structure level IDENTICAL to the semantic level, and has correspondingly NO interpretive semantic rules at all. [18]

In essence, the generative semanticists claim that there can be no difference between the deep structure of a sentence and its meaning representation, that what is generated initially must contain all the meaning it ever obtains, thus the name, Generative Semantics. (Remember that the semantic component in the standard theory is interpretive in nature; that theory is sometimes referred to as Interpretive Semantics.) Obviously Generative Semantics has moved away from the structuralists' requirement that the levels of analysis remain separate, which Chomsky's theories maintained. As Figure 1.11 shows, Generative Semantics starts with the meaning representation, interprets that to produce the surface structure, and applies the phonological rules to arrive at the phonological representation. The standard theory can be said to be *syntactically based*, whereas the Generative Semantics theory is *semantically based*.

According to Chomsky's 1965 theory, the deep structure of a sentence is the tree (called a *phrase-marker*), containing all the words that will appear in the surface structure of the sentence. Thus the subject, predicate, and other constituents are defined at the level of the deep structure. Since these concepts of subject, predicate, etc., carry some meaning, the deep structure includes that level of semantic information. The generative semanticists, on the other hand, believe that word selection is part of the transformational process, that the *underlying structure*, the Generative Semantics name for deep structure, contains the "sense-components", but not the actual words that will appear in the surface structure. The word *kill* would be inserted into the surface structure to replace the sense-components *cause, become, not*, and *alive* in the underlying structure. This substitution, *lexicalization*, would be only one of many transformations applied during generation of a sentence containing the word *kill*. See Figure 1.12.

The generative semanticists noticed the similarities between certain adjectives and verbs, as in the sentences:

The metal is hard.
The metal hardened.
The sauce is thick.
The sauce thickened.

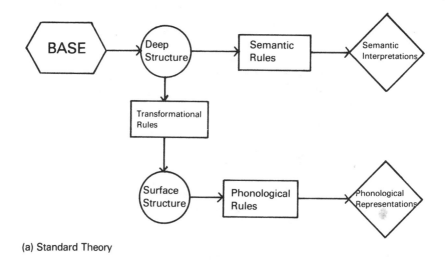

(a) Standard Theory

(b) Generative Semantic Theory

Figure 1.11   Comparison of Chomsky's Standard Theory and Generative Semantic Theory

These similarities could be explained by the Generative Semantics concept of lexicalization being a late transformation. Figure 1.13 shows the progression from the lowest level underlying structure to a high level underlying structure. In this interpretation, *thicken* means *to become thick*, which is indicated by the combination of the meaning, *thick*, and the verb features [+PRO] and [+INCHOATIVE], or progressive and initial or formative. In other words, the sauce thickens by moving progressively from an initial state to the state of being thick.

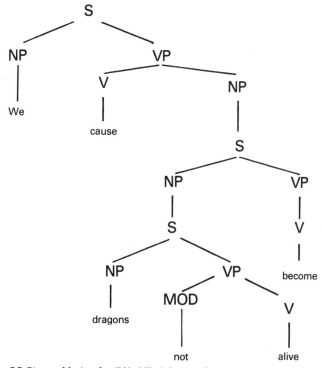

GS Phrase Marker for "We killed dragons"

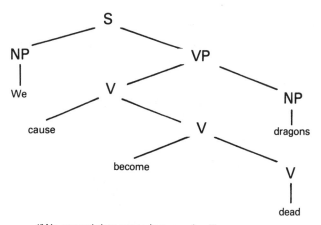

"We caused dragons to become dead"
"We caused dragons to die"

Figure 1.12   Generative Semantics Phrase Markers

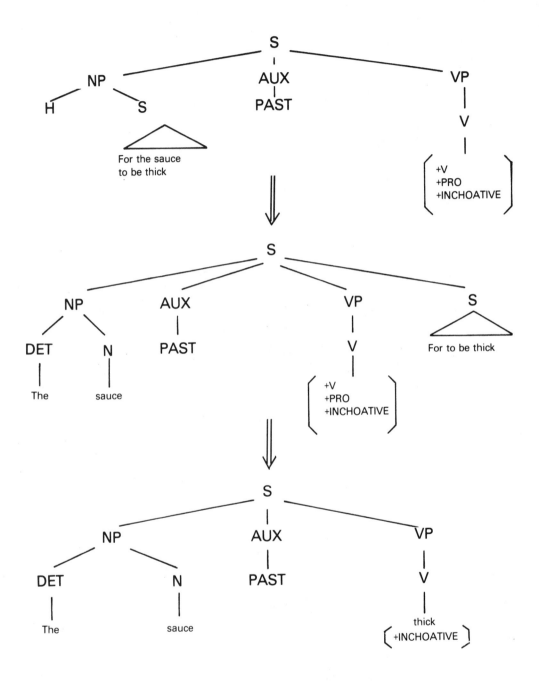

Figure 1.13   GS Phrase Markers for "The sauce thickened."

CHOMSKY'S EXTENDED STANDARD THEORY

There are a number of other differences between Generative Semantics and the Standard Theory, but there is still another theory that must be considered. Partly in reaction to the generative semanticists, Chomsky himself moved beyond the Standard Theory to what he calls the Extended Standard Theory, still a syntactically based theory, but allowing for the semantic interpretation of a sentence to apply to both the deep structure and the surface structure. In addition to the Projection Rules applied to the Deep Structure in the Semantic Interpretation Component, there are also semantic rules applied to the Surface Structure, i.e., after the syntactic transformational rules are completed. See Figure 1.14.

Chomsky is still actively revising his theories and undoubtedly will continue to do so. As of the late 1970's, the Extended Standard Theory could be represented as in Figure 1.15. The base operates similarly to the earlier base component; the transformational rules have been strengthened by further study; and various other rules and features have been added to the model. Translating the surface structure into a *logical form* before the semantic rules are applied developed out of the movement toward formal grammar, common among many linguists of the last few years. Although Chomsky has not specifically defined the syntax of the logical form, it is apparently similar to that of standard forms of predicate calculus. The rules between the Surface Structure and the Phonetic Representation—Deletion Rules, Surface Filters, Phonological Rules, and Stylistic Rules—are primarily a clearer delineation

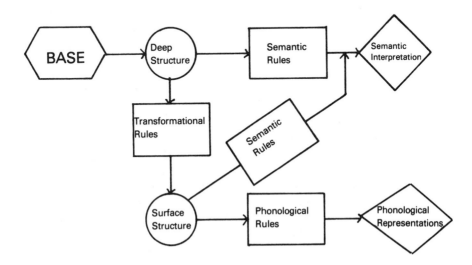

Figure 1.14   Chomsky's Extended Standard Theory

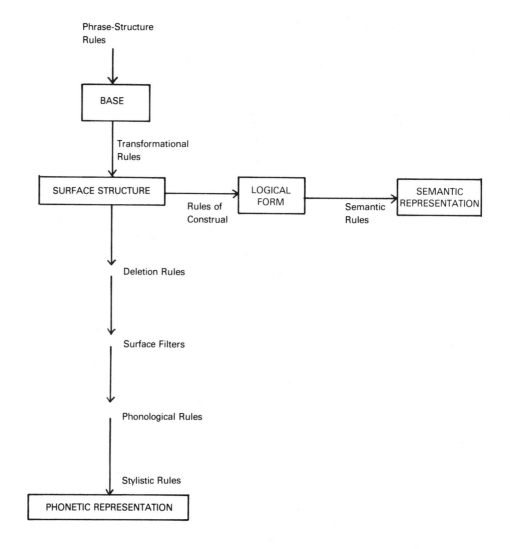

Figure 1.15   Late 1970s Picture of Chomsky's Conception of Grammatical Organization

and ordering of notions that have been discussed for a number of years. The important point in looking at yet another of Chomsky's theories is that linguistics is still a very dynamic field; there is much dispute over the proper approaches and methods for describing language. And, there will continue to be disagreement as the field progresses.

TEXT LINGUISTICS

All the grammars thus far described, fall into a category referred to as *sentence grammar*, in that the maximum unit of analysis dealt with is the sentence. Another approach to handling natural language is *text linguistics*, which produces *text grammars*, to deal with natural language. The objection that text linguists have with the Chomsky-style grammars is that often the meaning of a sentence cannot be determined from that sentence standing alone, and therefore the context of the sentence must be considered. For example, the sentence,

> He went there later.

does not reveal *who* we are talking about nor *where* he went nor *later* than what. However, if the sentence occurs in the context below, we know all these things.

> John told me that he was going to play tennis this morning, and I asked him if he would pick up the flowers for the party on the way back. He said he had promised to help Joe fix his car. But he did get to the florist. He went there later.

The context provides the information needed to interpret the individual sentence. Thus, for much use of natural language, looking at only one sentence will not reveal all the meaning contained in the sentence.

The notion of text as used in text linguistics refers to linguistic units larger than sentences which have structural aspects as phrases, clauses, and sentences do. One of these larger units is called a *discourse*. The study of discourse attempts to determine the well-formedness and appropriateness of a particular discourse, just as the application of grammars to sentences identifies them as well-formed and appropriate. The basic difference in text linguistics is the concept that text is more than sequences of sentences to be considered one by one. Rather text has its own structure and meaning which can be ascertained by the application of the proper rules.

Later chapters will reveal that interpreting language must often move not only beyond the sentence, but sometimes beyond the text itself to *understand* the language. However, since this book is an introduction to the subject and cannot possibly include all the techniques for and theories about manipulating natural language, the emphasis will be on sentence grammars and at appropriate points the weaknesses of that approach. Methods for using techniques of various sorts to represent the meaning of sentences and the knowledge derived from them will be examined in some detail.

Part II

Natural Language
Input and Output

Chapter 2

Text
Processing

Much of the information processed by computers is *text*, data of the type generally called *character* or *alphanumeric*. In natural language processing, all written material is text. Therefore, text processing and the input and output of text are important subjects in this book. This chapter will consider the general characteristics of textual material; equipment used for I/O, transmission, and storage of text; and some basic techniques for processing text.

CHARACTERISTICS OF TEXT

Dealing with text is both simpler and harder than manipulating numeric data. In terms of the physical characteristics, it is simpler in that text is linear; the first character is handled, then the second, then the third, until the last is reached. At that point the data is processed. But in logical terms, text is quite slippery. Generally, in the computer, numeric data is represented in a specific form: a number is given a fixed quantity of bits and a set format. All integers occupy the same amount of storage in memory in a particular computer, as do real numbers. (Of course, extended precision may increase the amount, but it is still a fixed amount.) Text, on the other hand, is made up of words and names and other strings of characters, which are many different lengths, and thus require differing amounts of memory for storage.

Connected text, such as this paragraph which you are reading, can be handled as a linear string of characters, then broken up into words of varying length, which could then be processed. A *word* is defined in text processing as the string of characters, usually alphabetic, that fall between *delimiters*: blanks, commas, periods, parentheses, and any other allowable punctuation marks that indicate the end of a word. This definition covers some forms of text besides connected text, such as business letters and mailing lists containing names and addresses, or bibliographic data with various fields separated by specific punctuation marks. Much of this type of data is not referred to as natural language because it is not in sentence form. However, parts of some fields look very much like natural language, such as titles of books. This type of textual data has been the primary object of text editors and word processing systems without much concern for the language involved. As we shall see in this chapter, many of the techniques for handling both types of data are the same, up to a point. Beyond that point, processing textual data requires an understanding of the language in which the information is expressed. This chapter will consider only the similarities: general text processing, the mechanics of dealing with text. The problems of understanding the language will be dealt with later.

STORAGE REQUIREMENTS FOR TEXT

Character information is usually stored with one character per byte or word. Sometimes the data must be packed to eliminate wasted space. For example in Pascal, character data is usually stored one character per word. If an array of characters is defined as packed, then it is stored one character per byte. The particular code for representing character data depends on the computer. The most common codes are ASCII, EBCDIC, and 6-bit BCD. Figure 2.1 shows these three codes. ASCII is a seven-bit code and can thus represent 128 different characters. Since no computer uses seven-bit bytes, on a machine with an 8-bit byte, ASCII allows an extra bit for whatever purpose the computer designers choose. On the Apple II computers, for example, the extra bit indicates normal (white on black) or *reverse video* (black on white). EBCDIC is an 8-bit code, designed originally by IBM for their System 360, the first computer to use 8-bit bytes. The 8-bit code allows for 256 combinations, or 256 different characters. The 6-bit BCD code allows 64 characters, which was somewhat restrictive for text processing. People complained about not having lower case letters and a larger choice of special symbols. In addition to these three common codes, there are other methods of encoding character data, as we shall see.

A major problem with text data is the incredible volume one must work with. So far this chapter, up through the end of the previous paragraph, contains over 4,000 characters, which is close to 4K of memory or secondary storage. If one assumes that a printed page of text in a book contains fifty lines, with an average of seventy-five characters per line, one page would occupy 3,750 characters or about 3.6K bytes. A 64K memory would hold about seventeen and a half pages; a 2.4M disk would hold 640 pages; and a 10M disk, 2,666 pages. Obviously text data takes up a lot of space.

CHAR-ACTER	ASCII	EBCDIC	BCD	CHAR-ACTER	ASCII	EBCDIC	BCD
a	01100001	10000001		F	01000110	11000110	110110
b	01100010	10000010		G	01000111	11000111	110111
c	01100011	10000011		H	01001000	11001000	111000
d	01100100	10000100		I	01001001	11001001	111001
e	01100101	10000101		J	01001010	11010001	100001
f	01100110	10000110		K	01001011	11010010	100010
g	01100111	10000111		L	01001100	11010011	100011
h	01101000	10001000		M	01001101	11010100	100100
i	01101001	10001001		N	01001110	11010101	100101
j	01101010	10010001		O	01001111	11010110	100110
k	01101011	10010010		P	01010000	11010111	100111
l	01101100	10010011		Q	01010001	11011000	101000
m	01101101	10010100		R	01010010	11011001	101001
n	01101110	10010101		S	01010011	11100010	010010
o	01101111	10010110		T	01010100	11100011	010011
p	01110000	10010111		U	01010101	11100100	010100
q	01110001	10011000		V	01010110	11100101	010101
r	01110010	10011001		W	01010111	11100110	010110
s	01110011	10100010		X	01011000	11100111	010111
t	01110100	10100011		Y	01011001	11101000	011000
u	01110101	10100100		Z	01011010	11101001	011001
v	01110110	10100101		0	00110000	11110000	000000
w	01110111	10100110		1	00110001	11110001	000001
x	01111000	10100111		2	00110010	11110010	000010
y	01111001	10101000		3	00110011	11110011	000011
z	01111010	10101001		4	00110100	11110100	000100
A	01000001	11000001	110001	5	00110101	11110101	000101
B	01000010	11000010	110010	6	00110110	11110110	000110
C	01000011	11000011	110011	7	00110111	11110111	000111
D	01000100	11000100	110100	8	00111000	11111000	001000
E	01000101	11000101	110101	9	00111001	11111001	001001

Figure 2.1   ASCII, EBCDIC, 6-bit BCD

Data Compression

Various solutions are available for solving the problems of the immense storage requirements of textual data in addition to ever increasing memory capacity. One is data compression, storing character data in less than the usual amount of space. Let's take EBCDIC on the System 370 as an example. There are only 99 symbols assigned out of the 256 combinations available. Only seven bits are required to represent those graphics. Since 26 of the symbols represent lower case letters, while another 26 represent upper case letters, quite a bit of redundancy exists in the 99 symbols. If a scheme is used to require two symbols for a capital letter, such that the first symbol indicates that the following symbol represents a capital letter and any character not preceded by the capitalization symbol is lower case, then the need for two sets of letters is eliminated. The basic set of codes required for the character set is reduced by 26, leaving 73. We have eliminated the second set of characters by using one additional character to indicate capitalization. If we eliminate some of the graphics not used in text (the APL symbols, for instance) and use one of the combinations as the *next-character-is-capitalized* symbol, then we can represent most of the 99 symbols with only six bits, saving 25 percent on every character. Figure 2.2 shows one possible set of six-bit codes for the character set. Since most input and output will require the 8-bit code, the input will have to be translated to the 6-bit representation for internal storage and then retranslated for output. This translation process might have to be done in machine-level code, since many high-level languages do not allow manipulation within a byte of storage. The savings in space can frequently make up for the increase in processing time.

Exercise: Write an algorithm for converting a regular character set (ASCII or EBCDIC) to compressed code.

Huffman Code

Another method for compressing data is based on the frequency of occurrence of each of the characters. If the letter E occurs most often, as it does in English, then E is stored in the fewest number of bits possible, and the other characters take more bits in order of their frequency. Therefore in English the letters J, Z, and Q, would take the most bits. Figure 2.3 contains a chart of the frequency of letters and the space for English text [1]. The code, called a Huffman code, is variable length, with the digits at the beginning of each code unique. These beginning digits can thus be used to distinguish among the characters. See Figure 2.4 for the Huffman codes generated from the list of frequencies in Figure 2.3. To show how the code works, let us look at an example. The word, *eagle*, would be encoded

000101111000010100000

Deciphering the code starts with looking for the shortest sequence of bits that form a valid combination. In this string, 000 is the code for the letter *e*. Starting from there, no three-bit code can be found so we look for a four-bit code and find 1011 for the letter *a*. We now have the following bits left:

CHARACTER	BINARY CODE	CHARACTER	BINARY CODE
space	000000	0	100000
a	000001	1	100001
b	000010	2	100010
c	000011	3	100011
d	000100	4	100100
e	000101	5	100101
f	000110	6	100110
g	000111	7	100111
h	001000	8	101000
i	001001	9	101001
j	001010	?	101010
k	001011	[	101011
l	001100	]	101100
m	001101	∧	101101
n	001110	—	101110
o	001111	'	101111
p	010000	!	110000
q	010001	"	110001
r	010010	#	110010
s	010011	$	110011
t	010100	%	110100
u	010101	&	110101
v	010110	'	110110
w	010111	(	110111
x	011000	)	111000
y	011001	*	111001
z	011010	+	111010
:	011011	,	111011
;	011100	–	111100
<	011101	.	111101
=	011110	/	111110
>	011111	next-char-caps	111111

Figure 2.2   Possible Character Set of Six-Bit Codes

11000010100000

Next we find no three, four, or five-bit code, but looking for a six-bit combination, the letter *g* is found. Then 10100 for the letter *l*, and we are left with only 000 for the letter *e*. Twenty-one bits were needed to contain the code for the word, *eagle*. Five 8-bit bytes would require 40 bits. If another fixed format had been used, with 27 characters, five bits would be required to store each

A	6.22
B	1.32
C	3.11
D	2.97
E	10.53
F	1.68
G	1.65
H	3.63
I	6.14
J	0.06
K	0.31
L	3.07
M	2.48
N	5.73
O	6.06
P	1.89
Q	0.10
R	5.87
S	5.81
T	7.68
U	2.27
V	0.70
W	1.13
X	0.25
Y	1.07
Z	0.06
(Space)	18.21

Figure 2.3   Frequency of Letters and Space (Adapted from Tanenbaum p. 38.)

character, and the word, *eagle* would take 25 bits. Twenty-one bits rather than 25 bits is a savings of 16 percent on this one word alone, and nearly 50 percent savings over a standard 8-bit code.

Exercise: Calculate the number of bits required to encode a piece of text containing 10,000 characters with the various characters occurring with the frequencies shown in Figure 2.3.

Exercise: Devise a Huffman code for a character set containing letters, numbers, and punctuation marks. Determine the frequencies from a sample text of at least 1000 words. One source that explains how to determine a Huffman code is Section 2.3.5 of *Structured Computer Organization* by Andrew S. Tanenbaum (Prentice-Hall, 1976). Calculate the savings of encoding the sample text in your Huffman code over using a 6-bit code and an 8-bit code.

CHARACTER	%	HUFFMAN CODE
(Space)	18.21	111
E	10.53	000
T	7.68	1101
A	6.22	1011
I	6.14	1001
O	6.06	1000
R	5.87	0111
S	5.81	0110
N	5.73	0100
H	3.63	11001
C	3.11	10101
L	3.07	10100
D	2.97	01011
M	2.48	00111
U	2.27	00110
P	1.89	00100
F	1.68	110001
G	1.65	110000
B	1.32	010100
W	1.13	001011
Y	1.07	001010
V	0.70	0101010
K	0.31	01010110
X	0.25	010101110
Q	0.10	0101011110
J	0.06	01010111110
Z	0.06	01010111111

Figure 2.4   Huffman Code for Frequency of Characters in Figure 2.3

Word Frequency Code

Another way to minimize the amount of storage taken by natural language data, is based on word frequency rather than character frequency. Several studies have been made of the words which are used most frequently in the English language, based on large amounts of text from various sources: literature, periodicals, etc. One of these studies produced the following list of the thirty most commonly used words: the, of, and, to, a, in, that, is, was, it, for, he, as, with, be, on, I, his, at, by, had, this, not, but, from, have, are, which, her, and she. [2] If each of these words were given one of the unused combinations in the 7- or 8-bit codes, then these commonly used words would be stored in a shorthand form which occupies only one character. Since each of the one-character shorthand codes would represent a word, the delimiters around them could be eliminated and they could serve as delimiters themselves. Even though most of these words are short, since they occur frequently and require no delimiters, replacing them with a one-byte code saves considerable storage.

Exercise: Select unused codes to represent these thirty function words, and encode a sample text. Determine the amount of savings in storage space. Is the saving worth the encoding and decoding? What effect would using both data compression and function word substitution have on storage saving? on processing time?

VARIABILITY OF TEXT

In addition to the problem of storage requirements, text also has the characteristic that it is variable. If it is continuous text, such as a story, it is made up of words of varying lengths, of sentences, phrases, and clauses of varying numbers of words, and varying numbers of paragraphs, pages, chapters, and so on. If the text is unconnected text, such as a name and address file or bibliographic reference, the fields within the record are often different lengths. In addition, there are often different fields required for different types of records in such data. For example, most addresses take three lines, but some take four or more. Some people use only first and last names, others use first and last names and a middle initial, and some have four names. In some instances, such as bibliographic references, many fields are optional. Look at the following examples of references:

> Robert F. Simmons, "Semantic Networks: Their Computation and Use for Understanding English Sentences," in *Computer Models of Language and Thought*, edited by Roger C. Schank and Kenneth Mark Colby (San Francisco, 1973).

> Mitchell Marcus, *A Theory of Syntactic Recognition for Natural Language* (Cambridge, Massachusetts, 1980).

> James L. Peterson, "Computer Programs for Detecting and Correcting Spelling Errors," *Communications of ACM*, Vol. 23, No. 12 (December, 1980), 676-687.

The first two of these refer to books, the first to a specific chapter in a collection; the other to a book written by a single author. The first requires a field for author and a field for editor (in this case multiple editors), two title fields, in addition to the date and location of publication. The second has no editor and only one title. The third cites an article in a journal, requiring two titles, volume number, issue, and page numbers. Thus, the format for bibliographic references must be quite flexible, in terms of variable length fields and also variable inclusion of fields.

Several methods for representing these variable features are available. One common method involves choosing a fixed size for a set number of fields, so that the data is coded to fit the format. This approach is commonly seen on forms that have a fixed number of squares in which data is to be recorded. If the systems analyst designing an application has decided that last names have ten characters, *Williamson* is in luck, *Jones* wastes five spaces, and *Dangerfield* gets no respect, the last letter must be chopped off. With this approach, every possible field must be included and left blank if it is not needed. Obviously, using a fixed format for variable data is not practical, in many circumstances.

If the application of the variable length data requires non-sequential access, which it frequently does, the implementation of the variable length format may take up as much storage as fixed format. For example, many file systems set up all variable length records in an area equal to the length of the longest individual record, thus requiring maximum amount of space. This problem can be overcome by adding the methods discussed in this section to the file management system, if they are not already included.

Having the text data represented in variable-length form is more efficient in terms of storage space, but will require more processing to access the fields or individual units in the data. Let us consider bibliographical references. If each reference is created as a separate record, then we can consider the record as a long string of characters, as many as needed for the particular reference. But there are many different fields to be distinguished. One method would be to use delimiters, characters which will not appear in the data used to indicate the end of the field. Thus, the program to access the fields begins with the first character and scans for the delimiter, counting each character as it scans. When a delimiter is encountered, the end of the field is found, and the number of characters in the field is known. Then the next field begins, and so on. If there are some fields which are not included in a particular reference, the delimiters would fall together with nothing separating them, thus indicating a null or empty field. In our example, a slash (/) is used to delimit fields, and the following fields are allowed, in this order:

Author

Editor

Primary title (of book or periodical)

Secondary title (of chapter or article)

Date of Publication

Place of Publication

Volume

Edition (or Number for periodicals)

Page numbers

The first citation given above would be encoded as:

/Robert F. Simmons/Roger C. Schank & Kenneth Mark Colby/Computer Models of Language and Thought/Semantic Networks: Their Computation and Use for Understanding Natural Language/1973/ San Francisco////

The second would be:

/Mitchell Marcus//A Theory of Syntactic Recognition for Natural Language//1980/Cambridge, Massachusetts////

The journal article would be as follows:

/James L. Peterson//Communications of ACM/Computer Programs for Detecting and Correcting Spelling Errors/ December 1980//23/12/676-687/

Less storage is required for each reference than with fixed format, and the delimiters do not take up many characters. Therefore it is efficient in terms of space requirements. However, each character must be accessed individually to find the various fields, a procedure that would be expensive in terms of processing time. And, keeping up with which field is being processed can be tricky. A method for indicating which fields are included in a particular record is a *bit map*. In a bit map one bit (binary digit) or Boolean variable is used to represent each field. If the field is in the particular reference, the corresponding bit is set on (to one); if it is not included, the bit is set off (to zero). The bit map is placed at the beginning of the record and is therefore accessible before any of the fields are processed. The specific form of the bit map is dependent upon the programming language and the computer system. If we use a string of one's and zero's to represent the bits, the bit maps for our three citations would be:

1) 111111000

2) 101011000

3) 101110111

Thus the author, editor, primary title, secondary title, date of publication, and place of publication are included in the first reference, but not the volume, edition, and page numbers, and so on.

A difficulty that the current format has is the problem of not knowing the length of a field without scanning the whole field. Rather than having just delimiters, we can add the field length at the beginning as well. Assuming we use a bit map also, our previous citations might be encoded as follows:

111111000/17/Robert F. Simmons/38/Roger C. Schank and Kenneth Mark Colby/39/Computer Models of Language and Thought/80/Semantic Networks: Their Computation and Use for Understanding English Sentences/4/1973/13/San Francisco/

Notice that delimiters (slashes) must be added around the field lengths, since some numeric data occurs in the record, and unused fields are not included. Processing the fields would require reference to the bit map to know which field was next.

Exercise: Design a format that uses field length instead of a bit map. Are delimiters still needed between fields? What is another solution to the problem?

MARC FORMAT AND WEBMARC

A format designed to handle the various problems of dealing with text was developed by the U.S. Library of Congress MARC (MAchine Readable Catalog) Project in 1967. The MARC format has been used for a variety of library projects including communication and information exchange among the many libraries with machine readable information. Donald Sherman adapted the MARC format for recording dictionary data, specifically Webster's Seventh Collegiate Dictionary (known as W7), which was originally recorded in machine-readable form by the Lexicographical Project at SDC. WEBMARC, Sherman's version of W7 in MARC format, contains 68,657 entries, each stored as a variable-length record representing the information about one word in the dictionary. To quote Sherman,

> The organization of MARC structure records is divided into three distinct areas: *leader*, *directory*, and *data fields*. The leader is an initial fixed area, and contains general record status and identification information. The directory functions as a table of contents which inventories all the data fields in a record. The motivation for an independent directory is to simplify first level retrieval operations. The final record area contains only data fields, with one data field corresponding to each directory entry. The first two characters of each data field are reserved for indicator codes; the remainder of the field contains the texts and codes which comprise the data base. [3]

In WEBMARC, the leader is the first 24 characters in each record and contains fixed-length fields recording the record length, status (F for full record), source of data (W7), record extension number (usually 0, for non-extended record, 1, 2, ... for entry requiring more space than one physical record), an address pointer to the data part of the record, and a record identification number. The record directory follows the leader and is made up of a series of fixed-length (12 character) segments containing a tag identifying each part of the lexical entry, the address of the first character in that part, and the length of that part. The tag fields are three-digit numbers, the first digit of which identifies the type of the field. See Figure 2.5 for the table of tags. The main spelled form of the entry is always 100, the definition is 200, and so on. Variant forms of the main entry are identified by adding to the unit's position of the tag; run-on entries by adding to the ten's position of the tag. A sample directory segment from the word, *abaca*, is

```
100 0014 00022
```

The main spelling entry starts in the fourteenth position relative to the beginning of the data area and extends for 22 positions.

The data area is broken up into subfields with a variety of codes for identifying the subfields. The subfield begins with a two-character indicator to describe the information in the field, then follows a subfield code identifying the data in the subfield, and then the data element, which is variable length and terminated by a field terminator code. The subfields included in a field depend upon the type of field. For example, the spelling field contains the general word class as the two-character indicator; the subfields are the spelled form of the entry in upper-case, the hyphenation points in the word, accent mark information, alternate word class code and a status byte, indication of type of entry (e.g., slang, dialect, etc.), and information about variants (if the entry is a variant of another entry). The field containing the definition has subfields to give sense number, text of the definition, synonymous cross-reference, usage notes, and so forth. The full pronunciation field contains appropriate subfields. Other fields are included for synonomy, etymology, and partial pronunciation.

The WEBMARC format illustrates several of the methods described for recording variable data, such as dictionary entries and bibliographical citations. It is not especially efficient in that no data compression is used and many of the code fields take up more space than required. The description given here ignores many details to concentrate on the format scheme.

Exercise: Design a simplified dictionary format for recording the spelled form, hyphenation points, general word class (part of speech), definition, and synonyms, using the methods discussed in this chapter for using available storage space as efficiently as possible. Record a sample of entries by choosing words from a dictionary.

Exercise: Discuss the tradeoffs in storage space versus processing time involved in the various schemes for recording text data described in this chapter.

EQUIPMENT FOR TEXT I/O

From the earliest days of computers, most input and output was in character form. Teletype, paper tape, and of course, punched cards were, for many years, the primary means of communicating with computers. In each of these

DATA CATEGORIES

ENTRY TYPES	SPELLED FORM	DEFINITION	FULL PHONETIC	PARTIAL PHONETIC	ETYMOLOGY	SYNONYM
main	100	200	400	800	600	500
1st variant	101		401	801		
2nd variant	102		402	802		
.	.		.	.		
.	.		.	.		
.	.		.	.		
1st run-on	110	210	410	810		
2nd run-on	120	220	420	820		
.	.	.	.	.		
.	.	.	.	.		
.	.	.	.	.		

(a)

Spelled Form (tags 100, 101, 110 . . .)
$a — spelled form
$b — hyphenation points
$c — accent codes
$d — alternate word class status
$e — alternate word class code
$i — variant type
$s — variant status
$1 — label
indicators — word class code

Definition (tags 200, 210 . . .)
$a — sense and subsense data
$d — text of single definiens
$1 — label
$s — synonymous cross-reference
$u — usage note
$v — verbal illustration
$w — directional cross-reference type
$x — directional cross-reference word
indicators — word class code

Full Phonetic (tags 400, 401, 410 . . .)
$a — 1st consonant cluster
$b — 1st vowel cluster
$c — 2nd consonant cluster
$d — 2nd vowel cluster
.   .
.   .
.   .
$v — optional segment code
$w — label
$x — vowel nasalization code
$y — syllable division code
$z — canonical word shape code
1st indicator — stress position
2nd indicator — number of syllables

Synonym (tag 500)
$a — text of synonym paragraph
$w — type of synonymy cross-reference
$x — synonymy cross-reference word
indicators — blank

Etymology (tag 600)
$a — text of etymology paragraph
indicators — blank

(b)

Figure 2.5   (a) Table of WEBMARC Tags. (b) Outline of WEBMARC Subfields

devices, a code was used to represent each individual character, which was internally converted to whatever form was necessary for processing. Even numeric information was recorded as strings of numeric characters, then converted in the computer to fixed-point binary or floating-point representation. Printers were frequently not even attached to computers, but might be available for listing the contents of punched cards. (One device for listing the contents of cards was the IBM 407 Accounting Machine, which was often retained for that purpose after its accounting days were past.) More recent computer systems use interactive terminals, some producing hard-copy much as a printer does, but many displaying character output on a CRT screen.

All of the input devices mentioned have one characteristic in common; they all require a human to visually read the original source data and translate it into machine readable form by striking the appropriate keys of a keyboard attached to a recording device. An alternative to human keying of data is optical input, in which a machine "sees" and records the characters without human intervention. Devices to sense the presence or absence of marks in specific locations on a sheet of paper have been available for many years. We are undoubtedly all familiar with standardized tests requesting us not to make stray marks, to fill in the space completely, and to erase thoroughly. These instructions are intended to produce acceptable input for mark-sense readers. More sophisticated optical devices recognize characters as well as marks: numbers and letters, primarily. Some of them can handle handprinted characters with somewhat lower reliability, but handwriting, or cursive writing, is still too complex to decipher. One device that *reads* characters in many different type styles (called *type fonts*) is the Kurzweil Reading Machine. One version of the Kurzweil machine designed to aid the visually-impaired reads the text and *speaks* the words, albeit in a very strange voice. Other versions of the Kurzweil are being used as input devices to a computer system to translate large volumes of textual data into computer readable form. The Oxford University Computing Centre and the Brigham Young University Humanities Research Center are using them to read literary material into the system. Since the Kurzweil goes through a "training session" during which characters that it does not recognize can be identified for it, the reading machine is capable of reading text in many different fonts.

Whatever form of input is used for getting text data into a computer system, once it is there, it can be stored as text data or converted into another form, such as one of the numeric representations or a compressed form to conserve space. It can be processed in memory or placed in secondary storage (disk, tape, bubble memory, etc.) for retention. If the data needs to be available for human reading, it must be output in an appropriate form, which is a visual image such as characters printed on paper or displayed on a video screen.

In this chapter so far, we have made two assumptions: first, that the data we are concerned with is in written form rather than spoken form and second, that the language of concern is English. Assuming that the data is in English oversimplifies the situation in that the English writing system allows words to be written as a linear string of characters. In languages such as Chinese or Japanese that use pictographs, transcribing text is an entirely different matter. In addition to the pictographs, the Japanese language has an alternate writing system called Katakana, in which the syllables of the spoken word are transcribed. Katakana is easily transformed into computer readable form, but it is not the preferred method of writing for most Japanese people. Perhaps a graphic input and output system which refers to the larger meaning constructs of the pictographs would be more appropriate for such languages.

Exercise: Consider the problems of input and output of a language which uses a non-Roman alphabet, such as Arabic or Cyrillic. What problems are associated with optical reading of such a language? How has the problem been solved by people using the language?

Exercise: Design a method for input and output of a pictographic language, such as Chinese or Egyptian hieroglyphics. Investigate books or articles written describing other schemes for dealing with such languages.

TEXT PROCESSING TECHNIQUES

Representation of textual data in a particular programming language is dependent upon the data types and structures provided by the language. Some languages include a full complement of string manipulation features for defining and operating upon strings as dynamically defined variable-length data structures. Many languages, however, do not handle strings as built into the language, and text data must be defined with arrays of characters. Because only a few recently designed computers recognize strings as a hardware feature, in most implementations at the primitive level, strings will be handled as successive bytes of characters. The question of whether string definitions and functions are provided by the programming language or defined by the programmer is a matter of who does the work. Of course, it is easier for the programmer if the language defines the features, but sometimes the language which must be used does not have the functions needed.

The characteristics of text described earlier, relate to the data types and functions required for manipulating text. At the lowest level, a character must be defined, with a specific set of graphic symbols and other necessary codes corresponding to each of the bit combinations allowed in a character. For example, in a Pascal implementation which uses the ASCII character set, defining a variable as

```
var ch : char
```

allocates a whole word, then uses only one byte of that word for the character. The use of ASCII determines the set of graphics—letters, numbers, and special characters—available, and also determines the collating sequence: the order in which the codes occur in the set of characters relative to the beginning of the set. The position of a character in the set is the *ordinal* value of the character. See Figure 2.6 for the ordinal values for the ASCII character set. The collating sequence allows relational comparisons to be made: is ch equal to G, is ch greater than Z and so forth.

In addition to the basic character type, data structures holding characters must be definable. The most common is the array of characters:

```
var line : array[1..80] of char;
```

Here line is defined as an array of 80 elements, each of which is a character. Generally, accessing line is limited to one element of the array at a time so reading character values from a line of data into line for example, would require a repetition:

```
var i : integer;
    line : array[1..80] of char;
    .
    .
    .
    for i := 1 to 80 do
       read(line[i]);
    readln;
```

(The readln with no parameter list is required in Pascal to advance to the next line of input data.) Defining the array as packed would conserve storage space, but would not necessarily change the processing required. Some implementations of Pascal do allow a packed array of characters to be read with a single statement:

```
var line : packed array[1..80] of char;
    i : integer;
    .
    .
    .
    readln (line);
```

A major problem with defining text data as we just did is that an array is static and usually fixed length. The memory required for static data is allocated at the beginning of execution of the program (or a module within the program), and a fixed number of bytes are provided, which will remain allocated whether they are needed or not. But text is not static nor is it fixed length, usually. Therefore, another representation would be better.

Languages which define strings as a built-in data type provide the flexibility needed. Using UCSD Pascal which includes strings as a built-in data type, our previous example would be:

CHARACTER	ORDINAL VALUE	CHARACTER	ORDINAL VALUE	ORDINAL CHARACTER	VALUE
NUL	0	+	43	V	86
SOH	1	,	44	W	87
STX	2	–	45	X	88
ETX	3	.	46	Y	89
EOT	4	/	47	Z	90
ENQ	5	0	48	[	91
ACK	6	1	49	\	92
BEL	7	2	50	]	93
BS	8	3	51	∧	94
HT	9	4	52	—	95
LF	10	5	53	,	96
VT	11	6	54	a	97
FF	12	7	55	b	98
CR	13	8	56	c	99
SO	14	9	57	d	100
SI	15	:	58	e	101
DLE	16	;	59	f	102
DC1	17	<	60	g	103
DC2	18	=	61	h	104
DC3	19	>	62	i	105
DC4	20	?	63	j	106
NAK	21	@	64	k	107
SYN	22	A	65	l	108
ETB	23	B	66	m	109
CAN	24	C	67	n	110
EM	25	D	68	o	111
SUB	26	E	69	p	112
ESC	27	F	70	q	113
FS	28	G	71	r	114
GS	29	H	72	s	115
RS	30	I	73	t	116
US	31	J	74	u	117
SP	32	K	75	v	118
!	33	L	76	w	119
"	34	M	77	x	120
#	35	N	78	y	121
$	36	O	79	z	122
%	37	P	80	{	123
&	38	Q	81	~	124
'	39	R	82	}	125
(	40	S	83		126
)	41	T	84	DEL	127
*	42	U	85		

Figure 2.6   Ordinal Values of ASCII Character Set

```
var line : string;
      .
      .
      .
readln (line);
```

Since **string** is a built-in type, then **line** can be treated as one element. The storage required for a string is allocated at the time it is needed (rather than at the beginning of execution of the program or module) and the number of bytes allocated is determined by the value being assigned. Thus if **line** were 80 characters long, 80 bytes would be allocated; if **line** were 12 characters long, only 12 bytes would be allocated. A string in UCSD Pascal is represented as a packed array of characters, thus conserving storage, and there are built-in functions for manipulating strings.

Everyone is familiar with the basic operations applied to numbers: addition, subtraction, multiplication, division, and relational comparisons of equality, greater than, less than, and so on. There are also primitive operations for string data, ways of operating on the data to break it up and put the pieces together in various ways. The basic operations on strings are:

Creation of the string

Determining the length of the string

Concatenation of two or more strings

Pattern matching

Relational operations

Creation of a string involves allocating storage and assigning a value to a string, which can be done with the assignment operation:

```
var  str : string;
      .
      .
str := 'any characters';
```

A string can also be created by an input operation:

```
var str : string;
      .
      .
readln(str);
```

The string created by assignment or input occupies only the number of bytes equal to the number of characters in the string; therefore, a function to return the length of a string provides access to the number of characters in the string at a specific moment that the **length** function is invoked. The **length** function returns an integer value, since it is a count of the number of characters.

Putting strings together is called concatenation, which means to link together as in a chain. Concatenation joins two strings, the second is linked onto the end of the first to form a new string, the length of which is the sum of the lengths of the original strings. For example, if we define two strings and assign values,

```
var sl,s2 : string

sl := 'abcd'; (* length = 4 *)

s2 := 'xyz'; (* length = 3 *)
```

then by concatenating s1 and s2, the resulting string is abcdxyz which has a length of 7.

When text data is fixed-format, i.e., when a particular piece of information is always at the same location in the string relative to the beginning of the string, breaking strings up only involves knowing the exact position of the information in question. However, since most text processing deals with data which is both variable length and variable format, breaking the text into its constituent parts requires the operation of pattern matching. An example using pattern matching is manipulation of a string containing a name, entered last name first followed by a comma, as in:

Jones, Susan M.

Locating the comma in the string determines the position of the last character of the last name. In most implementations of strings, a primitive form of pattern matching is used to provide the location of the beginning of a pattern; this operation is called position or index and returns an integer value. Thus if name is defined and assigned a value,

```
var name :   string

name := 'Jones, Susan M.'
```

then the position of the comma , within name is 6. Using the value 6, the substrings preceding and following the comma can be copied (using the copy or substring function) into other strings to be processed. To illustrate:

```
var name,last,first : string;
    index : integer;

begin
    name := 'Jones, Susan M.';
    index := pos(',',name);
    last := copy(name,1,index-1);
    first := copy(name,index+2,length(name)-index-1);
    writeln('First Name: ',first);
    writeln('Last Name : ',last)
end.
```

This segment of code would print:

```
First Name: Susan M.
Last Name : Jones
```

Further processing could divide up the field first into first name and middle initial by scanning for blanks, if more breakdown were needed.

In some programming languages such as SNOBOL and ICON, pattern matching functions are quite involved, in that in addition to matching a pattern, the pattern can be replaced by some other string. Also patterns can be quite complex with *wild card* options and alternative selection of parts of the pattern. We will look at some examples later in the chapter.

Relational operations for string data are comparable to those for numeric data.

=	equality
<>	inequality
<	less than (the left comparand is closer to the beginning of the collating sequence than the right comparand)
>	greater than (the left comparand is farther from the beginning of the collating sequence than the right comparand)
<=	less than or equal to
>=	greater than or equal to

Strings can be tested and manipulated accordingly. If we are processing a story that we know ends with the string, The End., then finding that string will indicate the terminating condition:

```
if text = 'The End.'
    then writeln('The story is completed');
```

Relational operations are required for many kinds of processing, including alphabetizing. If we are sorting names into alphabetical order, then comparing the names determines whether they are in proper sequence. For example, if we want to print two names in alphabetical order:

```
var name1, name2 : string;
    .
    .
    .
if name1 > name2
    then writeln(name2,name1)
    else writeln(name1,name2);
```

As we shall see in the examples, there are many reasons for needing the relational operations on strings.

UCSD PASCAL STRING FUNCTIONS

In UCSD Pascal a string is assumed to be a maximum of 80 characters unless a length indicator is included in the declaration:

```
var str1 : string;
    str2 : string[255];
    str3 : string[4];
```

Thus, str1 has a maximum length of 80 characters; str2, 255 characters; and str3, 4 characters. The absolute maximum string length allowed is 255 because the length will be stored in a single eight-bit byte. The built-in string functions defined in UCSD Pascal are concat, copy, insert, delete, pos, and length. They will be explained in turn. In all these examples, assume the following variable declarations:

```
var str1,str2,str3 : string;
    index1,index2 :   integer;
```

```
function concat (strs) :   string
```

The function concat can have any number of string arguments, variables, or constants, separated by commas; it returns a single string in which the string arguments have been concatenated in the order given in the function call.

If the following assignments are made:

```
str1 := 'data';
```

```
str2 := 'structures';
```

```
str3 := concat(str1,'#',str2)
```

str3 ends up having the value data#structures

```
function copy(strg, index, count) : string
```

Copy will return as its value the substring found starting at position index and extending for count characters. The arguments can be variables or constants.

```
str1 := 'artificial intelligence';
str2 := copy(str1,5,6);
```

The value in str2 is ficial.

```
procedure insert (substr, strg, index);
```

The substring substr is inserted into the target string strg at position index. For example,

```
strl := 'any string of characters';
insert('***',strl,8);
```

strl ends up with the value **any str***ing of characters**. Substr and index may be constants or variables; **strg**, the target string, must be a variable.

```
procedure delete (strg, index, count);
```

Delete removes characters from a string starting at the position **index**, removing **count** characters.

```
strl:='abracadabra';
delete(strl,2,5);
```

strl is left with the value **adabra** and a length of 6.

NOTE: Copy and **concat** are functions which return a string value; **insert** and **delete** are procedures which modify a string variable. The last two string functions **length** and **pos** return integer values because they refer to character positions in a string.

```
function length (strg) : integer;
```

The function **length** returns the number of characters in the string **strg** at that time. Because strings are variable length, **length** may return different values at different times as the value of the string changes.

```
strl := '9 letters';
i := length(strl);   (* i = 9 *)
strl := concat(strl,' or numbers');
i := length(strl);   (* i = 20 *)
```

```
function pos (substr, strg);
```

The function **pos** returns the character position of the substring **substr** within the string **strg**, if the substring is found. If it is not in the string, **pos** returns the value zero.

```
strl := 'elephant';
i := pos('ant',strl); (* i = 6 *)
j := pos('pant',strl); (* i = 0 *)
```

In addition to these functions and procedures for operating on strings, a string can also be indexed to return a single character within the string. Given these variables,

```
var strl : string;
    ch   : char;
```

then with the following statements:

```
str1 := 'abcd';
ch := str1[3];
```

the character in the third position, which is c, is assigned to ch.

IMPLEMENTING STRING FUNCTIONS WITH ARRAYS

Other programming languages which handle strings have different sets of functions, but the set included in UCSD Pascal is representative. However in programming languages which do not provide strings as a built-in type with built-in functions, including Standard Pascal, these functions can be simulated by the user with arrays of character.

First the data type string is defined:

```
const strlen = 80;
type string = record
                 str :  array[1..strlen] of char;
                 len :  integer
              end; (* string record *)
```

This declaration means that 80 positions will be allocated every time a string is declared. However, since the length field will contain the number of characters assigned in the "string", we can consider the definition *semi-static*; the storage allocated is static, but the data will be dealt with dynamically. Before a value is assigned to str within a string, the value of len is set to zero.

The first procedures to be defined are length, readstr, copystr, and writestr.

```
function length (s : string) : integer;
begin
   length := s.len
end; (* length *)
```

```
procedure readstr (var s : string);

var index : integer;

begin
  index := 0;
  while not(eoln(input)) do
     begin
        index := index + 1;
        read(s.str[index])
     end;
  readln;
  s.len := index-1
end; (* readstr *)
```

```
procedure writestr (s : string);

var index : integer;

begin
    if length(s) <> 0
      then for index := 1 to length(s) do
                write(s.str[index]);
    writeln
end;  (* writestr *)
```

Exercise: Note that readstr and writestr make certain assumptions about the position of a string; in both procedures the string being read or written is the only item on the line. Write additional procedures that would allow the programmer control over whether the string is on a line by itself or part of another line.

```
procedure copystr (var s1 : string;
                        s2 :  string;
                        index : integer;
                        count : integer);

var index1,index2 :  integer;

begin
    index2 := length(s2);
    if (index2 <> 0) and (index+count-1<index2)
      then begin
                index1 := 1;
                while (index <= count) do
                      begin
                          s1.str[index] := s2.str[index];
                          index1 := index1 + 1;
                          index := index + 1
                      end
                s1.len:= count
           end
      else begin
                writeln('error in copystr -- no copy done');
                s1.len := 0
           end;
end; (* copystr *)
```

Note that the copystr procedure functions like a regular assignment statement only in that one string can be assigned the value of another string. However, the copystr procedure cannot be used to assign a literal value to a string. Many versions of Pascal require that assigning a literal value to a string must be done one character at a time:

```
strl.str[1] := 'h';
strl.str[2] := 'a';
strl.str[3] := 'l';
strl.str[4] := 't';
strl.len := 4;
```

All these statements would be required to assign the value halt to strl. (With real string functions and some implementations of Pascal, this could be done with strl := 'halt', and the length would be handled automatically.) As we have defined the copystr procedure, the primary method for assigning a value to a string would be reading it in.

The concat procedure will use the function length defined previously. concat must be a procedure rather than a function because in Pascal, user-defined functions can only return simple data types and a string is not a simple data type. The value "returned" will be in strg.

```
procedure concat(var strg : string;
                     sl,s2 : string);

var indexl,index2,lenl,len2 :   integer;

begin
   lenl := length(sl);
   len2 := length(s2);
   (* copy first string *)
   for indexl := 1 to lenl do
       strg.str[indexl] := sl.str[indexl];
   indexl := lenl + 1;
   index2 := 1;
   repeat (* copy second string *)
      strg.str[indexl] := s2.str[index2];
      indexl := indexl + 1;
      index2 := index2 + 1
   until (index2>len2) or (indexl>strlen);
   (* set length of new string *)
   if lenl+len2 > strlen
     then begin
          writeln('error -- data lost in concatenation');
          strg.len := strlen
        end
     else strg.len := lenl + len2
end; (* concat *)
```

The procedures insert and delete will use previously defined functions and procedures.

```
procedure delete(var strg : string;
                     index : integer;
                     count : integer);
var sl,s2 :  string;
    index2 :  integer;
begin
  (* copy part before deletion *)
  copystr(sl,strg,1,index-1);

  (* copy part after deletion *)
  index2 := length(strg) - (index+count)+1;
  copystr(s2,strg,index+count,index2);

  (* concatenate two parts *)
  concat(strg,sl,s2)
end; (* delete *)
```

```
procedure insert(sub : string;
                    var strg : string;
                    index : integer);
var sl,s2 :  string;
    index2 :  integer;
begin
  (* copy part of original before insertion *)
  copystr(sl,strg,1,index-1);

  (* concatenate insertion *)
  concat(sl,sl,sub);f

  (* copy part of original after insertion *)
  index2 := length(strg) - index + 1;
  copystr(s2,strg,index,index2);

  (* concatenate all parts *)
  concat(strg,sl,s2)
end; (* insert *)
```

The function pos will determine the location of a substring within a string.

```
function pos (substr, strg : string) : integer;
var index1,index2,index3,index4 :  integer;
    match    : Boolean;
begin
  (* index4 :  last position in strg for substr to start *)
  index4 := length(strg) - length(substr) + 1;
```

```
pos := 0;
index1 := 1;
match := false;

repeat (* until match is found or end of string *)
    while (strg.str[index1]<>substr.str[1])
        and (index1 > index4) do
            index1 := index1 + 1;

    if index1 <= index4
    then begin
            index3 := index1; (* save position of first character *)
            match := true;
            while (index1 <= index2)
                and (index2<=length(substr))
                and match do
                  if (strg.str[index1] = substr.str[index2])
                    then (* characters match *)
                      begin
                          index1 := index1 + 1;
                          index2 := index2 + 1
                      end;
                    else match := false (* characters do not match *)
        end
until match
    or (index1 > index2);  (* end found before match *)

if match (* substr found in strg *)
    then pos := index3;
end; (* pos *)
```

Since the declaration of the string type sets the length of the array allocated to 80 characters, use of these functions certainly allows much less flexibility than real built-in strings. Every string will require 80 characters, no more, no less. It might be useful in some circumstances to implement short strings and long strings in addition: say, for example, strings of 16 characters for holding individual words, and strings of 255 characters for longer text. The functions would have to be modified or extended to handle the different lengths.

Exercise: Implement shortstrings with a maximum length of 16 characters, modifying the functions or creating new functions as necessary.

In addition to the functions defined above, relational operations are also necessary for any significant text processing. Therefore, three more functions will be discussed: eqstr, gtstr, and ltstr. These are all Boolean functions with two string arguments, returning true if the first string is equal to the second, greater than the second, or less than the second, respectively. If the appropriate condition does not hold, each function will return false.

```
function eqstr(sl,s2:string):Boolean;

var short,long,temp : integer;
    match : Boolean;

  function eqchrs:Boolean;
    var index : integer;
        eq : Boolean;

    begin
       eq := true;
       index := 1;
       repeat
         if sl.str[index] <> s2.str[index]
             then eq := false;
         index := index+1
       until (index>short) or not(eq);
       eqchrs := eq;
    end; (* eqchrs *)

  function blanks(strg:string): Boolean;
    var index :  integer;
        blnk :  Boolean;

    begin
       blnk := true;
       index := short + 1;
       while (index<long) and blnk do
           begin
             if strg.str[index] <> ' '
                 then blnk := false;
             index := index+1
           end;
         blanks := blnk
    end; (* blanks *)

begin
  long := length(sl);
  short:= length(s2);
  if long = short
     then match := eqchrs
     else if long > short
             then if eqchrs
                     then match := blanks(sl)
                     else match := false
                  else begin
                     temp  := long;
                     long  := short;
                     short := temp;
                     if eqchrs
                         then match := blanks(s2)
                     else match := false
                  end;
```

```
    eqstr := match
end; (* eqstr *)
```

Exercise: Write the following functions:

```
function gtstr(s1,s2:string):Boolean;

function ltstr(s1,s2:string):Boolean;
```

This set of pseudo-string functions will not be as useful as built-in string functions; however, having them will eliminate some of the tedium of implementing these operations over and over.

STRING PROCESSING LANGUAGES

Whereas most programming languages either have no string processing built in or allow strings as one of several data types, there are a few languages with strings as the primary data type, most notably SNOBOL and its successor, ICON. SNOBOL was developed in the early 1960's at Bell Telephone Laboratories; it was *a string manipulation language* designed to improve upon some of the inherent deficiencies of an earlier string-oriented language, COMIT. The version of SNOBOL now in general use is SNOBOL4. ICON is similar to SNOBOL, but includes more modern control structures. [4]

The basic statement in SNOBOL is in the format:

```
label string-reference pattern = replacement-expression :go-to
```

(The `string-reference` is also called the *subject*; the `replacement-expression` is also called the *object*.) Several parts of the basic statement are optional: `label`, `pattern`, and `go-to`. Any statement may be labeled by starting the `label` in the first position of a line. For example, in the following statement, `loop` is a label.

```
loop text = text word
```

An asterisk in the first position indicates the line consists only of a comment.

```
* this line is a comment.
```

A period in the first position indicates continuation of the previous line.

```
str1 '$' = str2 str3
                :(loop)
```

An unlabeled statement must begin past position one.

```
$str = $str + 1
```

`String-reference` indicates the string which is being operated upon; it can be a data name referring to a string or a more complex combination of references. The pattern is the sequence of characters being searched for in the string-reference. For example, in the statement below (assuming there is no label),

```
strl '**' . . . . .
```

the object of the operation is to locate the pattern of two successive asterisks in the string strl. If the pattern is found in the string, the pattern matching operation is said to succeed; otherwise it fails. An equal sign in a statement indicates the replacement operation. If the statement is in the form:

```
subject = object
```

the effect of the replacement is the same as assignment: the value of the subject is replaced by the value of the object. Thus

```
strl = 'abc**xyz'
```

assigns the literal value indicated to the string strl. If the pattern is included, then the part of the subject string being replaced is the substring matched by the pattern; if the pattern match fails, then no replacement occurs. Thus, if strl has been assigned the value abc**xyz, then the statement

```
strl '**' = '????'
```

would remove the two asterisks matched and replace them with the literal string ???? giving abc????xyz. Note that the length of the object does not have to be the same as the length of the substring matched. Another version of this statement has a blank object:

```
strl '???' =
```

The substring matched will be replaced by the null string; i.e., it will be deleted. Assuming strl had the value abc????xyz, the statement above would remove three of the four question marks, leaving strl as abc?xyz.

One important operation on strings is concatenation, which is indicated in SNOBOL by writing strings to be concatenated one after another with blanks separating them. In the sequence of statements,

```
str2 = 'data'
str2 = str2 ' structures'
```

the result in str2 is data structures. Thus the string structures is concatenated onto the original value assigned to str2. If a blank occurs immediately following the subject string (when there is no equal sign), the data object which follows is assumed to be a pattern. For example, in the statement,

```
str2 str3 . . .
```

str3 is a pattern which will be searched for in str2. In this instance the blank indicates pattern matching rather than concatenation.

A large part of the power of SNOBOL is derived from the various forms of patterns allowed. Patterns can be defined as variables and can be given names. Various alternative sequences of characters can be included in one pattern so that a single statement can check for several different combinations of characters at one time. For example,

```
patt = (',' | ';' | '.' | '?')
```

would match the first of any of the punctuation marks, ',', ';', '.', or '?'. Thus,

```
text patt =
```

would remove the first of those punctuation marks. In another example, the following sequence of statements,

```
patt = (','|';'|'.'|'?')
text = 'What? A boy, a baby boy.'
text patt =
```

would result in text being,

```
What A boy, a baby boy.
```

In order to remove all the punctuation, we must use the go-to part of a statement.

The go-to part of a SNOBOL statement is used to transfer control within the program; it can be an unconditional transfer:

```
text patt =    :(loop)
```

or a conditional transfer. Conditional transfers depend on the success or failure of the statement. For example, in the statement

```
str '$' =     :s(money)f(broke)
```

if the string str contains a dollar sign, it will be removed and control will be transferred to the statement with the label money. If the string does not contain a dollar sign, control will be transferred to the statement labeled broke. The following sequence of statements can be used to remove all punctuation marks from text as mentioned before.

```
     patt = (','|';'|'.'|'?')
     text = 'What?  Another silly, stupid example?'
loop text patt =       :s(loop)
```

The statement labeled loop will succeed as long as it finds a punctuation mark; when all punctuation has been removed, the statement will fail and continue to the next statement.

Statements can succeed or fail for a variety of reasons. In addition to pattern matching, there are numerous functions for string analysis and manipulation. The program segment below provides several examples.

```
      pat = break(',. ').word span(',. ')
begin text = text trim(input) ' ' :s(begin)
match text pat = dict word      :s(inc)
add   dict = dict word ' '
inc   $word = $word + 1          :(match)
```

The functions break and span are used to move the pointer through the subject string. Break finds the first instance of any of the characters indicated (here a comma, a period, or a blank), then places the substring preceding that character into the variable word. Span then moves the pointer past the character found. The statement labeled begin reads in all the data. The function input gets the next record; **trim** removes all trailing blanks; and the resulting string and a blank are concatenated onto **text**. If the input operation succeeds, the statement is repeated. When all the data has been read, the input will fail and control will pass to the next statement. The statement labeled **match** applies the pattern **pat** to **text**, which places the next word into **word** and removes it from **text**. The next statement looks for the word in **dict**, the dictionary, where the words are being accumulated. If the word is not in the dictionary already, it is added. If the word is found, it will not be added again, but will be counted. The last statement counts each occurrence of a word by incrementing the variable which has the same name as the word. The dollar sign preceding the variable name indicates indirection: if the variable **word** has the value **the**, then a variable named **the** is used to count the occurrence. To print out the words with their frequency count in the order in which they occur, these additional statements are used:

```
     output = 'frequency count'
loop dict pat =                                              :f(end)
     output = 'the word ' word 'occurred ' $word 'times.':(loop)
end
```

Exercise: Revise the SNOBOL program to print out the words and their frequencies in alphabetical order. Printing out the words and their frequencies in alphabetical order would require finding the *lexically smallest* word in the dictionary (using the **lgt** [lexically greater than] function for comparison), printing it out and removing it from **dict**. Then this operation would be repeated until the dictionary was null.

Exercise: SNOBOL also has numeric relational operators, **eq**, **ne**, **lt**, **gt**, **le**, and **ge**, for comparing numeric values. Revise the SNOBOL program, above, to print out the words in order of their frequency.

SNOBOL also allows definition of arrays and user-defined data structures. One strong feature of the language is the flexibility of function definitions. Because of its many features for processing strings, SNOBOL has often been used for text processing and other non-numerical applications.

Many of the functions available in SNOBOL would be useful in other programming languages. Examples are **break** and **span** which are implemented below. This particular implementation is not identical to the SNOBOL functions, but provides operations frequently required when **break** and **span** are used. First, assume that a set of characters has been declared:

```
type charset = set of char;
```

Charset would have to be initialized to a particular set of characters at the beginning of the program. (The restriction that sets in Pascal must have a base type of scalar or subrange limits this implementation to single characters rather than strings, which would be more useful in many cases.) The definition for break is:

```
procedure break(var strg  : string;
                    patt      : charset;
                    var subst : string);

var i : integer;

begin  (* break *)
   i := 1;
   while not(strg[i] in patt) and (i<length(strg)) do
       i := i+1;
   if i > 1
       then begin
               subst := copy(strg,1,i-1);
               delete(strg,1,i-1)
             end
       else subst := ''
end;   (* break *)
```

The procedure moves through the string until a character is found which is in the set **patt**. At that point, all preceding characters are copied into the substring **subst** and deleted from **strg**. If none of the characters in **patt** are found, **strg** is unchanged and **subst** is set to the null string.

The procedure **span** also uses sets to locate the first character which is not in **patt**.

```
procedure span(var strg : string;
                  patt : charset);

var over : Boolean;

begin (* span *)
   over := false;
   while (not over) and (length(strg)<>0) do
       if strg[1] in patt
           then delete(strg,1,1)
           else over := true;
end; (* span *)
```

Span functions by testing each character from the beginning of the string **strg**; if that character is in the set of pattern characters, it is deleted from **strg**. As soon as a non-pattern character is encountered, the loop is terminated and the procedure is finished. By defining these SNOBOL-like functions in Pascal, string processing can include some of the features of SNOBOL.

Exercise: Pattern matching and replacement capabilities are particularly useful features of SNOBOL. Implement comparable functions in Pascal, or other general-purpose programming language.

LINKED LIST OF WORDS

As a final example of text processing, let us develop a procedure for inputting text data and converting it into a form that will be useful to later stages of processing, such as syntactic analysis or semantic analysis. Assume that the data is in a disk file, stored line by line. To analyze the text lexically, the words will be broken out one by one and stored into a linked list of words. To simplify the problem, only the word will be saved. (In reality when the word is found, it would be checked against the dictionary and appropriate features would be attached. Thus, the information part of the linked list would be more complex than indicated here.) First let us define the file and the variables to hold each line and each word found:

```
var  textfile : text;  (* file of characters *)
     word,line : string;
```

The linked list will be a dynamic data structure allowing easy insertion and deletion of words, which will be useful in the syntactic and semantic stages of processing. Each element of the linked list consists of two parts: the information part and a pointer to the next element. Thus each element, called a node, can be defined as:

```
type nodeptr = ^node;
     node = record
        info : string;
        next : nodeptr
     end;  (* node record *)
```

The nodeptr is a data element of type pointer, which is the memory address of a piece of data. In this case, the location of the piece of data will not be known until execution time (for flexibility). When a node is needed, a request is made for the storage required.

```
var p : nodeptr;
    .
    .
    .
    new(p);
    .
```

Since p is declared as a pointer to a node, new(p) will allocate the required amount of memory for a node and assign its location to p. By chaining the nodes together, the entire linked list can be accessed by linking through from the first node, to the next, and so on. See Figure 2.7 for a diagram of a linked list of the words of a sentence. As each word is encountered, it will be added to the linked list. Assuming that the additional variables, p, q, and list are defined as nodeptrs, the linked list will be initialized:

```
new(q);
list := q;
```

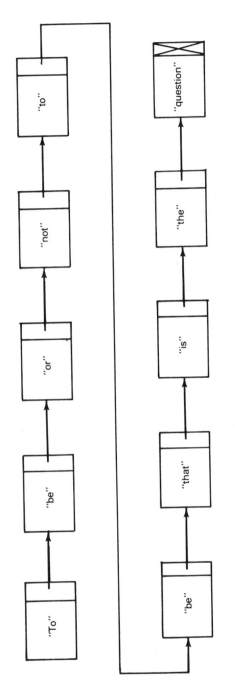

Figure 2.7   Linked List of Words in a Sentence, "To be or not to be, that is the question."

Then to add each word:

```
q^.info := word;
q^.next := nil;
if q <> list
    then p^.next := q;
p := q;
new(q)
```

A node is created initially and list is assigned to point to the first node. Then as each word is found, it is placed at the end of the linked list by assigning the value of word to the info field pointed to by q and setting the next pointer to nil, indicating that nothing follows it in the list. Then if the node being added is not the first in the list, the next field of the previous node, pointed to by p, is set to q, thus pointing to the newly created node. Then the pointer to the new node is saved in p.

To put all the pieces together, the program to read the text data, place it into a linked list, and then print out the linked list would be as follows:

```
program lexlist;

type nodeptr = ^node;
    node = record
        info : string;
        next : nodeptr
    end; (* node *)
    charset = set of char; (* used by break and span *)

var infile : text; (* file of characters *)
    word,line : string;
    inname : string; (*name of input file *)
    list,p,q : nodeptr;
    pat : charset;
    i : integer;

    procedure break(var strg : string;
                    patt : charset;
                    var subst : string);


(***********************************************************)
(*  break locates the first character in patt in the string strg,*)
(*        places all characters preceding that character into    *)
(*               subst                                           *)
(*        and removes the characters placed in subst            *)
(*  if none of the pattern characters are found, the entire strg *)
(*        is placed in subst and removed.                        *)
(***********************************************************)


    (* as defined earlier *)
```

```
        procedure span(var strg : string;
                        patt : charset);

(*********************************************************)
(*       span removes all instances of characters in patt    *)
(*                 found at the beginning of strg            *)
(*********************************************************)

  (* as defined earlier *)
begin  (* lexlist *)
    (* initialize set of characters in pat *)
    pat := [',','.','?',' '];

    (* input file and reset disk file*)
    write('enter input file name:');
    readln(inname);
    reset(infile,inname);

    (*  initialize linked list *)
    new(q);
    list := q;

    (*  read and process each line of text until all the file is processed *)
    while not(eof(infile)) do
        begin
          readln(infile,line);
          while line <> '' do
            begin
              break(line,pat,word);
              span(line,pat);
              if word <> '' (* if word exists add to list *)
                  then begin
                          q^.info := word;
                          q^.next := nil;
                          if q <> list
                              then p^.next := q;
                          p := q;
                          new(q)
                       end
          end
        end;
    writeln('all input read and added to list');
    p := list;
    while p <> nil do
        begin
          writeln(p^.info);
          p := p^.next;
        end;
    writeln('all words in list written');
end.  (* lexlist *)
```

Exercise: Define a text file with words from the lists in the appendix. Rewrite the program lexlist to include the features in the linked list.

Exercise: Pascal pointers only refer to a location in memory set up for a particular execution of a program and therefore cannot be written to a disk file for storage. Define the linked list in an array with an index indicating the next node in the list, and modify the program lexlist to write the list to a disk file.

Chapter 3

The
Lexical
Phase

The lexical phase of a natural language processing system involves the mapping between the input or output stream and the lexical items to be manipulated by the system. On input, lexical analysis breaks the input stream into lexical items—morphemes, words or other linguistic units. On output the lexical phase selects appropriate words to convey the intended meaning. Chomsky and other linguists separated the various phases of analysis and maintained the separation throughout processing. In other words, a linguist began with the phonological stage, then dealt with the lexical (or morphological) stage, then the syntactic stage, and finally the semantic stage. For the sake of clarity this chapter will primarily consider the lexical stage as distinct from the others, although in actual processing the various stages are generally integrated.

Since the phonological stage precedes the lexical phase, it will be considered briefly. Phonology is the study of the sounds which make up a spoken language, including how each sound fits together with others to produce larger linguistic units. The smallest distinctive unit of speech in a language is called a *phoneme*. A phoneme may in fact be a group of sounds, but whether it is one or several, the phoneme is recognized as different from other phonemes by speakers of that particular language. For example the initial sounds of the words *pin* and *bin* are different phonemes, but the *p* sounds in the words *pin*, *spin*, and *tip* are the same phoneme. If you listen carefully, you can hear a difference in the *p* sounds; saying the word *pin* produces a little puff of air when the *p* is pronounced whereas the other *p* sounds do not. Thus a phoneme is a class of sounds which is distinguished from other classes of sounds in a particular language. Each language contains a set number of phonemes with which the spoken language can be described. Phonemes do not carry meaning in the usual sense, but must be combined into established patterns to produce meaningful units.

The minimal meaningful unit in language is called a *morpheme*. If a morpheme can function alone, such as the word *dog*, it is called a *free morpheme* or free form. Other morphemes cannot be used by themselves, such as the plural ending *-s* in *dogs* or the past tense ending *-ed* in *jumped*; these are called *bound morphemes*. Bound morphemes in English serve as suffixes and prefixes on a root form. Words are made up of morphemes in several ways. A single free morpheme, called a *simple form*, is a word. A *complex form* is a single free form combined with one or more bound forms, such as *uninterested* (*un + interest + ed*) or *running* (*run + ing*). A complex form may also be several bound forms which together produce a free form, such as *conversation* (*convers + ation*) or *ineluctably* (*in + eluct + able + ly*). Notice that sometimes the combination of forms requires spelling changes. A *compound form* can be made up of two otherwise free forms, such as *catbox* (*cat + box*); in this situation each of the morphemes could stand alone as well as in the compound form.

Phonology only applies to speech, but text data has a comparable aspect. Each character (sometimes called a grapheme) works like a phoneme in speech. Like phonemes, individual characters in English do not carry any meaning. (Chinese characters, on the other hand, do.) Combined together the characters make up morphemes. Text input can be mapped into lexical items—words—fairly easily by scanning the input stream for delimiters—spaces and punctuation marks (as we did in Chapter 2). Breaking the lexical items, or words, up into morphemes is more complicated. Speech is more difficult to analyze initially than text because the word boundaries in speech are not as clearly delineated. Look at a sentence in your book; the words are easily identified as the characters between blank space and punctuation marks. Try reading the sentence aloud. If you read aloud smoothly, there is no silence between words. Try reading the sentence again, but this time put breaks between the words. The result sounds quite unnatural, doesn't it? Unlike speech, text is made up of discrete characters, some of which serve as delimiters, thus simplifying the task of analysis.

Discovering the morphemes within a text or utterance is a major part of lexical analysis. Free forms are easily located, since a free form corresponds to a word, delimited by spaces and/or punctuation marks. Compound forms are fairly easily identified also, since they are made up of simple free forms. Bound forms, however, require more processing since they are parts of words. Morphological analysis then involves locating the morphemes, free and bound, within a text. One scheme for isolating morphemes assumes every word is in the following form:

PREFIX* + ROOT + SUFFIX*

(The asterisk [known as a Kleene star] indicates that the item can be repeated zero or more times.) The word is scanned for prefixes and suffixes, and what remains is the root. Many words have no prefix or suffix, and some have several. The rule given above generates quite a number of patterns, such as:

```
0 + ROOT + SUFFIX
0 + ROOT + 0
0 + ROOT + SUFFIX + SUFFIX
```

and so on. (The 0 [zero] indicates a null item.) Unfortunately the process is not quite as simple as it seems. One cannot simply look up the prefixes and suffixes in a list and compare them with the beginning or ending characters of a word. For example *in-* is a proper prefix, as in *inadmissible*. However the word *informed* should be divided as *inform* + *ed*, not *in* + *form* + *ed*. *Un* can be a prefix as in *unusual* (*un* + *usual*), but it is not always, as in *under*. So the forms must continually be compared against the acceptable vocabulary list to determine when an actual morpheme has been isolated.

Natural language systems do not always include morphological analysis. The alternative is to put all possible forms of every word into the dictionary. However storing all possible variant forms is inefficient and unnecessary; many variant forms can be derived by simple spelling rules, such as plurals formed by adding *-s* or *-es* or past tense formed by adding *-ed*. Therefore an analysis routine to handle regular variants can save considerable storage since only the irregular forms need to be saved. Another advantage to analyzing words to find the morphemes is that the affixes (prefixes and suffixes) often relate to the use of the word. The suffix *-ly* often signals an adverb, as in *quickly*, the prefix *in-* usually indicates negation, as in *inadvertent*, and so on. Other affixes, such as plural or third person singular endings, provide syntactic information. The variant forms which are stored in the dictionary can point to the root form, rather than constituting a separate entry in the dictionary. For example there would be a primary entry for the word *go*, and entries for *went* and *gone* would point to *go*. In addition, the entries for *went* and *gone* could include identification of the variant form: past tense for *went* and past participle for *gone*.

The algorithm for isolating morphemes within forms containing regular changes is basically as follows:

```
repeat
    look for word in dictionary
    if not found,
        then modify the word
until word is found or no further modification possible
```

Compound forms would have to be handled somewhat differently. If the whole word is not found, then start from the first looking for a free form; if one is found, then try to identify the remaining letters as another free form. This method would work for *catbox*, *houseboat*, and *doorknob*. The entire word must be sought before the decomposition process begins, to avoid problems with words such as *catalog* or *rationalize*. A simpler solution would be to store all compound forms as free forms; although more storage would be required, the processing would be simplified. If compound forms are to be processed rather than stored, the algorithm for analysis becomes:

```
look for word in dictionary
if not found,
    then is it a compound form?
if not compound
    then while not found and more modifications possible
        modify the word
        look for word in dictionary
```

The order in which affixes are removed is important, and sometimes more than one is present. In addition certain spelling changes may be required. The outline below illustrates some multiple step suffix removals. [1] After each step the dictionary would be checked again for the resulting string of characters. (The number sign [#] identifies the final form located in the dictionary.)

```
1.  -s   endings (cf. hats, catches, ladies)
    a)   take off -s (#hat, catche, ladie)
    b)   take off -e (#catch, ladi)
    c)   change -i to -y (#lady)
2.  -ed  endings (cf. hoped, picked, cried, hopped)
    a)   take off -d (#hope, picke, crie, hoppe)
    b)   take off -e (#pick, cri, hopp)
    c)   change -i to -y (#cry, hopp)
    d)   if doubled letter, take off second (#hop)
3.  -ing endings (cf. hoping, jumping, hopping)
    a)   take off -ing and add -e (#hope, jumpe, hoppe)
    b)   take off -e (#jump, hopp)
    c)   if doubled letter, take off second (#hop)
```

This table does not include all possible suffixes that might need to be removed. Other frequent endings are *-er* and *-est* which identify the comparative and superlative forms of adjectives and *-ly* which changes an adjective to an adverb. In all of these instances if the word is very short, then the combination of letters is probably not a suffix, as in *best* or *only*. In other cases the rules just do not work; for example when the suffix *-ly* is removed, an *-e* is generally added. Thus *wholly* becomes *whol* + *e*, which is *whole*, but *fully* becomes *ful* + *e*, which is *fule*, instead of *full*. Some of these problems are left as exercises for the reader.

Exercise: Write a morphological analyzer to handle regular changes for forming plurals (*-s, -es*), possessives (*-'s, -s'*), past tense (*-d, -ed*) and progressive tense (*-ing* endings). Test the program on a text of at least 1000 words. How successful is your analyzer? What percentage of variants are not found?

Exercise: The suffix *-ly* often changes an adjective to an adverb. What spelling changes must be made for it to function well?

A-	HYPER-
ANTE-	IN-
ANTI-	INTER-
ARCH-	MAL-
AUTO-	MIS-
BE-	NON-
BI-	POST-
CO-	PRE-
COUNTER-	PRO-
DE-	RE-
DIS-	SEMI-
EM-	SUB-
EN-	SUPER-
EX-	TRANS-
EXTRA-	ULTRA-
FORE-	UN-

Figure 3.1   Common English Prefixes

Exercise: Figure 3.1 contains a list of common English prefixes. How many of them should be added to the morphological analyzer? In other words consider whether knowing that *forewarn* is made up of *fore-* + *warn* provides any useful information. Notice that *im-* as in *impossible*, and *ir-* as in *irresponsible* are not in the list because they are spelling variations of *in-*. What are the rules for determining that *im-* and *ir-* are alternate spellings of *in-*? Are there exceptions to the rules?

Exercise: Figure 3.2 contains a list of common English suffixes. Add them to the morphological analyzer. Which ones cause spelling changes? Are there any patterns in these spelling changes?

Exercise: Modify the morphological analyzer to recognize compound forms as well as simple and complex forms.

Irregular Forms

Let us consider some of the irregular morphemes. Plurals are not always formed simply by adding an -*s* to a noun. Some nouns are the same in singular and plural (*sheep*, *deer*), while others are formed by an internal change in the word (*mouse*, *mice*). A few words form the plural by adding a suffix other than -*s*, such as *ox* → *oxen* or *child* → *children*. Formation of the plural can be thought of as a process, in which one of these three changes occur:

```
1) addition of a suffix     dog  → dogs
                            ox   → oxen

2) zero modification        sheep → sheep + 0

3) internal change          mouse → mice
```

A process similar to internal change also occurs with other word classes. This process, known as *suppletion*, involves the substitution of a different base of the word; for example, the adjectives, *good, better, best*, and the verbs, *go, went, gone* or *be, am, is, are, was, were*. Words which change base usually must be handled as separate forms, by storing the variant in the dictionary with a pointer to the primary entry, as explained before.

-ABLE	-ITY
-IBLE	-IZE
-AGE	-LESS
-AL	-LIKE
-ANCE	-LY
-ATION	-MENT
-CY	-NESS
-DOM	-OUS
-ED	-S
-EN	-'S
-ENCE	-S'
-ER	-SHIP
-EST	-SOME
-FUL	-STER
-HOOD	-WARD
-ING	-WAY
-ISH	-WISE
-IST	

Figure 3.2   Common English Suffixes

Morphological vs. Syntactic Analysis

The difference between morphological analysis and syntactic analysis is not always immediately evident, but the distinction will be explained. [2] Morphologically, form classes can be defined by the composition of the lexical items. In other words, the bound morphemes attached to a root often identify the word class of the resulting complex form. For example, items which include plural or possessive bound forms must be nouns; a verb (*grow*) will have different forms for third person singular (*grows*), present participle (*growing*), past participle (*grown*), and past tense (*grew*). Adjectives form comparative and superlative by adding *-er* and *-est*, and adverbs are produced by adding *-ly* to an adjective.

Syntactically, form classes are defined by the distribution of the forms. Essentially form classes (comparable to parts of speech) are all the forms which can be used in a particular circumstance. For example, in the sentence

I saw the -----.

any form which can be used properly in this sentence can be called a noun (or a nominal—a noun substitute).

I saw the ship.

I saw the fifth running of the Crescent City Classic.

I saw the location of the Battle of Bunker Hill.

A distinction can be made that the terms, *noun, verb*, etc. are morphological and that the terms, *nominal, verbal*, etc. should be used for forms which substitute for nouns, verbs, etc. Thus in the sentence,

Swimming is fun.

the word *swimming* is a nominal, rather than a noun, since it is a verb form used in the place where nouns are found. Only certain forms can substitute for the various form classes: noun substitutes include pronouns, prepositional phrases, relative clauses, etc. Adjective substitutes can be nouns (*manhole* cover), verb forms such as participial forms (the *singing* waiter), and pronouns (*my* book). Prepositional phrases and relative clauses can also modify nouns, thus serving the adjectival role. Adverb substitutes include prepositional phrases and subordinate clauses.

A *construction* is two or more linguistic forms which function in a sentence as a single form. The noun phrases used in the examples above are considered constructions. If all the parts of a construction are required, it is called *exocentric*; if only one part is required and the other parts are optional, it is called *endocentric*. Examples of exocentric forms are as follows:

Noun + Verb	Mark runs.
Preposition + Noun	in water
Article + count Noun	the peach

Endocentric constructions consist of a *center* plus optional additions or expansions. The following examples in which the center is italicized illustrate the concept:

Adjective + Noun	tall *trees*
Noun + Noun	chicken *house*
Verb + Adverb	*sleep* soundly
Adverb + Adverb	very *quietly*
Adverb + Adjective	dark *red*
Noun + Relative clause	*men* who go to sea
Noun + Adjectival phrase	the *house* on the corner

Parsing natural language input requires discovery of these constructions and identification of their function within the sentence in which they occur.

Basic Forms of English Sentences

English sentences, as in most languages, can be extremely complicated, but consist primarily of a few relatively simple forms. The following abbreviations apply to the following examples:

N—noun

IV—intransitive verb

LV—linking verb

TV—transitive verb

Be—any form of the verb TO BE

X, Y, Z—nouns

x, y, z—adjectives

The basic forms of English sentences are:

1)	N + IV	(X happened)
2)	N + LV + N	(X became Y or y)
3)	N + TV + N	(X made Y)
3a)	N + TV + N (+ N)	(X made Y for Z) or (X made Z a Y)
3b)	N + TV + N + N	(X made Y into Z or z)
4)	N + Be + N	(X were Y or y)

Examples of these forms are as follows:

1)   Birds fly.

2)   John became a director.
     John appeared fat.

3)   Tom made a cake.

3a)   Tom made a cake for Jane.
      Tom made Jane a cake.

3b)   Terry made the basement into a study.
      The rain made the grass greener.

4)   The girls were softball players.
     The children are healthy.

Verbs with a linking function used in 2) are *seem, appear, smell, taste, grow, sound, cost, weigh, resemble, feel,* etc. Verbs used in category 3b) include *choose, elect, proclaim, consider, crown, believe, call, suppose,* and *name.*

In addition to the basic forms there are some standard variations. These include negative statements, questions, and passives. The transformational rules for forming them follow:

NEGATIVES

1, 2, 3) N + V (+ N) → N + do + not + V(infinitive) (+ N)

4)   N + be + N → N + be + not + N

QUESTIONS

1, 2, 3) N + V (+ N)   →   do + N + V(infinitive) (+ N)

4)   N1 + be + N2 → be + N1 + N2

PASSIVES

3)   N1 + VT + N2 → N2 + Aux + V(past participle) + by + N1

3a) N1 + VT + N2 + N3 → N2 + Aux + V(past participle) + N3 + by + N1

Later chapters will refer back to these basic sentence forms.

Other Aspects of Analysis

Several other aspects of an input text in addition to linguistic aspects can contribute information useful to the analysis phase. Punctuation is the most obvious. A punctuation mark always serves to delimit a word, in the same way that a blank does. The end of a sentence is almost always identified by the presence of an end-punctuation mark: a period (.), a question mark (?) or an exclamation mark (!). Within sentences punctuation may or may not be useful at the lexical stage, since many times punctuation is more closely related to sentence structure, i.e. syntax, than morphology. In addition, punctuation can be somewhat ambiguous. Semicolons (;) are generally used to separate clauses,

The boys went to the river; the girls went to the mountain.

but sometimes substitute for commas (,) when the phrases to be separated themselves contain commas.

John, the oldest student; Tom, the tallest student; and Jane, the smartest student, went to visit the state capitol.

Commas are frequently optional and therefore cannot be relied on to provide much information.

Many texts contain structural information in their encoding. For example, paragraph breaks and page breaks are frequently marked by inclusion of certain codes in the machine-readable form of the text. Poetry will generally be broken into lines and stanzas, in addition to the information available from basic punctuation. In more complex discourse analysis the presence of certain words will assist in the analysis of the text. For example, if several sentences begin, *first*, *second*, and *finally*, one could assume that the sentences are parallel in meaning and perhaps in structure. In-depth discussion of such concepts is beyond the scope of this book.

THE DICTIONARY

Once the morphemes have been isolated within the input stream, they are identified with regard to their function and meaning in the context of the sentence. Some information can be derived from morphological analysis, but most of it must be obtained from the dictionary. In addition to being just a vocabulary list to recognize the morphemes, the dictionary contains syntactic information to identify the structural function of each item and semantic information to determine the meaning. Other information is included for some types of systems, as we shall see in later chapters.

The dictionary largely determines the capabilities of the NLS, and must be appropriately structured to assure efficiency. The problems of the format and structure of the dictionary are closely related to the general problems of storage of text discussed in Chapter 2. As with storage of any textual information, there are tradeoffs to consider. For example if the text is compressed to optimize storage space, then the processing time is increased to compress and expand the data. The organization of the entries within the dictionary determines the speed with which any individual entry can be accessed. These points will be taken up in turn.

The format of each dictionary entry depends, of course, upon the information needed by the system. The most obvious data item within each entry is the morpheme itself, called the *head*. The head is the specific string of characters which is matched to locate a particular entry and is sometimes referred to as the print image. There may be more than one entry with the same head, as in the case of homographs, in which two words have the same spelling. For example, the sentences,

The *bear* is in the zoo.

and

The women *bear* their loads on their heads.

illustrate the need for two entries with the same head. These might be distinguished internally as *bear1* and *bear2*, but the part of the entry used for matching the input stream must include both simply as *bear*. The methods for distinguishing which entry is actually appropriate will be discussed later. An internal identifier is necessary in addition to the head to distinguish among multiple entries. This identifier could be similar to the external form, such as *bear* (external) and *bear1* (internal), but it need not be. *Bear* might be identified internally as B243 or with some other scheme. One way of identifying an entry is to save the location of that entry. In this way the internal identifier is also a pointer to the location of that entry in storage (either primary or secondary memory). Whatever the form of the internal identifier, it will enable the system to access the specific dictionary entry during processing.

The syntactic information required in each entry depends upon the method of analysis to some extent, but certain data will frequently be included. The grammatical functions which the word can perform will be identified. Thus *bear1* would be marked as a noun, and *bear2* as a verb. Other syntactic information might be useful; for example prepositions might include restrictions about what kind of object they work with. The preposition *inside* refers to physical location; knowing that can assist in analyzing the rest of the sentence. In the phrase

inside the state

knowing that the preposition takes a physical location as its object would determine the particular meaning of the word *state* in this sentence. The format of the syntactic information is also dependent upon the processing, but several general schemes can be mentioned. Once again the specific string of characters can be used to identify syntactic features; the first instance of *bear* in the example above might be encoded as

bear bear1 noun

or

bear bear1 n

or

bear b243 s1

where b243 identifies the first sense of the word and s1 is a code to identify nouns. Another scheme would be to include a pointer to a block of code that processes nouns. This scheme would be useful in that all noun entries would automatically be handled by the same piece of code, which might improve efficiency.

The meaning of each entry is also represented in some way. The word *state* illustrates this requirement well; *state* can be a location, such as

the state of Virginia

or a set of circumstances at a given time such as

his mental state

or a condition such as

a state of melancholy

The difficulty in distinguishing among these different meanings is that more is required than simply the word class. In all these examples the word *state* is used as a noun; in the first example the word is used in a physical sense; in the last two it is used in an abstract sense. Various levels of meaning are represented in different systems, as we shall see in Unit III. The amount of meaning to be represented determines the power of the resulting system. Chapter 9 will review the meaning representations discussed in Unit III.

STRUCTURE OF THE DICTIONARY

The structural organization of the dictionary influences the overall efficiency of the NLS. An ordinary dictionary is arranged in alphabetical order (more or less) according to a particular algorithm decided by the publishing company. Imagine how difficult locating a particular word would be if the entries were put in randomly. Alphabetical order is one option for a NLS lexicon since that arrangement would allow a binary search on the elements in the file. A binary search is similar to a method of dictionary search sometimes taught in elementary school. When searching for a particular word, you open the dictionary in the middle and determine which half will contain the word you seek. Then the appropriate half is divided in half. This procedure continues, dividing each section in half until the proper page is found.

Binary Search

Implementing a binary search requires that the items be arranged in a vector in sequential order, usually ascending. If the vector contains n elements in the range [1..n], the middle element is n **DIV 2** (n divided by 2, using integer division). Comparing the item at that position with the search key will determine one of three things:

1. the middle element contains the search key
2. the middle element is less than the search key, which means that the key will follow the middle element in the vector
3. the middle element is greater than the search key, and the key falls before the middle element in the vector.

If 1 occurs, then the element is found and the search is over. If either of the other situations occur, then the range of the vector being searched is changed, and the procedure continues. If the variables `first` and `last` are used to index the first and last elements of the section of the vector being searched, `mid` is the middle element of that section, `found` is a Boolean variable used to signal when the search key is found, and `key` is the search key, then the algorithm for a binary search of a vector `v` of n elements arranged in ascending order is as follows:

```
(* initialize variables *)

first ← 1
last ← n
found ← false
```

```
(*        loop while search key not found      *)
(*            and more elements to examine      *)
while (not found) and (first <= last) do
    begin
        mid ← (last + first) div 2;
        if (key = v[mid])
            then found ← true
            else if (key < v[mid])
                    then last ← mid - 1
                    else first ← mid + 1
    end
```

The calculation of MID is an algebraically simplified form of the following:

```
mid ← (last - first) div 2 + first
```

which is half of the difference between the positions of the first and last elements added to the beginning point of that part of the vector. Notice also that the loop will be terminated when the search key is found or when first is greater than last, which means that all the elements have been checked.

A binary search can be quite efficient since so few elements are examined. If the entire dictionary could be stored in memory, the binary search would be an acceptable situation, but if it is stored on disk, even the small number of disk accesses to locate an entry would reduce the efficiency of the system.

Indexing

Indexing the dictionary can improve search time. If the first level of indexing is a breakdown into the twenty-six letters of the alphabet (similar to the thumb tabs in an ordinary dictionary), then the number of probes into the dictionary is greatly reduced. Having additional levels of indexing can further reduce the number of probes. Even with a very large dictionary, several levels of indexes can be stored in memory. Thus the initial stages of the search for an entry would be in memory, which is fast, and the final stage would be on disk, which is slower. Figure 3.3 illustrates a multiple level index to a dictionary. Notice that the first level breaks the dictionary into parts based on its initial letter. A one-character table-driven search could be used at that point. The first character of the word is pulled off, then manipulated using the characteristics of the ASCII character set to convert it into its ordinal position in the alphabet, as follows:

```
ch ← first letter of word
p ← ORD(ch) - ORD('A')
```

The variable p now contains the position of the letter within the alphabet. The function ord returns the decimal ordinal value of a character within the 128 ASCII characters. For example, the character E is the sixty-ninth ASCII character, and the letter A is the sixty-fifth. Therefore if we subtract the position of the first letter of the alphabet from the position of the one we are dealing

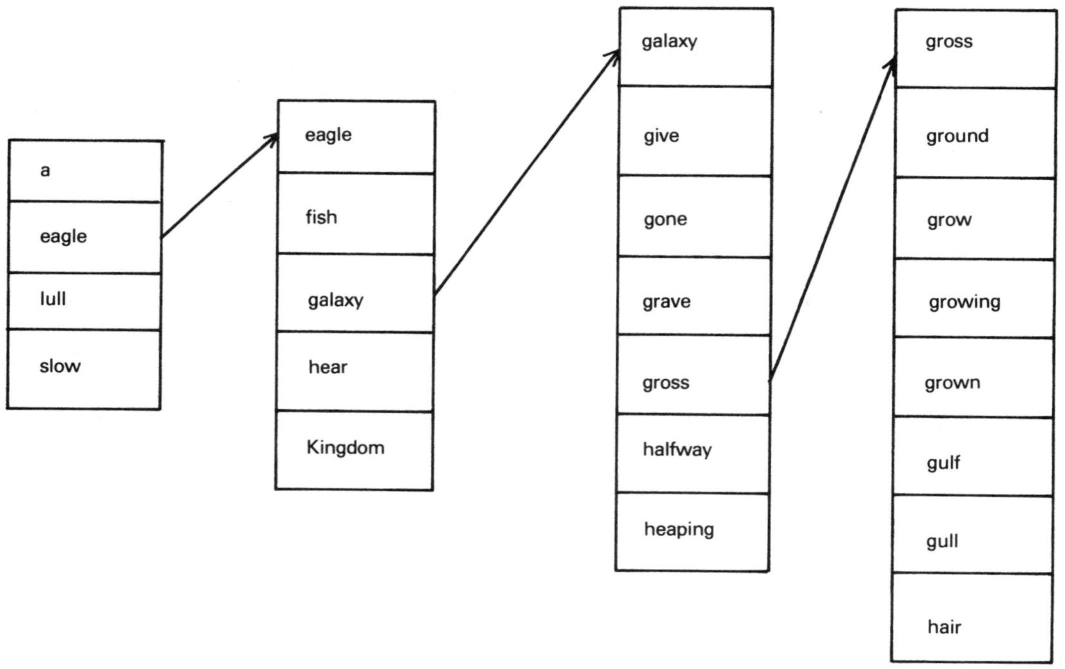

Figure 3.3   Multiple-Level Index to a Dictionary

with, the result is the position of the character within the alphabet, counting from zero to twenty-five $(0 \ldots 25)$. Adding one to the difference changes the range to one to twenty-six $(1 \ldots 26)$. To illustrate more clearly,

```
ch ← 'E'
p  ← ORD(ch) - ORD('A') + 1
p  ← 69 - 65 + 1
p  ← 5          (* 'E' is the fifth letter of the alphabet*)
```

However, this calculation only works for capital letters; the algorithm to use with either capital letters or lower case letters would have to test to determine which one the character is. The algorithm for both would be as follows:

```
ch ← first letter of word
q  ← ORD(ch)
if (q <= ORD('Z'))
   then p ← q - ORD('A') + 1
   else p ← q - ORD('a') + 1
```

The variable p can now be used to index a table containing pointers to the second level of indexing. At each successive level of indexing after the first, either a linear search or a binary search can be used, depending on the size of the dictionary and thus the size of the index. Let us investigate this concept.

A hypothetical dictionary contains 10,000 entries, arranged alphabetically. If we assume that the entries are evenly distributed across the alphabet, then each letter will average 385 entries. (This is obviously not a reasonable assumption since the letters J and X, for example, do not occur initially nearly as often as S or C. But for our immediate consideration, we will make the assumption anyway.) Each element in the twenty-six element table of initial characters would contain a pointer to the appropriate second-level index. In the second level each element would contain the word which began that section of the dictionary (see Figure 3.3.). A linear search starts comparing the search key (the item we are looking for) with the first element in the index, and proceeds one by one sequentially through the index. Since the search argument may not be in the index (since the index points to the beginning of sections of the dictionary), the comparison would be looking for the element which is greater than the search key, in which case the previous element would point to the proper section. For example, if part of the index contains the words,

> FLUID
>
> FOLK
>
> FORBIDDEN
>
> FOUL

and the search key is FOOT, then the comparison with FORBIDDEN would tell us that the word FOOT is in the section pointed to by FOLK because FOOT is greater than FOLK, but less than FORBIDDEN. A linear search of 385 [10,000/26] items will average 193 comparisons [ROUND(385/2)]. The worst case would occur if the key were in the last position; in the worst case 385 comparisons would have to be made.

The worst case for a binary search of 385 elements would be log2(385), which is 9, significantly better than even the average case with a linear search. Only when the index becomes quite small would a linear search be better, since the algorithm for a linear search is quite simple compared to a binary search. If, on the other hand, the 385 elements were broken up into several more levels of indexes, the search efficiency can be improved without using a binary search. For instance, the index could be three-level, as follows:

FIRST LEVEL	26 elements ('A'..'Z') [each indexes 385 entries]
SECOND LEVEL	7 elements [each indexes 55 entries]
THIRD LEVEL	7 elements [each indexes 8 entries]

The worst case for a linear search on each level would be 58 probes [26 + 7 + 7 + 8], and the average could be assumed to be about half that, or 29. That is not as efficient as a binary search, but significantly better than a linear search on a second-level index of 385 elements. If the initial letter is used to index the first level, as described above, then the worst case would be 22 probes [7 + 7 + 8], and the average would be 11, which is not much different from a binary search. The memory requirements for these two methods would be minimal; enough storage would be needed to hold 40 index elements [26 + 7 + 7] containing the head and a pointer to the next level. The lowest level index would contain the disk address, requiring only one disk access.

Exercise: Calculate the relative advantages of these three search methods—binary search, linear search on multiple level index, and linear search on second through nth levels of multiple level index with ordinal calculation used on first level—for dictionaries containing 1000, 50,000, 100,000, and 1 million entries. Test the multiple level index with 2, 3, and 4 levels.

Exercise: Calculate the frequency of occurrence as the initial character in a word of each letter of the alphabet, using a text of several thousand words. Assuming that the sample text used is representative, how many entries would occur for each letter of the alphabet in a dictionary of 10,000 entries? How would this uneven distribution affect the search methods chosen? What changes should be made to the algorithm to improve the search?

Exercise: Evaluate the search for a dictionary entry which uses the ASCII ordinal value calculation for every letter of a word. What are the advantages and disadvantages of such a search?

Trie Searching

A method of searching which capitalizes on the position of characters within a key is the *trie* search. The name *trie* is derived from re*trie*val. [3] A lexical trie is set up by arranging a given set of words first according to their initial letters, as we did for the index described earlier, but then continuing to group the words by the common letters in the second and succeeding positions. Let us use the list of the 31 most common English words described in Knuth [4], to illustrate building a trie for retrieval purposes. Figure 3.4a contains the list of words alphabetically, and Figure 3.4b lists them in order of frequency.

INDEX	WORD	INDEX	WORD
1	a	17	in
2	and	18	is
3	are	19	it
4	as	20	not
5	at	21	of
6	be	22	on
7	but	23	or
8	by	24	that
9	for	25	the
10	from	26	this
11	had	27	to
12	have	28	was
13	he	29	which
14	her	30	with
15	his	31	you
16	I		

(a) Most Common English Words, Ordered Alphabetically.

FREQUENCY	WORD	FREQUENCY	WORD
1	the	17	be
2	of	18	not
3	and	19	by
4	to	20	but
5	a	21	have
6	in	22	you
7	that	23	which
8	is	24	are
9	I	25	on
10	it	26	or
11	for	27	her
12	as	28	had
13	with	29	at
14	was	30	from
15	his	31	this
16	he		

(b) Most Common English Words, Ordered by Frequency

Figure 3.4

(Compare this list with the list given in Chapter 2 of 30 most common words in British and American English compiled in the 1970's by the Norwegian Computing Centre for the Humanities.) The first step in building a trie is to create a matrix with 27 rows. There is a row for each letter of the alphabet plus one to represent a blank. The first column of the matrix groups the words by their initial letter. If only one word exists with that initial letter, such as *not* and *you*, then the word is placed in that slot. If there is more than one word with the same first letter, then the slot in the matrix contains an index to the next available column, which is used to sort the words on their second letter. If more than one word has the same first and second letters, then there will be an index to another column to sort the words on their third letter.

Figure 3.5 shows the trie for the 31 most common English words. Notice that the words beginning with A—*a, and, are, as,* and *at*—are sorted in the second column. The word *a* falls into the first row since its second letter is a blank, i.e., it has no second letter; the word *and* falls into the N row, and so on. The words beginning with H—*had, have, he, her,* and *his*—are not completely sorted by their second letter. Because there are multiple words with the same first two letters, additional columns are needed. The A row of column 5 contains (10), which is an index to column 10. In column 10 the words *had* and *have* are sorted by their third letters. Similarly the E row of column 5 contains (11), which sorts the words *he* and *her* by their third letters. Although the actual word is seen in the trie representation shown in Figure 3.5, in the internal representation that position in the trie would contain a pointer to the location of the dictionary entry for that word. The trie would contain only the most common words, providing quick access to words occurring the majority of the time. For a word used less frequently, after searching the trie and not finding it, the next level of search—using an index or some other method—would be tried.

There are several advantages to using a trie structure to search for particular words. Perhaps the most obvious is that one can quickly determine when the word sought is not in the trie. For example, only one probe of the trie in Figure 3.5 would be required to know that any word beginning with one of the letters C, D, E, G, J, K, L, M, P, Q, U, V, X or Z is not in the list. If the word sought were *thistle*, three probes would be needed to find *this*, and since *this* is found, no other word exists which begins with that sequence of letters, and thus *thistle* is not in the trie. With this particular group of words three probes would be the worst case since only three levels of sorting are needed. With a larger word list more duplicate letters would occur, and more probes would be needed to move through the trie.

Exercise: Develop an algorithm to build the trie shown in Figure 3.5 from the list of 31 most common English words.

Exercise: Develop an algorithm to access the trie built by the previous exercise.

FIRST LETTER		SECOND LETTER								THIRD LETTER		
		A	B	F	H	I	O	T	W	HA	HE	TH
	(1)	(2)	(3)	(4)	(5)	(6)	(7)	(8)	(9)	(10)	(11)	(12)
þ		A				I					HE	
A	(2)				(10)				WAS			THAT
B	(3)											
C												
D										HAD		
E			BE		(11)							THE
F	(4)						OF					
G												
H	(5)							(12)	WHICH			
I	(6)				HIS				WITH			THIS
J												
K												
L												
M												
N	NOT	AND				IN	ON					
O	(7)			FOR				TO				
P												
Q												
R		ARE		FROM			OR				HER	
S		AS				IS						
T	(8)	AT				IT						
U			BUT									
V										HAVE		
W	(9)											
X												
Y	YOU		BY									
Z												

Figure 3.5   TRIE for 31 Most Frequent English Words

Exercise: Develop an algorithm to build a trie from a list of any number of words provided as input to the program. Test the algorithm with lists of 50, 100, and 1000 words. What are the relative efficiencies of a trie for these different sizes of word lists?

Exercise: Develop an algorithm to access the trie built by the previous exercise.

Exercise: Since the matrix in which a trie is represented is frequently rather sparse, would an algorithm to store the trie in a sparse matrix be more efficient? Why?

Hashing

Another method for accessing the dictionary is called *hashing*. This method involves manipulating the search key in some way, often mathematically, to derive an address within the dictionary at which to find the entry being sought. The dictionary (or just its index) is first built using the hash function, and later accessed with the same hash function. The best hashing method is easily calculated, has a high success rate (in terms of locating the item sought on the first attempt), and produces a fairly even distribution of addresses.

Let us consider an example of hashing to locate a dictionary entry. If the search key is a word to be matched with the head form of a specific dictionary entry, the letters of the word can be considered numeric values. One possible value for a letter is its position within the alphabet, as used for the first level index earlier in the chapter. A simple hash function then would be the sum of the ordinal values of the letters in the key. Thus the hash value for the word *dog* would be $4 + 13 + 7$, which is 24. However the hash value for *cat* is $3 + 1 + 20$, which is also 24. This situation in which two keys hash to the same number and thus into the same position in the word list is called a *collision*. Since two words cannot occupy the same position, some means of finding another location for one of them must be found; for example, the procedure could be to move sequentially from the position where the collision occurred down through the list until an empty position is found. Another possibility is to apply another hash function to find a new location. However, resolving collisions can be expensive, so a more appropriate solution is to use a better hash function.

Another method for assigning a value to a letter would be to find its relative frequency of occurrence, as described in Chapter 2. (See Figures 2.3 and 2.4.) Let us consider an algorithm based on the relative frequency of letters in a word being sought. [5] From the information in Figures 2.3 and 2.4 the table in Figure 3.6 can be constructed. If we assume that the table in Figure 3.6 is called `freq` and the letter is upper case, then the value for the letter is calculated as follows:

LETTER	FREQUENCY
A	3
B	18
C	10
D	12
E	1
F	16
G	17
H	9
I	4
J	25
K	22
L	11
M	13
N	8
O	5
P	15
Q	24
R	6
S	7
T	2
U	14
V	21
W	19
X	23
Y	20
Z	26

Figure 3.6   Frequency of Letters in English Text (Based on Figures 2.3 and 2.4)

```
function val (ch:  alpha);
begin
   val := freq[ord(ch)-ord('A')+1]
end;  (* val *)
```

(Adapting this function to work with lower case letters is left as an exercise for the reader.) This value based on frequency of occurrence can then be used in various ways to establish a hash value.

1. The values for all the letters of a word are added together:

    CAT: 3 + 1 + 20 → 24

2. Only the first and last letters are used:

    DOG: 4 + 7 → 11

3. The second and fourth letters (or some other combination) are used:

    TREE: 18 + 5 → 23

4. Word length is added in:

    MOUSE: 11 + 13 + 21 + 19 + 5 → 69 + 5 → 74

5. The product is used rather than the sum of the values:

CAT: 3 * 1 * 20 → 60

However, with any of these methods some words will still produce collisions, for example LOOP and POOL:

4)   LOOP: 12 + 13 + 13 + 14 → 52

POOL: 14 + 13 + 13 + 12 → 52

Even adding in the word length would not resolve the conflict. To resolve the difficulty, the letters could be weighted by their position within the word:

6)   LOOP: 12*1 + 13*2 + 13*3 + 14*4 → 131

POOL: 14*1 + 13*2 + 13*3 + 12*4 → 127

Whatever method is used, some collisions will still occur and must therefore be dealt with. One solution is to use different level hash functions; for example, if the sum of the first and third letters produce a collision, then try the sum of the second and fourth, and so on.

As with other methods of accessing the dictionary, hashing is perhaps most efficiently used on a subset of the entire list of words. Selecting the 31 most common English words to be hashed with the remaining words accessed through an index can produce quite efficient processing.

Exercise: Write procedures to test at least three of the hashing methods described. Test each method to determine how frequently collisions will occur by applying each method on lists of 100, 200, 500, and 1000 unique words. What factors determine successful hash functions?

Exercise: What other hash functions could be used to access a dictionary as efficiently as possible—using a simple calculation to result in a minimum number of accesses while maintaining a good distribution?

So far this chapter has been primarily concerned with the analysis phase of natural language processing, with what happens to the text when it is input. The output phase is just as important, in that the processing would be useless if no response is given. However, access of the dictionary during output depends greatly on the contents of the dictionary. If a word to be selected from the dictionary must carry a certain meaning, then selection of that particular word depends upon the type of semantic features identified and the method of organizing the words based on those semantic features. The final chapter of the book will reconsider the dictionary and its contents in light of the design of a natural language system.

Part III

Natural Language Structures and Algorithms

Chapter 4

Transformational
Generative
Grammar

In 1957 Noam Chomsky published *Syntactic Structures*, in which he defined *generative grammar* as,

> a rules system formalized with mathematical precision that generates, without drawing upon any information that is not represented explicitly in the system, the grammatical sentences of the language that it describes and assigns to each sentence a structural description, or grammatical analysis. [1]

This structural description is called a *phrase marker*, and is usually represented as a tree structure. As discussed in Chapter 1, the rules system or grammar is a series of rewrite rules defining the relations between elements in the language defined by the grammar. The first part of this section will consider the structural aspects of Chomsky's 1957 theories by dividing the problem in the following manner:

1. Define a representation for Phrase markers
2. Define a representation for Phrase Structure rules
3. Define a representation for Transformational rules

A sample Phrase Structure (PS) grammar is given in Figure 4.1. (None of the grammars given in this book are to be considered complete grammars of the English language, but rather are sample grammars used for specific illustrative purposes. Writing accurate and complete grammars of any type is an extremely complicated and time-consuming process requiring skill and experience.) One sentence which can be generated by this grammar is

The dog can run in the park.

$$S \rightarrow NP + VP \qquad (4.1)$$

$$NP \rightarrow Det + N \qquad (4.2)$$

$$VP \rightarrow VP\ ADV \qquad (4.3)$$

$$VP \rightarrow Aux + V \qquad (4.4)$$

$$ADV \rightarrow PP \qquad (4.5)$$

$$ADV \rightarrow Adv \qquad (4.6)$$

$$PP \rightarrow Prep + NP \qquad (4.7)$$

$$Det \rightarrow a,\ the,\ this,\ \ldots \qquad (4.8)$$

$$N \rightarrow dog,\ baby,\ park,\ \ldots \qquad (4.9)$$

$$Aux \rightarrow must,\ can,\ \ldots \qquad (4.10)$$

$$V \rightarrow run,\ smile,\ hurt,\ \ldots \qquad (4.11)$$

$$Adv \rightarrow quickly,\ slowly,\ \ldots \qquad (4.12)$$

$$Prep \rightarrow in,\ with,\ by,\ \ldots \qquad (4.13)$$

Figure 4.1   Phrase Structure Grammar

which has the phrase marker shown in Figure 4.2. This sentence was produced by applying the following rules:

$$S \rightarrow NP + VP \qquad (4.1)$$
$$NP \rightarrow Det + N \qquad (4.2)$$
$$Det \rightarrow The \qquad (4.8)$$
$$N \rightarrow dog \qquad (4.9)$$
$$VP \rightarrow VP + ADV \qquad (4.3)$$

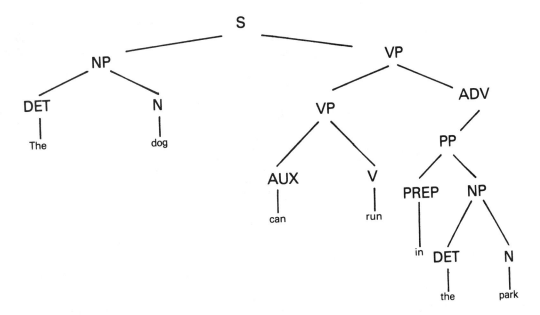

Figure 4.2   Phrase Marker

```
VP  →  Aux + V        (4.4)
Aux →  can            (4.10)
V   →  run            (4.11)
ADV →  PP             (4.5)
PP  →  Prep + NP      (4.7)
Prep →  in            (4.13)
NP  →  Det + N        (4.2)
Det →  the            (4.8)
N   →  park           (4.9)
```

Exercise: Determine whether there is a correspondence between the level of division within the tree and the number of rules which have been applied at that point.

In choosing a data structure to represent phrase markers, one must realize immediately that if a phrase marker is a tree structure, then the tree structure would be the most appropriate data structure available. [2]

It is not the only one; phrase markers can be represented as strings, in which case the various constituents selected (on the right hand side of the rule) by applying a specific rule would replace the preceding constituent (on the left hand side of the rule). However using strings as described here would obscure the hierarchical structure and the grammatical categories; thus the tree representation is better. If we assume (for the moment, at least) that PS rules have at most two constituents on the right hand side of the arrow, then binary trees will be a reasonable representation. A binary tree has two branches from each nonterminal node, and can be defined by the following type declaration:

```
type nodeptr = ^node;
     node = record
              info :  (* whatever the data is *)
              left :  nodeptr;
              right:  nodeptr;
          end; (*node record *)
```

(The notation `^node` means that `nodeptr` is defined as a pointer to a variable of type `node`.) A tree then consists of a root node, containing some piece of information, a pointer to a subtree branching to the left and a pointer to a subtree branching to the right. Each subtree also contains information, and left and right pointers. Finally the terminal nodes, called *leaves*, have null pointers since they do not point to another node. See Figure 4.3. Trees are dynamic data structures, in that the various parts of the tree are added as they are needed; the tree is built to fit the data it will contain. Not all binary trees are completely balanced with all branches present and extending the same length. In fact the phrase marker in Figure 4.2 is a binary tree even though the

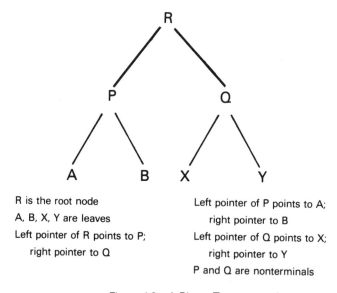

R is the root node
A, B, X, Y are leaves
Left pointer of R points to P;
    right pointer to Q

Left pointer of P points to A;
    right pointer to B
Left pointer of Q points to X;
    right pointer to Y
P and Q are nonterminals

Figure 4.3   A Binary Tree

right node is missing from the **ADV** node and several branches on the right half of the tree extend farther than the left half.

The only real difficulty of representing phrase markers as binary trees would occur if the restriction were lifted that the right side of a PS rule could contain only two constituents. For example if rules (4.3) and (4.4) were combined as

```
VP → Aux + V (ADV) (4.3&4)
```

then there are three constituents possible for a **VP**. However if the type definition for a **node** is modified to replace the **left** node with **daughter** and the **right** node with **next**,

```
type nodeptr = ^node;
    node = record
            info : (* whatever the data is *)
            daughter: nodeptr;
            next : nodeptr
        end; (*node record *)
```

then the problem is essentially eliminated. The first two constituents of **VP** rule are included in the **daughter** node of **VP** and the third element is pointed to by the **next** node of **VP**. Thus Figure 4.4 represents the phrase marker for the sentence,

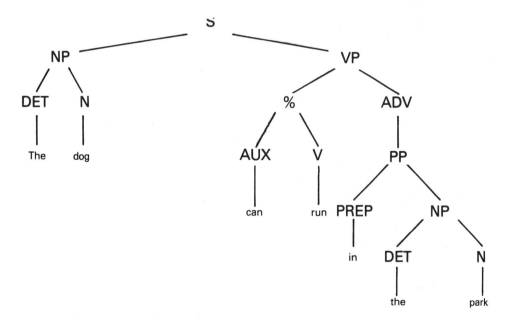

Figure 4.4   Phrase Marker with Dummy Node

The dog can run in the park.

using the combined (4.3 & 4) rule instead of (4.3) and (4.4). The only difference between Figure 4.4 and Figure 4.2 is the *dummy* node under **VP** which has no name, but is signified by the percent sign (%).

The **info** field of the **node** record must be determined. Two kinds of information occur in a phrase marker: at the root and at each non-terminal node only the type of constituent is needed; at the terminal nodes in addition to the type of constituent, the actual word selected must be included. Thus the type definition must be modified again to be a variant record with constituent type for all nodes and an additional field for terminal nodes.

```
type consttype = (S,NP,VP,Det,ADV,PP,Aux,V,Prep);
     nodetype = (root,terminal,nonterminal);
     nodeptr = ^node;
     node = record
                constit :  consttype;
                daughter:  nodeptr;
                next :  nodeptr;
                case nodetag :  nodetype of
                    terminal :  (word :  string);
            end; (*node record *)
```

Figure 4.5 shows the phrase marker from Figure 4.2 in the new format.

How is the information in the phrase marker to be accessed? Most linguistic references to constituents in a sentence start with the constituent type and then refer to the component parts. For example, a reasonable way to describe the constituents of the sentence,

The dog can run in the park.

would be:

[S [NP [Det,N], VP [VP [Aux,V], ADV [PP [Prep, NP [Det,N]], nil]]]

which is standard *pre-order traversal* of a binary tree representation. Pre-order traversal is performed by the following operations:

1. Visit the root.
2. Traverse the daughter subtree in pre-order.
3. Traverse the next subtree in pre-order.

Thus we start with **S**, then taking the daughter subtree in preorder, obtain **NP**, followed by **Det** and **N**. Having completed the daughter subtree, we proceed to the **NEXT** subtree, obtain **VP**, then the succeeding **VP**, **Aux**, **V**, and so forth.

Exercise: Write out the complete path through the tree in Figure 4.4 in preorder. In addition to preorder, there are two other traversal methods: *inorder traversal* and *postorder traversal*. The rules for these are as follows:

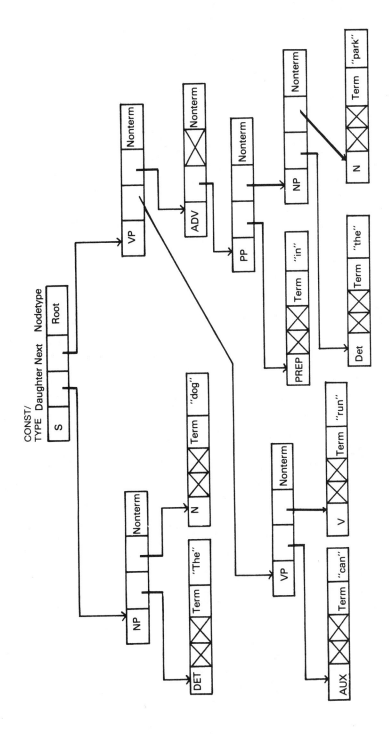

Figure 4.5   Phrase Marker of Figure 4.2 Defined by Type Definition 4.3

123

Inorder traversal:

1. Traverse the daughter subtree in inorder.
2. Visit the root.
3. Traverse the next subtree in inorder.

Postorder traversal:

1. Traverse the daughter subtree in postorder.
2. Traverse the next subtree in postorder.
3. Visit the root.

Write out the complete path through the tree in Figure 4.4 in inorder and postorder.

In traversing a tree in any order one must note that at certain points, the operation backs up. In other words, when a **daughter** node is reached, the location of the *parent* node that pointed to it must be available in order to obtain the pointer to the **next** node. And when the **next** node has been processed, the location of an *ancestor* node is required to continue the traversal. However we have no information about the location of preceding nodes because all the pointers point down toward the terminals. One solution to the problem is to make the tree a right in-threaded binary tree. (Another solution is to use a stack to keep up with the preceding pointers.) The term, *right in-threaded binary tree*, is a complicated name for a fairly simple modification to the tree. Referring to Figure 4.6, which is a right in-threaded version of Figure 4.2,

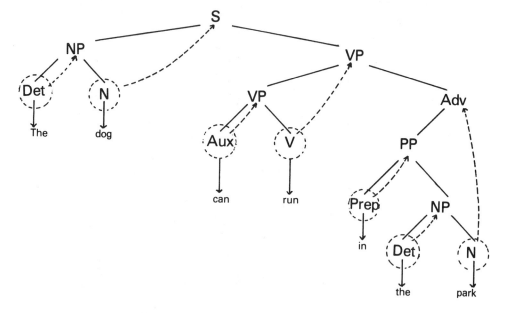

Figure 4.6   Phrase Marker with In-Right Threading

notice that the locations where backing up is necessary are only at the nodes with no successors, and these nodes have both pointers null. Thus, the next pointer is available for indicating the location of the ancestor node.

Implementing a threaded tree requires an indication in the node definition of whether each particular node is threaded or not; in other words, whether a pointer is a regular pointer to a successor node or a thread pointing back to a predecessor node. Therefore, the type definition must be modified once again.

```
type consttype = (S, NP, VP, Det, ADV, PP, Prep, N, Aux, V);
     nodetype = (root, terminal, nonterminal);
     nodeptr = ^node;
     node = record
                constit:consttype;
                daughter : nodeptr;
                next :   nodeptr;
                thread :   Boolean;
                case nodetag of
                     terminal : (word:string);
            end; (* node record *)
```

The Boolean item called thread indicates whether or not the next node which is our right node, points to a succeeding or preceding node. If thread is true, the node is threaded to point to an ancestor node; if thread is false, the node has regular pointers. Thus in Figure 4.6 the nodes, Det, N, Aux, V, Prep, Det, and N, would have thread set true; all other nodes would have thread set false. Figure 4.7 represents the phrase marker of Figure 4.6 in the structure of type definition given above.

One additional requirement for the type definition would be some delineation of the dummy node, which was used to allow more than two constituents on the right side of a PS rule. One approach would be to add a new nodetype called dummy, and modify the variant part of the node record to indicate that dummy nodes are regular nodes with no constituent type. Another approach would be to add dummy as a new constituent type. The decision of which approach is better and the implementation of dummy nodes is left as an exercise for the reader.

Next, methods for creating the nodes and pointers must be considered. Essentially three operations are required: first, creating a node and indicating the type of node; second, creating a pointer to a daughter node; and third, creating a pointer to a next node.

1. Creating a Node and Indicating the Type of Node

Since trees are dynamic structures, the only declaration is the pointer to the root node.

```
var phrasemarker :   nodeptr;
```

The actual creation of the nodes of the tree will occur during execution with a statement such as:

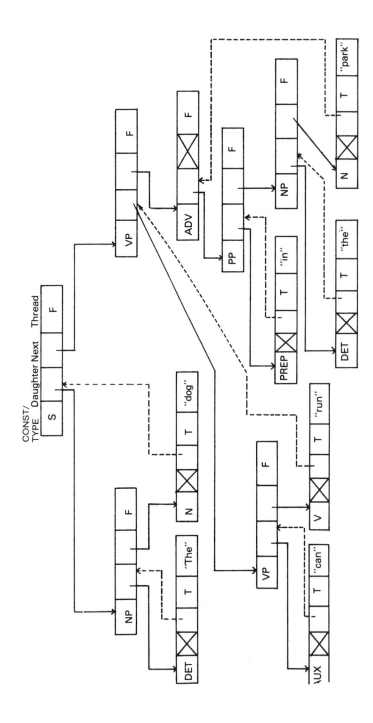

Figure 4.7 Diagram of Right In-Threaded Binary Tree Representation of "The dog can run in the park."

```
phrasemarker := makenode(S,root);
```

The function makenode is responsible for calling the standard procedure new, passing it the node type as a tag field in order to establish the proper format for the node. Assuming newnode is a working name for the node being created, in our case the statement would be:

```
new(newnode,root);
```

(For all the examples that follow, assume that newnode, oldnode, and tempnode are working variables of type nodeptr, used for the newly created node, the existing node, and a temporary node, respectively. Con is a working variable of type consttype.)

Separate calls to new would be required for terminal and nonterminal nodes. Makenode will also establish the constituent type. Thus in this example, phrasemarker is a pointer to the root node of the tree, and the value of this pointer is assigned after the makenode function creates the root node of constituent type S. The makenode function can also set the daughter and next nodes of the newly created node to nil, since it does not yet have any successors.

```
function makenode(con : consttype;
                  ntype :  nodetype)  :  nodeptr;

var newnode : nodeptr;

begin
    case ntype of
        root : new(newnode,root);
        nonterminal:new(newnode,nonterminal);
        terminal : new(newnode,terminal);
    end; (* case *)

    (* set constituent type *)

    newnode^.constit := con;

    (* set pointers to nil *)

    newnode^.daughter := nil;
    newnode^.next := nil;

    (* return value of function to new pointer *)

    makenode := newnode;

end; (* makenode function *)
```

The two procedures setdaughter and setnext will call makenode to create the new nodes to be pointed to.

2. Creating a Pointer to a daughter Node

Setdaughter will require three parameters: oldnode, the name of the existing node of which the daughter node is to be created; con, the constituent type for the new node; and STR, the value of the string to be assigned to word for terminal nodes. The constituent type can be used to determine the node type: S is a root node; NP, VP, PP, ADV are always nonterminals; and so on. In addition, the thread must be set. When a daughter node is created, the thread points back to the parent node; thus the first parameter, oldnode, becomes the thread. To illustrate, the daughter node of phrasemarker (as defined above) is to be created as a NP:

```
setdaughter(phrasemarker,NP,'');
```

(The null string must be included even though nonterminal nodes do not have a word field.) The setdaughter procedure will call makenode:

```
newnode := makenode(con,nonterminal);
```

Then the daughter pointer must be set to the new node:

```
oldnode^.daughter := newnode;
```

The new node must be threaded to point back to the old node:

```
newnode^.next := oldnode;
newnode^.thread := true;
```

3. Creating a Pointer to a next Node

The setnext procedure is similar to setdaughter: it has the same three parameters; it also calls makenode to create the appropriate type of node, and sets up the thread. However, there are some differences. The most obvious is that the next pointer is set to the new node instead of the daughter pointer. Also the thread must be handled differently because the next pointer of the new node will not point to the parent, but rather to some ancestor node preceding the parent node. It will however point to the node to which the parent node is threaded; therefore, the next node of the parent node must be saved to become the thread for the newly created node. In addition, the parent node is no longer threaded so thread must be set to false.

```
(* save the thread of the oldnode *)

tempnode := oldnode^.next;

(* unthread  oldnode *)

oldnode^.thread := false;

(* create next pointer *)

oldnode^.next := newnode;

(* thread newnode *)
```

```
newnode^.next := tempnode;
newnode^.thread := true;
```

The implementation of the complete definitions for the procedures **setdaughter** and **setnext** is left as an exercise for the reader.

Exercise: Include a more complex grammar with **S** as non-root and multiple constituents on right, etc. Modify type definitions and procedures to handle new aspects.

Exercise: What is the algorithm for traversing a binary tree using a stack rather than with threading?

PHRASE STRUCTURE RULES

Phrase structure (PS) rules are essentially rules for replacing a constituent named on the left side of the rule by the constituents named on the right side of the rule. Special cases of PS rules are the first rule in a grammar, which defines the **root** or starting point for the generation process; and the rules containing **terminals**, in which the constituents named are replaced by actual words rather than other constituents. PS rules are quite similar to BNF (Backus Naur Form) rules; in fact, BNF notation was derived from Chomsky's use of PS rules in the 1950's. (Only context-free PS rules are being considered here.)

There are two primary methods for representing PS rules in a program: (1) as data declared in the program or input to the program, and (2) as procedural elements of the program, either modularized procedures or sections of code. Researchers writing natural language processing systems have been arguing the merits of the two approaches for several years, and some have resolved the dilemma by adopting schemes for combining both methods. Let us consider the two primary methods.

If PS rules are defined as data, the two areas of concern are format of the data and the access of the data. One straightforward representation scheme would be to write the rules as text—strings of characters—in much the same form as shown in Figure 4.1, for instance, with one rule per record. Any access to the rules would require basic string manipulation operations (see Chapter 2), such as scanning the strings for particular delimiters (→ or +) and matching a string, such as a constituent name, in one rule with a string in another rule. String manipulation is fairly slow relative to other kinds of processing, but a storage technique of this sort would have the advantage that text strings are easily modified by the user; thus, different grammars and combinations of rules could be tried with minor effort. Certainly the programs would not have to be changed. In order to retain the flexibility of easily modifiable rules and also improve processing speed, the text strings can be written as an external form which is then converted to an internal form more easily accessed. In other words, the user could deal with PS rules in text form, but the program would access the rules only after they had been converted into another form, perhaps pointers or numerical codes.

On the other hand, constituents can be defined as procedure names, such that encountering a constituent immediately creates a call to the procedure which handles that type of constituent. This method works in programs written in languages that make little or no distinction between data and executable statements, such as LISP or SMALLTALK. Another level at which this approach works is in assembly language, where a procedure can be accessed by means of an address stored in a table. Then a table lookup operation functions in a manner comparable to a name which triggers a procedure call. See Figure 4.8.

In a Pascal-like language which makes a strong distinction between data and executable statements and does not allow manipulation of procedure addresses as described, the **case** statement provides an alternate control mechanism for this method. The recognition of a particular constituent triggers the selection of the appropriate case list element and thus execution of the relevant procedure. For example, assuming con is defined as **consttype** as described above, then the following **case** structure would implement our PS rules.

```
case con of

   S:(* sentence handling routine *)

   NP : (* noun phrase handling routine *)

   VP : (* verb phrase handling routine *)

   and so forth.

end; (* case *)
```

What do each of the routines do when they are executed? The answer to that question depends on the particular use of the PS rules. If the rules are being used to generate sentences, then each routine would have to call the routines which generate the sub-constituents of that constituent. For example the sentence handling routine would have to call the *noun phrase* handling routine and the *verb phrase* handling routine, which would in turn call the *determiner* routine and the *noun* routine, and so forth. When a terminal was reached, for instance, a noun, then the routine to handle that would select an actual word to fill the slot. All the routines could be defined as functions which return a pointer to the particular node generated.

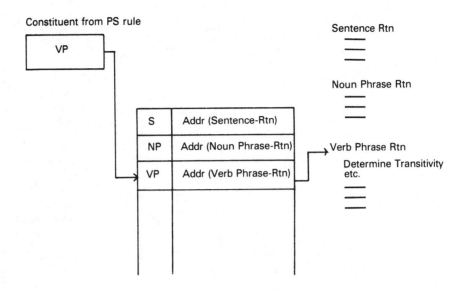

Figure 4.8   Table Lookup Operation

If the purpose of the system is analysis, breaking an existing sentence into its constituent parts, a different method would be required. In this situation a call to a particular routine, say a `Verb` routine or a `PP` routine, might require determination of whether or not the element under consideration is in fact a verb or a prepositional phrase. Syntactic analysis, also known as parsing, will be considered in detail in later chapters.

Exercise: (1) Write a procedure to create a phrase marker and assign values to terminals (input words from keyboard); (2) Write a procedure to access the phrase marker and write out the sentence; (3) Write a procedure to access the phrase marker and write out the analysis [S [NP . . . .]].

TRANSFORMATIONAL RULES

Transformational rules, described by Chomsky in *Syntactic Structures*, consisted of two components: the structural description (SD) and the structural change (SC). The structural description lists the constituents which must be present in a sentence in order for the sentence to be transformed by that particular rule. For example, the SD for the *passive* rule could be written:

```
[NP, Aux, Vt, NP, (Adv)]
```

which would be indexed as:

```
X1, X2, X3, X4, X5
```

to indicate the position of each constituent within the sentence. The SC would show the final position of each constituent by giving the index numbers:

```
X1 X2 X3 X4 X5  →  X4 - X2 - be + en + X3 - by + X1 - X5
```

Thus the sentence,

```
The car will hit that tree soon.

NP    Aux   Vt    NP    Adv

X1    X2    X3    X4    X5
```

would be transformed by this rule to:

```
That tree will be + en + hit by the car soon.
```

Another transformational rule would resolve be + en + hit into be hit to produce:

```
That tree will be hit by the car soon.
```

(The be indicates the inclusion of the proper form of the *be* verb; and the en + v says to include the past participle form of the verb, in this case *hit.*)

One way to represent T-rules for processing would be as follows:

```
const maxcon = 10; (* maximum number of constituents in transrule *)

type constituent : consttype;
     transrule = record
                  sd :  array[1..maxcon] of constituent;
                  sc :  array[1..maxcon] of integer;
                 end; (* transrule record *)
```

(The integers in sc refer to the index position of the constituents in the sd.) This form will not even handle the example given above because it has no provision for additional elements besides the original constituents in the sentence; in this case, be + en. It also does not deal with the combination of constituents which occurs in some T-rules. The rule called There-insertion illustrates the problems.

```
sd:  [NP      V       X]

      1       2       3

sc:  THERE+2  1       3
```

(The symbols, X, Y, Z, are used to indicate unknowns. X, Y, or Z match any constituent that happens to be in that position.) The word, *there,* is combined with the verb to produce the first element of the transformation. For example,

A tiger is in the cage.

is transformed into

There is a tiger in the cage.

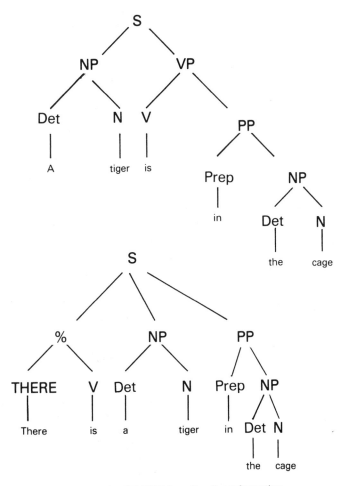

Figure 4.9   Example of THERE-Insertion Transformation

The plus sign (+) means *sister adjunction*; the two (or more) constituents will be combined under the same node of the phrase marker, on the same level, thus the notion of sisters. See Figure 4.9, for the phrase markers of the example before and after the transformation.

Some provision must be added to the declaration of **transrule** to represent added elements, such as literals or structural indicators, and adjunction. If the declaration of **constituent** is expanded to include a literal string instead of a constituent type, **transrule** will handle added elements.

```
type constituent = record
                   constit : consttype;
                   case nodetag :  nodetype of
                      terminal:(word :  string);
                   end; (* constituent record *)
        transrule = record
                   sd :   array[1..maxcon] of constituent;
                   sc :   array[1..maxcon] of integer;
                   end; (* transrule record *)
```

In order to deal with adjunction, the elements of the array in sc must be defined with a variant record as well. There are essentially three types of indexes possible: the regular index which refers to an element of sd, a null index which refers to a position in the sd which is now empty, and a complex element made up of multiple constituents combined by adjunction. Both of the first two indexes can be represented by an integer value; the first in the range of 1 to the number of constituents in the sd, the second as zero. However, the third must allow for more than one constituent.

```
type constituent = record
                   constit = consttype;
                   case nodetag :  nodetype of
                       terminal:(word :  string);
                   end; (* constituent record *)
        indextype = (regind, emptycon, multicon);
        index = record
                case ind :  indextype of
                   regind,emptycon :
                        (indx :  integer);
                   multicon :
                        (leftindx :  integer;
                         leftstr  :  string;
                         rightindx :  integer;
                         rightstr :  string);
                end; (* index record *)
        transrule = record
                   sd :   array[1..maxcon] of constituent;
                   sc :   array[1..maxcon] of index;
                   end; (* transrule record *)
```

(leftindx and rightindx would specify indexed items on either side of the + sign; leftstr and rightstr would hold inserted items such as the word *there* in the There-insertion rule.)

The specific rules can be defined in several ways. One "quick and dirty" way would be to assign the values to the array elements in assignment statements in the program. A neater way would be to read in values from a file (e.g., a disk file or interactive terminal) and assign them as input. This would have the advantage of allowing modification of rules and addition of new rules without modification of the program.

Exercise: The declaration of `index` above only handles two elements in combination in adjunction. Modify the declaration to handle any number of constituents in combination.

Exercise: Other types of adjunction exist besides sister adjunction: *mother adjunction* and *daughter adjunction*. Daughter adjunction causes the constituent moved to be placed under the constituent it is combined with. Mother adjunction causes the constituent moved to be made a sister adjunct to the node that dominates the constituent indicated. Using the symbols **&** and | to indicate daughter adjunction and mother adjunction respectively, the rules below would produce the trees shown in Figure 4.10.

```
[A   B   C   D]

 1   2   3   4

 1  4+2  3   0

[A   B   C   D]

 1   2   3   4

 1  4&2  3   0

[A   B   C   D]

 1   2   3   4

 1  4|2  3   0
```

Modify the declaration of `transrule` to indicate these three types of adjunction.

Exercise: Particle movement is one important transformation. Find the rule in a linguistics book on transformational grammar. Create values for the rule for Particle movement and write a procedure to implement the transformation.

Exercise: Using the procedure from the previous exercise, create a phrase marker for a sentence, apply the particle movement rule, printing out both versions. Apply other rules found in a linguistics reference.

CHOMSKY'S STANDARD THEORY

In discussing Chomsky's 1957 grammar, we have assumed that the *lexeme* (or word) chosen for a terminal constituent was selected from the appropriate lexicon in some unexplained manner, perhaps at random. Obviously that is not an adequate solution for a working system. Therefore additional information about the lexemes and their function in the sentence is required to permit a meaningful selection process. As we discussed in Chapter 1, Chomsky came to

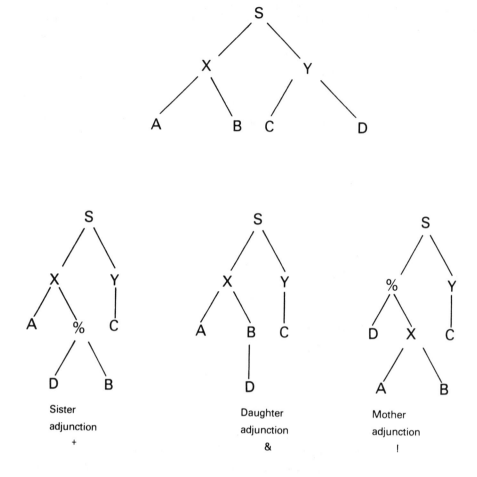

Figure 4.10   Three Types of Adjunction

the same conclusion after considering the work of other linguists, in particular, Jerrold J. Katz and Jerry A. Fodor. [3]

Katz and Fodor developed a theory of semantics that consisted of two components: a dictionary and a set of projection rules. The dictionary consists of entries for each word (or morpheme) of the language, comprised of a semantic portion, a grammatical portion, and a phonological portion. The primary element of concern in the grammatical portion for an entry would be the identification of the part of speech, or constituent type, that word could be. For example, the word *airplane* is a noun and could be used grammatically only in situations allowing nouns. Words which could be more than one constituent type, such as *plane*, which could be a noun (with two different senses) or a verb, would have more complex entries. For each sense or meaning of the word, the semantic portion of the dictionary entry would consist of two types of identifiers: semantic markers and distinguishers. Semantic markers would identify each word-sense according to a set of primitive features, such as *human, physical object, young,* and so on. The distinguishers would further differentiate between various senses of a particular word by describing additional aspects of each word-sense in order to make it unique. Various relations could be determined between different words; if the semantic markers of two different words are the same, then those two words are said to be *synonymous.*

Exercise: Make up a list of primitive features for nouns and adjectives. Would primitive features for verbs be different? In what way(s)?

The projection rules are used to combine the semantic markers of the individual constituents of a sentence to produce the meaning of the various complex constituents of the sentence. In other words, the semantic markers of the individual words of a noun phrase would be combined, and only those combinations that did not conflict would be retained to represent the meaning of the noun phrase as a whole. If we refer back to the example given in Chapter 1, the noun phrase, *the colorful ball,* would have several different possible meanings, but the notion of a cannonball with green and purple stripes is not likely and therefore would be discarded. Thus the projection rules can be thought of as being applied in a bottom-up manner first to the terminal nodes of the phrase marker, then to each group of nodes successively up the tree until the root node is reached. When the semantic markers have been combined for all components of the root node, we can say that the meaning of the sentence has been determined. To use linguistic terminology, a semantic interpretation of the sentence has been achieved.

Let us now turn to the problems of representing the dictionary entries. Each entry in the lexicon must contain the word—known as the *head*—to identify the entry. The other major components of the entry would be the grammatical part and the semantic part. (We shall continue to ignore the phonological part.)

```
type lexentry = record
                head : string;
                grampart : (* grammatical information*)
                sempart : (* semantic information *)
            end; (* lexentry record *)
```

The grammatical part would identify the constituent role this word could play in a sentence. Since some words can be different constituent types in different situations, each type would need to be identified. The semantic part then would be included with each different constituent type, much like a regular dictionary entry, which gives all the senses of the word for one part of speech, then all the senses for another part of speech, and so on. The semantic part would contain: 1) semantic markers indicating whether or not each primitive feature applied to this word, and 2) the distinguisher to make finer discriminations between words than are possible from semantic markers alone. Since each sense of the word would have a different set of semantic markers and distinguishers, the semantic part would be repeated for each word-sense.

A semantic marker will be one of three possible states for a particular word: + or -, if that primary feature applies or its reverse applies, respectively, or 0, if that feature is not applicable to this word. Thus, markers will be defined by the type,

```
type tristate = ('-','0','+');
```

The markers will be stored in an array indexed by the marker names; for now, they will be referred to merely by their position within the array—firstsm..lastsm. A possible representation for the dictionary entry as described so far is given below:

```
type posint = (1..maxint);
     tristate = ('-','0','+');
     markers = packed array[firstsm..lastsm] of tristate;
     lexentry = record
                    head :  string;
                    numconsttype :  posint;
                    grampart :  array[1..numconsttype] of consttype;
                    numsenses :  posint;
                    sempart :  array[1..numsenses] of
                              record
                                   semmarker : markers;
                                   distinguisher :  string
                              end (* sempart record *)
          end; (* lexentry record *)
```

Maxint is a constant equal to the maximum integer value for a particular implementation of Pascal. Notice that numconsttype and numsenses are defined as posint, positive integers; an upper bound allowing fewer possible elements would be appropriate. Note also that grampart and sempart are defined as variable dimension arrays, which are not a part of standard Pascal. In variable arrays the value of the dimensions are not defined until execution time. This structure is intuitively logical even though it cannot be defined in this way in the programming language. The distinguisher is defined as a string simply for convenience; its use has not been specified and therefore its structure is vague. The distinguisher string can be scanned as necessary when information from it is needed. Recalling the example shown in Figure 1.3 in Chapter 1, the distinguishers for the sense of the word, *bachelor*, which is [+human], [+male], are *who has never married* and *young knight serving under the standard of another knight*. If the interpretation of the sentence required information in addition to that in the markers themselves, the strings for the two distinguishers could be scanned.

Applying the Projection Rules produces the various readings of each sentence part, by building up a semantic interpretation for phrases, then for clauses, and then for the sentence as a whole. Quoting from Katz and Fodor (1964), the projection rule that would handle combining the markers from a noun and its modifier into the markers for a noun phrase is as follows:

(R1) Given two paths of the form

```
(1) Lexical String1 → syntactic markers of head →
(al) → (a2) → ... → (an) → [1] <set of strings
of markers OMEGA1>
(2) Lexical String2 → syntactic markers of modifier →
(bl) → (b2) → ... → (bm) → [2] <set of strings
of markers OMEGA2>
```

such that there is a substring OMEGA of the string of syntactic or semantic head markers and OMEGA [is an element of] OMEGA2. There is an amalgam of the form

```
Lexical String2 + Lexical String1 → dominating node
marker → (al) → (a2) → ... → (an) → (bl) →
(b2) → ... → (bm) → [[2] [1]] <OMEGA1>,
```

where any bi is null when (THERE EXISTS ai) (bi = ai) and [[2] [1]] is [1] where [2] = [1]. [4]

Essentially the semantic markers are combined in a manner that eliminates repetition, by union of the sets of markers. Thus any primitive which is + in either the first set or the second set of markers would be + in the resulting set of markers; any primitive which is + in both sets would be + in the resulting set, but would occur only once. In order to resolve conflicting combinations which could arise, such as + in one set and − in the other, one of the constituents in each pair can be considered primary, and the other secondary. In other words, for each combination of constituents, such as modifier and head, one of them can be considered a stronger type, the head. A table can be used to represent the possible choices from two sets of markers and the resulting markers:

PRIMARY	SECONDARY	RESULT
0	0	0
0	+	+
+	0	+
+	+	+
+	−	+
−	+	−
−	−	−
−	0	−
0	−	−

The two combinations (**+ -**) and (**- +**) are somewhat ambiguous in that these constituents have some marker in conflict. For example, in the phrase *small elephant*, the word *elephant* might include a marker [+SIZE] to indicate its largeness whereas the main meaning of *small* would be conveyed by [-SIZE]. Thus by our rules [+SIZE] and [-SIZE] would be resolved to [+SIZE] since the head is primary. However *small elephant* could refer to a tiny figurine of only a few inches as well as a live baby elephant of only a few hundred pounds. Obviously our method is not very precise in determining meaning. But the resolution of ambiguity of that sort requires consideration of context, not merely reference to a dictionary.

In a noun phrase such as *colorful ball*, the noun would be the *head* and the adjective, the *modifier*. If the noun phrase were *light red ball*, this rule could also be applied to the adjective phrase, *light red*, in which *red* is the head and *light* is the modifier; then the combined phrase would be the modifier of the noun *ball*. Similar rules explain the resolution of the semantic markers of an article and noun, of a subject and verb, of a verb and its object.

Exercise: Look through a dictionary for an entry with multiple senses. Write out the word using the form given in the declaration of `lexentry`. Consider whether a better design could be developed for `lexentry`. In what ways can it be improved?

Exercise: Make up projection rules similar to Katz and Fodor's above, for an article and noun, a subject and verb, and a verb and its object.

How can the semantic information of this type be linked to the representation of a sentence? The lexicon would probably be a mass storage file of records of `lexentry` type with one variable length record for each word. Within a phrase marker, as declared earlier in the chapter, each terminal node should point to a lexical entry rather than merely containing a string to represent the word. This change to the definition of `node` would give:

```
type node = record
              constit : consttype;
              daughter : nodeptr;
              next : nodeptr;
              thread : Boolean;
              case nodetag : nodetype of
                    terminal : (word : ^lexentry);
            end; (* node record *)
```

(Note that the pointer to `lexentry` would refer to a file and therefore would not be a pointer in the sense of a Pascal pointer as given here. The notation is used for convenience, not accuracy.) In addition, the `nonterminal` nodes need to be changed to include the collection of semantic markers derived from the subordinate parts of that constituent when the projection rules are applied. However the requirements differ for the various complex constituent types. For example in a noun phrase the semantic markers for the modifiers must agree with the semantic markers for the noun, but the combination will produce a synthesis of the modifier markers and the noun markers. Verbs, on the other hand, require a more complicated scheme. A transitive verb which takes a subject and an object requires two sets of semantic markers to show semantic requirements for the subject and object. An intransitive verb would only need one set for the subject; and a copulative verb would have one set which would be a combination of the subject and the predicate nominative. The various changes then that need to be made to the **node** declaration would also involve the different types of semantic sets for nonterminal nodes.

Complex Symbols

Chapter 1 described how Chomsky incorporated Katz and Fodor's semantic theory into his grammar. The *base* of the *syntactic component* included *phrase structure* rules to generate phrase markers and the *lexicon*, containing all the lexical items, or words, of the language. The lexicon also had rules of lexical insertion which were similar to projection rules, in that they stated the restrictions on how the semantic markers of the constituents had to match. In other words, the rules of lexical insertion stated that if the noun in the subject position was [+HUMAN], then the verb in the predicate had to accept a human subject. The sentence,

Colorless green ideas sleep furiously.

violates the selection restrictions in several ways. The verb *sleep* requires an animate subject, but *ideas* are abstract and not animate. Since *ideas* are abstract, they cannot be described as *green* because only *physical objects* can have color. In addition if something is described as *green*, it cannot also be *colorless*. And finally the word, *furiously*, is quite inappropriate for modifying the verb *sleep*.

Chomsky used the term *complex symbol*, to identify the combination of the markers from constituents under a common node. (See Figure 1.5 for an illustration.) Representing complex symbols as defined by Chomsky would entail having a different representation for each type of nonterminal node— noun phrase, verb phrase, etc.—and expanding the definition of the constituent V to enable differentiation between transitive, intransitive, and copulative verbs. Thus the declaration of the constituent types would be:

```
type consttype = (S, NP, VP, Det, Adv, PP, Aux, Art, N, Vt,
                  Vi, Vc, Adj, Prep, X);
```

Then the definition **node** would be expanded:

```
node = record
         constit : consttype;
         daughter : nodeptr;
         next : nodeptr;
```

```
thread : Boolean;
case nodetag : nodetype of
  terminal :  (word :^lexentry);
  nonterminal : record
                    case constag : consttype of
                      NP : (npmarker : markers);
                      VP : (vpmarker : record
                                          subjmarker :  markers;
                                          objmarker :  markers;
                                        end;(* vpmarker record *));
                      (* and so on for all nonterminal node types *)
                    end; (* nonterminal record *)
end; (* node record *)
```

The declaration for **node** given above only works for one reading of each constituent, therefore no ambiguity or even alternate readings would be allowed.

Exercise: Modify the declaration for **node** to handle as many readings as needed.

Another weakness with this representation for **node** is that verb types have not been differentiated. When the constituent type is **VP**, **vpmarker** is made up of **subjmarker** and **objmarker**. This arrangement would match transitive verbs, which have both a subject and an object. If we just ignore **objmarker** for intransitive verbs and use **objmarker** for predicate nominative or complement for copulative verbs, **vpmarker** would work. But a more sophisticated declaration would be more appropriate.

Exercise: Modify **node** to handle different types of verbs differently.

Verbs such as *give* which take an indirect object would not be covered by this representation of **node** even if it included three separate variant parts for transitive, intransitive, and copulative verbs. It should be obvious that continuing to add pieces to the declaration whenever an exception is encountered makes for a very messy declaration. A more appropriate approach would be to begin over with a different method, as many linguists have done.

CONCLUSION

Transformational generative grammar is not an elegant solution to the problems of linguists interested in using computers to test and implement their theories, although it has been important in theoretical linguistics. The phrase structure rules can be used to generate sentences, and the transformation rules can produce certain variations. However this type of grammar is not satisfactory. It is not symmetrical, in that the rules which work for generation of sentences cannot be reversed to apply to the analysis of sentences. Another weakness of transformational generative grammar is that it works too closely with the surface structure. According to the Generative Semanticists, the lexical selection is applied too early. Apparently transformational generative grammars are too syntactically oriented, without allowing for semantic concerns. These major objections have been dealt with by the methods to be considered next. Transition networks were designed to handle the problems of analysis that transformational grammars are unsuited for, and the problems of semantics are better dealt with by case grammar, semantic networks, and conceptual dependency theory.

Chapter 5

Transition Networks

Another approach to representing natural language structures uses the model known as *transition networks*. Transition networks are based on the application of the mathematical notions of graph theory and finite state machines to the study of grammars. There are several types of transition networks, which differ in complexity and effectiveness. [1]

A *finite state machine* is a theoretical (or actual) device which begins in a particular state and changes state when specific conditions occur. It is finite in that, at any point in its operation, the next state can be determined by knowing the current state and the conditions which can cause a transition. Since it is restricted in this manner, the number of states is known and therefore considered finite. The most basic network is the *finite state transition graph*, which consists of a group of nodes connected by directed arcs. Each node represents a state in a finite state machine, and the arcs show the transitions from one state to another. Each arc is labelled with the condition which causes the transition along that arc from its tail to its head. In computer science, networks made up of multiple nodes with multiple links are often represented as graphs. Rather than develop the theoretical and mathematical implications of graph theory, we will proceed with an intuitive notion of graphs as an important type of data structure. [2]

FINITE STATE TRANSITION NETWORKS

As the most basic level of transition network, the finite state transition graph can represent the sequence in which words can appear in a sentence by following the path through the graph. For example, a grammar which allows the sequence,

Article Noun Auxiliary Verb

such as in the sentence

The boy may swim.

can be represented by the finite state transition diagram in Figure 5.1. In the diagram the circles are the nodes and represent the particular state of the sentence recognizer or generator at that point. Each line between the nodes is an arc and indicates the terminal symbol (in this case, the word category) which will cause a transition from the current state to a subsequent state. Each arc has arrows indicating the direction of the transition, and thus this kind of diagram is called a *directed graph* or digraph. In the diagram, state Q0 is referred to as the initial state and Q5 as the final state. A transition network has only one initial state, but may have more than one final state. Notice that this diagram serves to describe other sentences as well, such as the following:

The brown dog runs.
The little children can sing.
A bad girl cries.

The information provided by the transition diagram can also be given in table form, indicating at each state a transition which is possible based on a particular symbol. Thus the information required to establish a transition network is a series of triplets of the form (Qi, C, Qj) where Qi is the current state, C is the condition (or symbol) which causes this transition, and Qj is the subsequent state. The triplets required to define the state diagram in Figure 5.1 are:

(Q0, ART, Q1)
(Q1, NOUN, Q3)
(Q1, ADJ, Q2)
(Q2, NOUN, Q3)
(Q3, AUX, Q4)
(Q3, VERB, Q5)
(Q4, VERB, Q5)

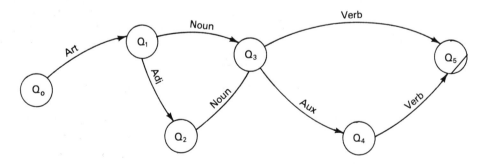

Figure 5.1   A Deterministic Finite State Transition Network

In this diagram at each node, a word of a particular class, such as a noun or an article, determines one and only one subsequent node; this type of state diagram is called *deterministic*. A non-deterministic network could have one word type causing more than one transition from a particular node, as shown in Figure 5.2. Here at state Q1, a verb can cause a transition to Q2, which is a terminal state, or to Q3 which expects a noun to follow (i.e., a direct object). Either path can produce a grammatically correct sentence. (This particular example can be rewritten as a deterministic model, as can all nondeterministic graphs.) From now on we will consider only deterministic transition networks.

Implementation of Finite State Transition Graphs in Pascal

One method for implementing the finite state transition graph is to use an integer array:

```
const maxelements = 100;
var finstategraph : array[1..maxelements] of integer;
```

The format of the elements within the array defines the graph. The first position of the array is the entry for the initial state; each node contains the following information:

```
State number (starting with 0)
```

```
Number of arcs leaving this state (n)
```

```
Repeat n times:
  Index of symbol causing transition (reference to symbol table)
  Index of next state if this arc is followed
```

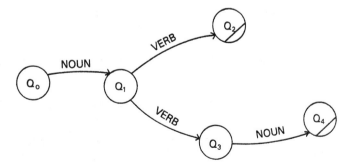

Figure 5.2   Non-Deterministic Finite State Transition Network

Since the array is integer, a symbol cannot be included; therefore a symbol table must be built to contain each of the valid symbols. For example the symbol table for the finite state transition diagram in Figure 5.1 would be:

Index	Symbol
1	ART
2	NOUN
3	ADJ
4	AUX
5	VERB

Using this symbol table, the finite state transition diagram in Figure 5.1 would be stored as:

Index	Integer value	Explanation
1	0	Q0
2	1	# of arcs
3	1	Index to ART in symbol table
4	5	Pointer to Q1
5	1	Q1
6	2	# of arcs
7	2	Index to NOUN in symbol table
8	15	Pointer to Q3
9	3	Index to ADJ in symbol table
10	11	Pointer to Q2
11	2	Q2
12	1	# of arcs
13	2	Index to NOUN in symbol table
14	15	Pointer to Q3
15	3	Q3
16	2	# of arcs
17	4	Index to AUX in symbol table
18	21	Pointer to Q4
19	5	Index to VERB in symbol table
20	25	Pointer to Q5
21	4	Q4
22	1	# of arcs
23	5	Index to VERB in symbol table
24	25	Pointer to Q5
25	5	Q5
26	0	# of arcs (0 indicates terminal state)

Exercise: Using the format for representing finite state transition graphs given above, write a program to accept triplets for defining a graph and build the symbol table and the array for the particular graph defined. (The format for inputting the triplets could use only the state number rather than the letter and number; e.g., 0 instead of Q0, 1 instead of Q1, etc. The symbol is the literal string of characters. Commas are not required, but may be used for delimiters.) Print out the triplets read, the symbol table and the array built to represent the graph.

The finite state transition network is actually quite limited for representing natural language grammars. Some language phenomena cannot be represented by finite state transition networks, such as matched parentheses. Also because each arc is identified by a terminal symbol, some common and fairly uncomplicated sentence structures require extremely complex graphs. For example, sentences containing noun phrases, such as an article followed by an optional adjective followed by a noun, would require the diagram representing the noun phrase to be repeated whenever it is needed—as the subject, as the object of the verb, as the object of the preposition. Another solution, the recursive transition network, allows arcs to represent entire complex constructions, with each construction having its own graph to represent it.

RECURSIVE TRANSITION NETWORKS

A *recursive transition network* is like a finite state network in that it has one start state and one or more final states. All the states and the arcs connecting them are named. In addition to these characteristics, the RTN can have arc names which are state names—names of RTN's, thus the term *recursive*. Essentially traversing the graph which represents an RTN, such as Figure 5.3, involves checking the arcs at each node, or state. If an arc is a terminal symbol (i.e., a lexical category), control moves to the node at the head of the arc and the process begins again. If the arc is a state name (such as NP, for noun phrase), it represents a complete RTN. Therefore control must pass to the initial state of the RTN named on the arc. In this lower-level RTN, control will move from arc to arc as before, until a final state is reached. If the final state is reached without error, then control returns successfully to the higher-level graph and continues as before. If the final state is not reached successfully, then either an error has occurred or, more probably, the arc being tested does not apply.

Using the RTN's in Figure 5.3 as an example, notice that the arcs labeled NP (for noun phrase) and PP (for prepositional phrase) are of particular interest and that each of these has its own graph. Essentially the processing proceeds from the start state by determining whether the first part of the sentence is a noun phrase or an auxiliary verb. The test for a noun phrase would be made by saving the position of the node at the tail of the arc in order to be able to restore it later, and transferring to the NP graph. If in fact a noun phrase is detected, then processing proceeds by finding the state saved, following the successful arc, and moving to the next state. If a NP was not found, then the test for AUX would be made and that arc followed if successful. If neither a

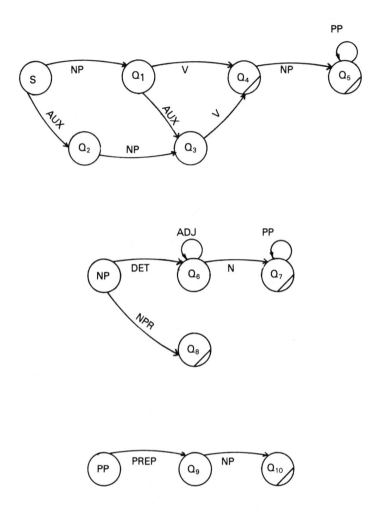

Figure 5.3   Recursive Transition Network (From William A. Woods, "Transition Network Grammars for Natural Language Analysis," CommACM, Vol. 13, October, 1970)

NP nor an AUX were found, then the string of symbols being tested would not be accepted as a sentence by this RTN.

Implementing RTN's

RTN's are obviously more complex than finite state transition graphs, and because of this complexity a different approach to their representation will be taken to provide greater flexibility. The graphs will be represented as linked lists which are dynamic structures rather than as arrays which are static structures.

Using a linked list implementation for the graph, each node will be represented by four elements: the information part of the node, a pointer to a list of all the arcs leaving the node, a pointer to another node if there is one, and an indication of whether or not this is a terminal node. Each arc in the linked list will contain a pointer to the head of the arc (i.e., the node reached by following that arc), the condition which causes transition along that arc (such as the symbols described earlier or the state names requiring recursion), and a pointer to another arc, if there is one. Figure 5.4 shows the general schema for the linked list representation and the particular representation of the NP part of the transition network in Figure 5.3.

In Pascal the arcs and nodes would be declared as follows:

```
type nodeptr = ^node;
     stateid = string;
     arcptr = ^arc;
     termsymbol = string;
     node = record
                info :   stateid;
                arclist :   arcptr;
                termnode :   Boolean;
                nextnode :   nodeptr
            end; (* node record *)
     arc = record
                arcinfo :   termsymbol;
                headnode :   nodeptr;
                nextarc :   arcptr
            end; (* arc record *)

     graph = nodeptr;

var  g : graph;
```

The variable g of type **graph** will be a pointer to the start state of the network. To initialize the first node of the network in the diagram in Figure 5.3, the following statements are needed.

```
var p,q : nodeptr;
    a,b : arcptr;

begin
  new(p);            (* get a new node          *)
  g := p;            (* set g to point to node  *)
  p^.info := 'S';    (* node name ← S           *)
  new(a);            (* get new arc             *)
  p^.arclist := a;   (* set ptr to arc          *)
  a^.arcinfo := 'NP'; (* arc name ← NP (state) *)
  new(q);            (* get new node            *)
  q^.info := 'Q1'    (* node name ← Q1          *)
```

node

nodeinfo	arclist	nextnode

where nodeinfo=state id
arclist=ptr to head of list of arcs
from the node
nextnode=ptr to another node
(or nil)

arc

arcinfo	head node	nextarc

where arcinfo=symbol or state id to cause transition
headnode=ptr to node at head of arc
nextarc=ptr to another arc (or nil)

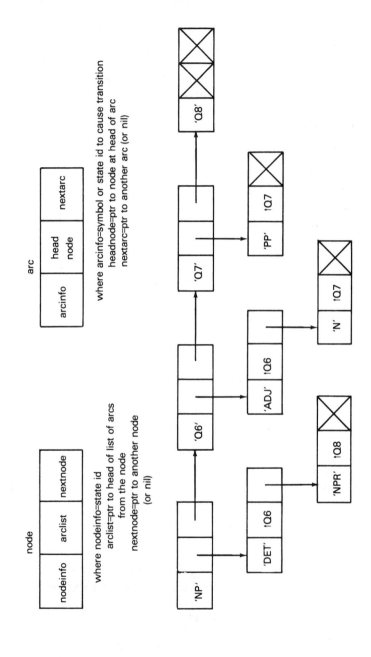

Figure 5.4   Linked List Representation of NP Part of Transition Network in Figure 5.3

```
p^.nextnode := q;      (* set ptr to next node    *)
new(b);                (* get new arc             *)
a^.nextarc := b;       (* set ptr to next arc     *)
b^.info := 'aux';      (* arc name ← AUX (state)*)
p := q;                (* save q as old ptr       *)
new(q);                (* get new node            *)
q^.info := 'Q2';       (* node name ← Q2          *)
p^.nextnode := q;      (* set ptr to next node    *)
        .
        .
        .
end
```

Obviously building the graph one node and one arc at a time is quite tedious and definitely not to be recommended. A general approach to building the graph would accept input data to define the graph, which could be built as the data is read.

Let us develop an algorithm to input quads (Qn C Qm F) where Qn is the node at the tail of an arc, C is the condition (terminal symbol or state name) causing the arc to be followed, Qm is the head of the arc, and F is the indicator for a final or terminal node. We will use the quads to build the graph to represent a recursive transition network. Each new graph within the RTN must be identified. There are two ways to identify them. The first would be to flag the input data so that the Qn for the first node of a graph is recognized as the name of the graph. Another way to locate the names of the graphs would be to match the C's, or conditions causing a transition, against the Q's, or state names, after all the quads have been input. Any condition which is the name of a node must have its own graph to represent the phrase. After entering all the quads for the example, the conditions possible should be saved in a symbol table with those which are state names flagged as such. The quads for the main graph of the diagram in Figure 5.3 would be:

```
S   NP   Q1   N
S   AUX  Q2   N
Q1  V    Q4   N
Q1  AUX  Q3   N
Q2  NP   Q3   N
Q3  V    Q4   N
Q5  PP   Q5   Y
```

For the NP part of the graph, these are needed:

```
NP  DET  Q6   N
NP  NPR  Q8   N
Q6  ADJ  Q6   N
Q6  N    Q7   N
Q7  PP   Q7   Y
Q8  NIL  NIL  Y
```

(The NIL's indicate a terminal node with no arc leaving it and therefore no head node.) Finally the PP part of the graph would require:

```
PP   PREP Q9   N
Q9   NP   Q10  N
Q10  NIL  NIL  Y
```

When these have all been input, the symbol table should include S, NP, AUX, V, PP, DET, NPR, ADJ, PP, and PREP. S, NP, and PP should be identified as state names since each begins a graph. Building the nodes and arcs for the graph proceeds as follows:

```
1) For the first quad of a graph, build the node and the arc
   emanating from it.
2) Repeat
        a) if the node does not already exist, build it, and
        b) build the arc needed.
   for each additional quad,
```

One tricky part of building the graph is connecting the arcs to the nodes to which they point since the head node descriptions generally follow the arc definitions. One solution might be to enter the quads in reverse order, but that would not guarantee success since sometimes the node definitions precede the arc definition (in normal order). A more reasonable approach would be to build the pointers to the heads of the arcs after all the quads have been entered and thus all the nodes are built. The pointers will combine the graphs when built correctly.

Exercise: Write a program to input the quads described above and build the graph. Test the program by traversing the graph to print out the name of each node and each arc leaving it. For the example used above, the output should begin:

```
NODE: S
      ARCS FOR S: NP
                  AUX
NODE: Q1
      ARCS FOR Q1: V
                   AUX
      .
      .
      .
```

Exercise: An alternative approach to building the graph is to produce the network from the BNF specification (or production system specifications) of the grammar. Design and implement a program for building the graph from the BNF representation of the grammar used above.

Sentence Analysis with an RTN

Using an RTN to analyze a sentence can determine whether the sentence is grammatical, according to the grammar represented therein. A sentence would be input, the lexical category of each word determined, and then these categories compared to the symbols on the arcs followed by moving through the graph. The usual way to determine the word type, or lexical category, is to look each word up in the lexicon where the information is stored. If, for example, the sentence input is

Can the yellow bird fly?

the lexical categories would be

AUX DET ADJ N V

Starting at S, the symbol AUX would take us to state Q2. From there, since the only option is NP, and the next word is identified as DET, the processing must go beyond that of the initial test. Here the new graph NP must be checked. Finding that the types, DET ADJ N, do indeed constitute an acceptable NP, we return to the higher level knowing that the arc with the state name NP is the one to take. Now at Q3, the symbol V moves us along the arc to Q4, which is a terminal node. Since all the words have been used and we have reached a final state successfully, the sentence can be declared grammatical. If at any point along the path through the graph, the word category did not match a possible condition along an arc or a subordinate graph tested could not be completed successfully, an error would have been detected. In some instances, the error situation can be resolved by backtracking, i.e., by moving back to preceding nodes and attempting a different direction. Backtracking is frequently required when a word is encountered which can be more than one word class, such as *state* or *bear*. Other sorts of errors would be detected upon reaching a terminal node with no arcs leaving it while there are still words to be checked, or running out of words before a terminal node is reached. Thus only successful completion of a path through the main graph and any subordinate graphs would signify a valid sentence.

This procedure for checking a sentence can be implemented in several ways. The most straightforward method uses a recursive function to check the validity of a group of words against a particular graph. This function would be called initially with the entire sentence. When an arc is encountered which contains a state name, the function is called again from that point in the sentence to check the words following against the subordinate graph. For example, when a check of the sentence,

The big brown dog barks at the cat.

is started, the first arc reached is NP. Therefore the function would be called, still pointing to the first word of the sentence. The function would then match the words,

> The big brown dog

against the NP graph and return successfully. Then the processing would be at node Q1 with the input pointer on the next word, *barks*. There the only option is the arc with the condition V which would be followed to node Q3. There a problem would arise: the function would be called to check whether the words,

> at the cat

constitute a NP. Since the first word, *at*, is a preposition, the check would fail and the function would return false. Since only one arc exists leaving this node, the sentence is not grammatical, according to the graph. (Notice that the sentence, *The dog barks the cat*, is grammatical, according to the graph.)

The function **checksentence** will be defined with two parameters: the name of the graph to be traversed, and the pointer to the part of the sentence to be checked. If the words and their corresponding types are stored in an array, the pointer to the part of the sentence would be an index to the position in the word array. It must be a variable parameter, since we are moving through the sentence and want to return from the function with the index updated, if the function is successful. In other words when we return from the function knowing that the phrase, *The big brown dog*, is a NP, the index should point to the word, *barks*, not back at *The* where it was at the time of the function call. The function **checksentence** will return a Boolean value of **true** or **false**, indicating in the former case that the sentence checks against the graph and in the latter, that it does not check, that a discrepancy has been discovered. The function definition line would be:

```
function checksentence (g : graph;
                        var wordindex : index) : Boolean;
```

(**Index** is a subrange type defined to allow only non-negative integers for the variable. **Maxint** is a constant containing the maximum integer value for a particular implementation of Pascal.)

```
type index = 0..maxint;
```

The initial call to the function would be:

```
wordptr := 1;
okay := checksentence(S,wordptr);
```

where **okay** is a Boolean variable, **S** is the name of the whole graph, and **wordptr** is given a value of one to indicate the first word of the sentence. Other calls would be made inside the function definition itself. For example if an arc is encountered with a state name rather than a terminal symbol, the function should call **checksentence** with a pointer to the graph representing the state name and a pointer to the next word in the sentence. If processing is at node Q2 in the state diagram in Figure 5.3, then, when it is determined that the arc contains a state name, the location of the NP graph will be used as the first parameter of the call to the function `checksentence`. The second parameter is the index to the position in the sentence where the function should begin matching words against the elements of NP. As explained before, the result of this recursive call will be a Boolean value indicating the validity of the phrase. If the recursive call fails, in other words the phrase being tested does not match the grammar, then the `checksentence` function has two options: if there are additional arcs, they must be tested as well. However, if that is the only choice, the only arc from the node, then the entire sentence fails. Thus, using a recursive function simplifies the analysis of a sentence.

Exercise: Write a program to analyze a sentence by matching the lexical categories against a grammar stored in a graph as described above. Write the procedure `checksentence` as a recursive function.

Exercise: Rewrite the program in the exercise above to handle a non-deterministic grammar as described earlier in the chapter. The program must be able to *backtrack* to test new possibilities if one path proves to be unsuccessful.

Implementing RTN's with Stacks

An alternative method for this situation is the traditional approach of simulating the recursion by using a stack. This method is the one described by William Woods in his article, "Transition Network Grammars for Natural Language Analysis," in *Communications of ACM* in 1970. Because we need to be able to stack the node pointers, to save the location of the current node while checking to see if a state found on an arc will cause a transition, a stack and its related functions must be defined.

```
const maxstack = 100;
type stkindex :  0..100;
     stktype : nodeptr;

     stack = record
               top :   stkindex;
               stk :   array[1..maxstack] of stktype
             end; (* stack record *)
```

`Top` is an index to the element of `stk` which is on the top of the stack. Any time an element is added to the stack, i.e., `pushed` onto the stack, `top` is incremented by one, then the element is put into `stk[top]`. When an element is `popped` off the stack, the element `top` points to is removed and `top` is decremented by one. Thus, the last element added to the stack is the first one removed—last in, first out. The main functions needed to manipulate the stack are `pop`, `push`, and `empty`. These functions will be defined generally so that they may be used with multiple stacks within a program.

Let us define the function `empty` first.

```
function empty (st : stack) : Boolean;

begin
    empty := (st.top = 0)
end; (* empty function *)
```

The value of the function `empty` is assigned a Boolean value depending on whether or not `st.top` is zero. The element `top` within a stack must be initialized to zero and will remain zero until an element is pushed onto the stack. It would also become zero when the last element is popped off the stack.

Push will be defined as a procedure which increments `top` and adds an element to the stack, if there is room left.

```
procedure push (var st : stack;
                    x : stktype);

begin
   with st
      if top = maxstack
         then writeln('attempt to overflow stack')
         else begin
                 top := top + 1;
                 stk[top] := x
              end
end; (* push procedure *)
```

Pop will use the function `empty` to determine whether there is an element to be removed from the stack. If an element is on the stack, it will be removed and returned and `top` will be adjusted.

```
procedure pop (var st : stack;
                   x : stktype);

begin
   with st
      if empty(st)
         then writeln('attempt to remove element from empty stack')
         else begin
                 x := stk[top];
                 top := top - 1
              end
end;  (* pop procedure *)
```

Exercise: Write the function `tos` (Top-Of-Stack), which returns the top element on the stack without popping it.

Using the definition of a stack and the functions for manipulating it, the process of analyzing a sentence proceeds as follows:
At each node,

Repeat
> If the lexical category of the next word matches the
> condition on an arc,
>> then if it is a terminal symbol, move to the next node;
>>> if it is a state name, push the pointer to the next node
>>> onto the stack and process the graph beginning with that state.

for all arcs.

If no match has been found, an error situation exists.

Exercise: Write a program to analyze a sentence by matching the lexical categories of the words against the grammar stored in an RTN as described above. Include a procedure which uses a stack to simulate the recursive function checksentence.

Problems with RTN's

Several weaknesses of using recursive transition networks are apparent if we recall the earlier discussion of Chomsky's work. Remember that there was considerable controversy over whether a sentence and its transformation should be equivalent. For example, are the two sentences,

> Can the little dog bark?

and

> The little dog can bark.

equivalent except for the fact that the first is interrogative and the second, declarative. The general consensus developed that the deep structure would be the same except for the classification: interrogative or declarative.

> Q + the little dog can bark

and

> DCL + the little dog can bark

If these sentences are equivalent except for one feature, then the representation for the two would be expected to be the same except for that one feature. That capability is not available with RTN's.

In addition and perhaps more importantly, when a sentence has been analyzed with an RTN, all we know is whether or not the sentence is grammatical, not what the constituent parts of that sentence are. Since determining that a sentence is grammatical is quite mechanical and of little use, a more complex analysis must be developed. After all, sentence analysis is only useful if information about the sentence can be accessed when the analysis is completed. Augmented transition networks, ATN's, are an extension of RTN's which can handle many of these problems and provide more significant information about a sentence. The first important test of ATN's was in a query system developed by William Woods to answer questions about lunar rocks.

AUGMENTED TRANSITION NETWORKS

ATN's are basically like RTN's with more conditions and actions for moving through the network. As mentioned, rather than just accepting or rejecting each word or phrase as it is encountered, the structure of the sentence is built up in the parse tree as input words match the elements of the network. The various parts of the sentence are held in *registers* until the structure of the sentence as a whole can be determined. For example, when a verb is encountered, it is stored in the V register; similarly all the words of a noun phrase would be saved in the NP register. A special language has been developed for specifying the grammar rules for ATN's. This language was presented in Woods' article on ATN's and has been modified slightly to simplify the explanation. The specification for the language we will discuss is as follows:

```
<transition network>→(<arc set><arc set>*)

<arc set>→(<state><arc>*)

<arc>→(CAT <category name><test><action>*<term act>)|
      (PUSH <state><test><action>*<term act>)|
      (TST <arbitrary label><test><action>*<term act>)|
      (POP <form><test>)

<action>→(SETR <register><form>)|
         (SENDR <register><form>)|
         (LIFTR <register><form>)

<term act>→(TO <state>)|
           (JUMP <state>)

<form>→(GETR <register>)|
       *| (* This is not to be confused with the repeat character *)
       (GETF <feature>)|
       (APPEND <register><form>)|
       (BUILD <fragment><register>*)
```

Remember that in a BNF-type grammar, the vertical bar indicates alternative selections, and the asterisk (Kleene star operator) * indicates a repeatable element in the language specification, not to be confused with the * used for the current input value. The words **PUSH** and **POP** were originally derived from the stack implementation of transition networks described earlier in this chapter and have been retained to conform with the traditional usage.

Following the language specification, a transition network is defined to be one or more arc sets, where an arc set is a state and its associated arcs. An arc set is comparable to a node and its arcs in the RTN scheme. Arcs are more involved than before in that there are now four types of arcs.

> CAT is like the original arc with a terminal symbol identifying the word class or category that causes that arc to be taken.

> PUSH is like an arc with a state name. Requesting the function PUSH means to move to the lower level transition network beginning at the state name specified.

> TST allows an arc to be taken based on any arbitrary condition; thus following an arc is not determined only by the specific word class found next in the sentence. A couple of examples of the type of tests that might be made are whether the sentence is passive or interrogative and whether a negative indicator had been encountered. TST can be used to allow tests on parts of the sentence already built.

> POP is a dummy arc used to determine if a terminal state has been reached and if so, what the final construction will be.

In the first three arcs, CAT, PUSH, and TST, at least one action and a terminal action occur.

The three possible actions, SETR, SENDR, and LIFTR, are used to build parts of the sentence.

> SETR immediately assigns a value to the register specified.

> SENDR passes the value down to the next lower level for assignment to a register.

> LIFTR passes the value up to the next higher level for assignment.

The terminal actions, TO and JUMP, specify whether processing is finished with the current word or phrase, whether the pointer to the input should be moved or remain where it is, and which state is to be processed next.

> TO indicates that the input pointer is to be moved and that processing is to proceed at the node indicated.

> JUMP means to continue processing at the node indicated without moving the pointer to the input; in other words, the words in the input have not yet been matched.

The forms are used to describe the data being handled.

> GETR returns the value contained in a specific register.

> * is the current input word or phrase—the item being worked on.

GETF determines the value for a specific feature for the current input word.

APPEND is used to add additional values onto the value currently in the register specified. One use for **APPEND** would be add a prepositional phrase onto the end of a noun phrase which is already formed and placed in the NP register.

BUILD builds parts or all of the final parse of the sentence from the contents of the registers specified.

The **BUILD** statement specifies first the fragment being built, then one or more plus signs (+) to indicate the number of nodes to be included, and finally the names of the features and registers from which the values are to be derived. For example, the statement

```
(SETR VP (BUILD (VP (V +) *) V))
```

first builds the **VP** fragment by placing the current input value into the position of the *, and the contents of the **V** register in the position of the +, and next assigns that fragment to the **VP** register. In a sentence, such as

The child eats the ice cream.

this statement would be reached after the first noun phrase, *The child*, had been assigned to the SUBJ register, and the verb, *eats*, to the V register. Then after determining that the current input, *the ice cream*, is an NP, the rule above is encountered, building the verb phrase, *eats the ice cream*. Notice that the form of the structure being built follows the parenthesized form described in Chapter 1. In this form the sentence would be represented as:

(S (NP *The child*) **(VP** *eats*) **(NP** *the ice cream*)))

A partial ATN grammar will be given in the ATN specification language to illustrate further the use of the language. It corresponds to the top level of the network in Figure 5.3, with nodes S/, Q1, Q2, Q3, Q4, and Q5, without the arc PP from Q5 to Q5. (See Figure 5.5.) (The slash following the state name indicates that it begins an ATN and thus is the name of a transition network.)

```
 1    ((S/ (PUSH NP/ T
 2              (SETR SUBJ *)
 3              (SETR TYPE "DCL")
 4              (TO Q1))
 5         (CAT AUX T
 6              (SETR AUX *)
 7              (SETR TYPE "Q")
 8              (TO Q2))

 9    (Q1 (CAT V T
10              (SETR AUX NIL)
```

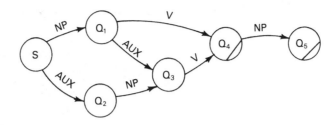

Figure 5.5   Top Level of Transition Network in Figure 5.3 (Without PP Arc)

```
11              (SETR V *)
12              (TO Q4))
13         (CAT AUX T
14              (SETR AUX *)
15              (TO Q3)))

16    (Q2 (PUSH NP/ T
17              (SETR SUBJ *)
18              (TO Q3)))

19    (Q3 (CAT V T
20              (SETR V *)
21              (TO Q4)))

22    (Q4 (POP (BUILD (S +++(VP +)) TYPE SUBJ AUX V) T)
23         (PUSH NP/ T
24              (SETR VP (BUILD (VP (V +) *)V))
25              (TO Q5)))

26    (Q5 (POP (BUILD (S ++++) TYPE SUBJ AUX VP) T)))
```

Let us go through the grammar line by line.

1. Starting at S, which is the beginning of the ATN, move down a level to the NP ATN to test whether it is true (T) that a noun phrase exists in the input. If NP is true, then execute 2, 3 and 4.

2. Set the register SUBJ to the current value of *, which will be the noun phrase.

3. Set the register TYPE to DCL for declarative.

4. Move the input pointer past the noun phrase dealt with and continue processing at node Q1.

5. If NP was false, check whether the category of * is AUX, for auxiliary. If AUX is true, then do 6, 7, and 8.

6. Set the register AUX to the current value of *, the auxiliary verb.

7. Set the TYPE register to Q, for question.

8. Move the input pointer past the auxiliary and continue with node Q2.

9. Node Q1 tests first for a verb; if V is true, then do 10, 11 and 12.

10. Set AUX register to nil, since no auxiliary was found.

11. Set the V register to the current value of *, the verb.

12. Move the input pointer and proceed with Q4.

13. If V was false, then if AUX is true, execute 14 and 15.

14. Set register AUX to *.

15. Move to Q3 after advancing the input pointer.

16. After the auxiliary, check for a noun phrase. If NP is true, then do 17 and 18.

17. Set the SUBJ register to the noun phrase in *.

18. Proceed with Q3 after moving the input pointer.

19. At Q3, check for a verb. If V is true, then do 20 and 21.

20. Set V register to *.

21. Move input pointer and proceed with Q4.

22. Since Q4 can be a terminal node, a sentence structure can be built here. If it is terminal, then BUILD will create a structure for the sentence such that the values of the registers TYPE, SUBJ, and AUX follow the state name S. Then VP follows with the value of the V register. For example, in the sentence,

The cat can climb.

the registers would contain the following values:

TYPE	DCL
SUBJ	*The cat*
AUX	*can*
V	*climb*

and the structure built would be:

(S DCL (NP *The cat*) **(AUX** *can*) **(VP** *climb*)))

23. If there is still more input and it is therefore not a terminal state, determine whether we have a noun phrase. If NP is true, then do 24 and 25.

24. Build the verb phrase (as described earlier) and assign that fragment to the register VP.

25. Move the input pointer and proceed with node Q5.

26. Since Q5 is the terminal node when it is reached, BUILD will create the entire sentence structure from the contents of the registers. Since nothing follows Q5, execution stops.

Implementing Augmented Transition Networks

The first approach to implementing ATN's will be somewhat restricted. Initially we will develop an interpreter for a specific grammar which is defined below. Later we will consider a generalized approach so different grammars can be used.

A complete grammar will be given to be implemented. In context free format, the grammar, which only handles simple declarative sentences, is:

S → NP VP
NP → DET (ADJ)* N / NPR
VP → (AUX) V (NP)

The same grammar written in ATN specification language is:

```
((S/  (PUSH NP/ T
         (SETR TYPE "DCL")
         (SETR SUBJ *)
         (TO Q1)))

 (Q1  (PUSH  VP/ T
         (SETR VP  *)
         (TO Q2)))

 (Q2  (POP (BUILD (S + (NP +)(VP +)) TYPE NP VP) T))

 (NP/  (CAT DET T
         (SETR DET *)
         (SETR ADJ NIL)
         (TO Q3))
       (CAT NPR T
         (SETR N  *)
         (SETR DET NIL)
         (SETR ADJ NIL)
         (TO Q4)))

 (Q3   (CAT ADJ T
         (APPEND ADJ *)
         (TO Q3))
       (CAT N T
         (SETR N *)
         (TO Q4)))

 (Q4 (POP (BUILD (NP +++) DET ADJ N) T)))

 (VP/  (CAT V T
         (SETR AUX NIL)
```

```
                    (SETR V  *)
                    (TO Q6))
               (CAT AUX T
                    (SETR AUX  *)
                    (TO Q5)))
          (Q5  (CAT V T
                    (SETR V  *)
                    (TO Q6)))
          (Q6  (POP (BUILD (VP ++) AUX V) T)
               (PUSH NP/ T
                    (SETR OBJ  *)
                    (TO Q7)))
          (Q7  (POP (BUILD (VP +++) AUX V OBJ) T)))
```

Exercise: Study the grammar carefully in order to understand it fully. Then write sentences with as many different structures as the grammar will allow. There are at least 16 different structures possible.

The first problem to consider in implementing this grammar as a program is how the data will be stored. The primary data items and/or structures to be designed are:

1. the sentence being input

2. the current word or phrase being analyzed
   (the register referred to as * in the grammar)
   with information about its word class

3. the various registers for storing parts of the sentence
   including the sentence as a whole.

The input string can be handled as in the RTN algorithm: the whole sentence is input and saved; then it is tokenized, i.e., broken into words. Because the word class is so important to the process of recognizing the structure of a sentence, it should be determined as soon as each word is found. For convenience, a function called **getnextword** should be written to return the next word and its category information in the **star** (*) register. The structure of the **star** register, as well as the other registers, is a problem. Each of the registers can hold a single word or a whole phrase or a series of phrases. Therefore the registers must be able to hold dynamic data. One alternative would be to use strings to represent the data, but, although they would be easy to build, the strings would have to be rescanned every time an access was made. Another possibility would be linked lists, which can be implemented in several ways—with arrays or with dynamic structures such as binary trees. The binary tree implementation used in Chapter 4 to represent phrase markers is quite appropriate for this problem. (Review the section of Chapter 4 on right in-threaded binary trees and their associated functions, `makenode`, `set-daughter`, and `setnext`.) The data types to be used include:

```
type consttype = (S, NP, VP, DET, ADJ, N, NPR, AUX, V);
     nodetype  = (root, nonterminal, terminal);
     nodeptr   = ^node;
     node      = record
        constit : consttype;
        daughter: nodeptr;
        next    : nodeptr;
        thread  : Boolean;
        case nodetag of
           terminal : (word : string)
     end;  (* node record *)
```

Using these type definitions, the registers can be implemented as `nodeptr`s. Then whether a single word or an entire sentence is to be stored, the register can hold it. Thus the register definition would be:

```
type register : nodeptr;
```

The `star` register is somewhat more involved and must also contain the word class for the next input word. Thus `star` could be defined as:

```
var star : record
             reg : register;
             cat : consttype
           end;  (* star record *)
```

The other registers needed would be defined as:

```
var sreg, npreg, vpreg, detreg, adjreg, nreg, auxreg, vreg, typereg : register;
```

The category field is not required for these registers since the specific register only holds one type of data, and thus the category is implicit.

The next concern in implementing the grammar is the design of the program itself. At the top level the program might be:

```
begin
   getsentence;
   sreg := analyze(S);
   printanalysis(sreg)
end.
```

The first procedure `getsentence` would input the sentence, break it into individual words and determine the word class for each word. (Whether the scanning for words and obtaining the word class is done in `getsentence` or in the function `getnextword` is not important to the current discussion; that design choice will be left to the reader.) The function `analyze` is the heart of the program. The last procedure `printanalysis` would print out the bracketed structure returned by `anaylze`. If this application were more realistic rather than simply an exercise to illustrate ATN's, the last procedure would be where the sentence analysis is used. In other words, at that point, processing could begin on the information input in sentence form. Thus the first two sections, getsentence and analyze, are merely the front end for some program with a specific need for the parse tree, such as a query system or an information retrieval system.

Let us now investigate the organization of the function analyze. The major structure of analyze will be a case statement determining which of the three ATN's in the grammar is being considered: S, NP, or VP. Thus we have:

```
function analyze (atnname : consttype) :  register;

begin
    case atnname of

        S  : (* find the parts of sentence  *)
        NP : (* determine the structure of the noun phrase *)
        VP : (* determine the structure of the verb pahrse *)
    end;  (* atn case *)
end;  (* analyze function *)
```

The S section would call NP, set typereg to "DCL", and set the npreg to the noun phrase found. Then it would call VP and set vpreg to the verb phrase found. The final step is to build the sentence structure from the values in npreg and vpreg and return this structure as the value of the function.

The NP section of the case statement would check for the constituent parts of a noun phrase and assign those parts as the value of the function. The VP section is comparable. The three routines, S, NP, and VP, will not be complete unless each one checks for errors. The first function of the sentence analysis program is still to determine whether the sentence input is correct. Thus at each point when the various checks are made for a particular word type or phrase type, the program must determine whether one of the alternatives has been found. If not, an error has occurred. An error routine with two functions will be part of the program; first, it would print out a message identifying the error, and second, set a flag, errorflag, to indicate to the program that an error has occurred.

With some of the functions and procedures needed for a complete implementation merely referred to, the grammar program now consists of the following:

```
program atn;

type consttype = (S, NP, VP, DET,ADJ, N, NPR, AUX, V);
     nodetype = (root, nonterminal, terminal);
     nodeptr= ^node;
     node = record
                 constit :consttype;
                 daughter:  nodeptr;
                 next :nodeptr;
                 thread :  Boolean;
                 case nodetag : nodetype of
                      terminal: (word: string)
            end;  (* node record *)
```

```
          register = nodeptr;
          starreg = record
                        reg : register;
                        cat : consttype
                    end; (* starreg record *)
var star : starreg;
    sreg, npreg, vpreg, detreg, adjreg, nreg, auxreg, vreg,
         subjreg, objreg, typereg :  register;
    errorflag : Boolean;

procedure error(msg : string);
(* definition of error routine *)

function build (ctype : consttype;
                   r1, r2 : register) : register;
(* definition of build function *)

function append (r1, r2 : register) : register;
(* definition of append function *)

procedure getnextword (star : starreg);
(* definition of getnextword routine *)

procedure getsentence;
(* definition of getsentence *)

procedure printanalysis(sreg : register);
(* definition of printanalysis routine *)


function analyze (atnname :  consttype) : register;
begin
   case atnname of
        S  : (* find the parts of sentence *)

            begin (* S *)

                npreg := analyze(NP);
                if not errorflag
                   then vpreg := analyze(VP);
                if not errorflag
                   then analyze := build(S, npreg, vpreg)
                   else analyze := nil

            end; (* S *)
```

```
NP : (* determine the structure of the noun phrase *)

    begin (* NP *)

        getnextword (star);
        if star.cat = DET
            then begin
                    detreg := star.reg;
                    getnextword(star);
                    adjreg :=nil;
                    while star.cat = ADJ do
                        begin
                          adjreg := append(adjreg,star.reg);
                          getnextword(star);
                        end;
                    if star.cat = N
                        then nreg := star.reg
                        else error('no noun phrase found')
                 end
            else if star.cat = NPR
                then begin (*proper noun *)
                        nreg := star.reg;
                        detreg := nil;
                        adjreg := nil
                     end
                else error('no noun phrase found');
        if not errorflag
            then analyze := build(NP,detreg,adjreg,nreg)
            else analyze := nil;

    end; (* NP *)

VP : (* determine the structure of the verb phrase *)

    begin (* VP *)

        getnextword(star);
        if star.cat = V
            then begin
                    auxreg := nil;
                    vreg := star.reg
                 end
            else if star.cat = AUX
                    then begin
                            auxreg := star.reg;
                            getnextword(star);
```

```
                              if star.cat = V
                                 then vreg := star.reg
                                 else error('no verb in verb phrase ')
                           end
                        else error('verb phrase not found');
                 if not errorflag
                    then begin
                         getnextword(star);
                         if star.reg <> nil
                            then begin
                                 npreg := analyze(NP);
                                 analyze := build(VP,auxreg,vreg,npreg)
                                 end
                            else analyze := build(VP,auxreg,vreg)
                         end
                    else analyze := nil

          end;  (* VP *)

   end;  (* atn case *)

end;  (* analyze function *)

begin  (* atn analysis program *)

   getsentence;

   sreg := analyze(S);

   printanalysis(sreg);

end.  (* atn analysis program *)
```

Exercise: Write the function getnextword.

Exercise: Write the build function. Note that it has a variable number of parameters as used in the partial program above, which will not work in Pascal. Develop some method for handling the problem.

Exercise: Write the append function.

Exercise: Write the error function.

Exercise: Combine the additional procedures, functions, and any data elements required to complete the program for the grammar described above.

Exercise: Modify the grammar to include prepositional phrases as in the NP graph in Figure 5.3. How would the analyze function above be changed?

Exercise: Modify the grammar to include questions as well as prepositional phrases, as in the entire graph in Figure 5.3. Modify the analyze function to handle the new grammar.

The approach taken for implementing the particular grammar will, of course, only work for that specific grammar. The program would have to be rewritten to modify or extend the grammar to handle a more extensive set of sentences. In some applications the input could probably be restricted enough that a limited number of sentence structures would be adequate. However, since ATN's are often used for experimentation in linguistic research, the program for implementing them could be controlled by a grammar stored as data, rather than incorporating a specific grammar into the program. Thus the grammar could be changed without having to rewrite the program. Our next consideration then is the implementation of a general ATN grammar program.

Implementing a General ATN Grammar Program

An important consideration in implementing ATN's concerns the flexibility allowed by the implementation, as mentioned above. Achieving this flexibility requires creation of two phases in the program. The second phase is a program which inputs sentences for analysis and performs the analysis based on a specific grammar. In order to create the environment which allows any grammar to be used, the first stage must be a compiler to generate the tables which the interpreter uses for the second stage. As with earlier implementations, certain constraints will be placed on the type of grammar that can be handled properly. The most important constraint for right now is that the grammar be deterministic, in order to avoid the problems of backtracking.

Implementing an ATN primarily involves creating an interpreter for a particular grammar; this grammar will be written in the specification language described above, which is based on LISP, a programming language designed for list processing, which uses parentheses to combine elements to form lists. Thus the parentheses in the ATN specification language show groupings of the various parts of the statements, and become important delimiters in scanning the grammar. At the highest level of the parentheses, a grammar consists of a list of arc sets, which are nodes and the description of conditions and tests imposed on them. Within each arc set following the state name, the next level of parentheses defines a list of possible arcs. Each arc in turn gives the list of actions to be done if that arc is taken. The actions are concluded by a terminal action.

LISP would be a good language in which to write the interpreter because it has the advantage of allowing a data item to operate as a function call. Thus when a command is encountered in the grammar, it can be called as a function. However a similar effect can be achieved in Pascal with table look-up. The command names are stored in a table; when a command is encountered in the grammar, it is found in the table and its index will be used to direct execution to the appropriate part of a case statement which contains all the possible operations. The command table is not dependent on the specific grammar since the commands are taken from the specification language. The program will consist of two stages: the first inputs the grammar and builds the necessary tables, and the second actually executes the grammar, given an input sentence, by interpreting the tables built by the compiler. The earlier implementation of ATN's for a specific grammar was essentially the second stage here, with the first stage having been done by hand.

For the first stage of the program, each arc set will be read in and the state name saved with a pointer to the beginning of the list of arcs for that set. Since one of the constraints is that the grammar be deterministic, only one of the arcs will be possible at each node. The one arc to be taken determines the actions to be performed and the node to process next.

The same node type used in the specific grammar implementation above could serve our purposes for creating lists. However, since the grammar specification language uses list notation as defined in LISP, list structures implemented in Pascal directly will be somewhat easier to handle. Only those list structures and functions necessary for this problem will be developed now. As shown in Figure 5.6, in LISP any element of a list can be a list itself. Therefore, the new node type lnode will include the information contained in the node, a link to the rest of the list in this node, and a link to the next node. If the element is a single item, the link to the rest of the list in the node will be nil. The type definition for lnode is

```
type infotype = string;
     lnodeptr = ^lnode;
     lnode    = record
                     linfo :  infotype;
                     lrest :  lnodeptr;
                     lnext :  lnodeptr
                end; (* lnode record *)
```

Functions must be defined to manipulate lnode's and the lists created with them. Thus functions are needed to create lnode's, to return a part of a list, to test an element in a list, and to create lists and add to lists already created.

The function makelnode will create a node and initialize its parts.

```
function makelnode (x : infotype) : lnodeptr;

var newlnode : lnodeptr;

begin (* makelnode *)

  new(newlnode);
  n^.linfo := x;
  n^.lrest := nil;
  n^.lnext := nil;
  makelnode := newlnode

end; (* makelnode *)
```

(Dogs can chase cats)

((The cat) (will hide))

(Fido (can eat) (in (the kitchen)))

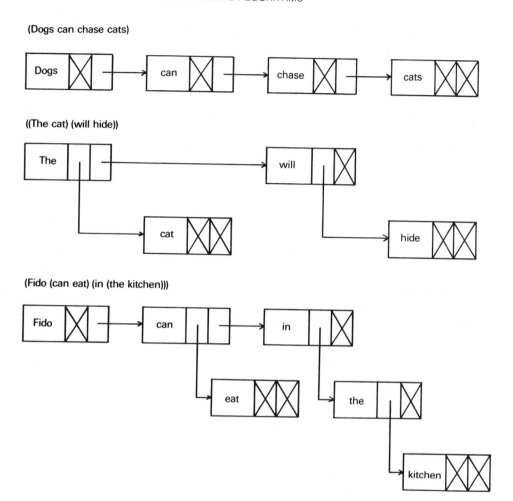

Figure 5.6   Examples of Linked Lists

The information is stored in the new node, and the pointers are set to nil. The function returns the pointer to the new node.

The routine **first** returns a pointer to the first node of a list (If you know LISP, you should recognize **first** as being comparable to **car** in LISP). Since that node may be the first of a list itself, the value returned may point to a single node or a list. The data in the first node will be copied into a new node.

```
function first (l : lnodeptr) : lnodeptr;

var newlnode : lnodeptr;

begin (* first *)

   new(newlnode);
   newlnode^.linfo := l^.linfo;
   newlnode^.lrest := l^.lrest;
   newlnode^.lnext := nil;
   first := newlnode

end;   (* first *)
```

The function rest will return a pointer to the node following the first one in the list (comparable to cdr in LISP). No data is copied.

```
function rest (l : lnodeptr);
begin (* rest *)
   rest := l^.lnext
end;   (* rest *)
```

Atom is a Boolean function which will return true if the first element of the list is a single element.

```
function atom (l : lnodeptr) : Boolean;
begin (* atom *)
     atom := (l^.lrest = nil)
end;   (* atom *)
```

The function to append a node or list onto the end of an existing list would have the following definition line:

```
function append (n,l : lnodeptr) : lnodeptr;
```

where n points to the node or list to be appended and l points to the list to which it is to be added. The value returned is the same as the original value of l. The procedure list will link the parameters specified together into a list.

Exercise: Write the function append as described above.

Exercise: Write the procedure list. Hint: the procedure list is quite similar to build in the previous section.

To return to writing the compiler to translate a grammar into a language analyzer, let us look first at the problem of inputting and storing the grammar. Since the specification language is in LISP list notation, the grammar can fairly easily be stored in list format. With the set of list processing functions, the grammar can be interpreted from the list structure during the second stage. The state names and the register names also need to be stored as the grammar is input. In addition, the location of the node which begins the arc set identified by the state name must be saved as the node is built.

Scanning the grammar as it is input in order to store it in list form requires finding the left and right parentheses. A left parenthesis begins a new list, and a right parenthesis ends the current list. Thus the grammar at the highest level is a list of arc sets; each arc set is a list in which the first element is a state name and the other elements are arcs. The program will therefore operate recursively, building various levels of lists as the grammar is input.

Exercise: Write the procedure necessary to input the grammar in list notation and store it in list form.

There will be four major tables created by the first phase to be used by the second phase: a table of command names whose indices will correspond to the appropriate part of a case structure to execute that command, a state name table with pointers to the appropriate nodes, a table containing all the ATN's and their locations, and a register table which will contain all registers used by the grammar. The register values will be added during the second phase. Let us define these tables one at a time.

The table of command names `commtab`, will have the following form:

```
const numcomm = 14;

type identifier = string[8];
     commname : identifier;

var commtab : array[1..numcomm] of commname;
```

This table would be initialized by a routine that stores the values:

```
procedure initcommtable;

begin (* initcommtable *)
    commtab[1] := 'CAT';
    commtab[2] := 'PUSH';
    commtab[3] := 'TST';
    commtab[4] := 'POP';
    commtab[5] := 'SETR';
    commtab[6] := 'SENDR';
    commtab[7] := 'LIFTR';
    commtab[8] := 'TO';
    commtab[9] := 'JUMP';
    commtab[10] := 'GETR';
    commtab[11] := '*';
    commtab[12] := 'GETF';
    commtab[13] := 'APPEND';
    commtab[14] := 'BUILD'
end; (* initcommtable *)
```

The state name table, the ATN table and the register table would be initialized as the grammar is read. Each type of item is easily identifiable by its location. A state name is the first element of an arc set. If the convention of placing a slash (/) after a state name which is also the name of an ATN is followed, then ATN names can be identified by the slash. Register names occur in action statements and several of the forms. These three tables would be defined as:

```
type tablerec = record
                  name : identifier;
                  ptr  : lnodeptr
                end;  (* table record *)

var  statetable : array [1..maxstates] of tablerec;
     atntable : array [1..maxatns] of tablerec;
     regtable : array [1..maxregisters] of tablerec;
```

Maxstates, maxatns, and maxregisters are constants with appropriate values.

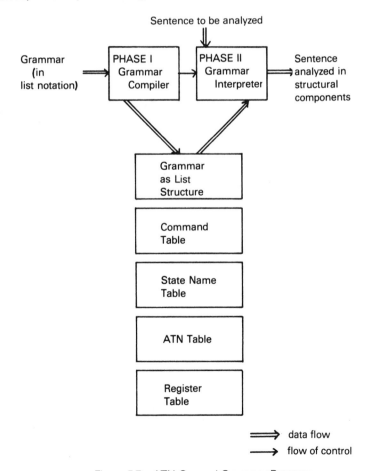

Figure 5.7   ATN General Grammar Program

Once the grammar has been stored in list form and the tables have been built, the first phase is completed. The second phase then is an interpreter which uses the list formatted grammar to control analysis of the sentence input by accessing the tables built in the first phase. See Figure 5.7 for a schematic of the program. The key to the execution is the case statement indexed by the commands. A location counter is needed to indicate where the next node to be processed is located. The location counter is started at the beginning of the grammar and is updated to point to the next node by assigning the value of the lnext field of the current node being handled. When a terminal arc is reached, either TO or JUMP, the state name from that arc will be found in the state name table and the node pointer which corresponds will be made the new value of the location counter. At the top level, the case structure for the command executor would be as follows:

```
procedure command (index : indexrange);

begin

case index of

      1 (* CAT  *) : (* routine to execute the CAT test *);
      2 (* PUSH *) : (* routine to execute the PUSH test *);
      3 (* TST  *) : (* routine to execute the TST test *);
      4 (* POP  *) : (* routine to decide on termination and call BUILD *);
      5 (* SETR *) : (* routine to set the value of a register *);
      6 (* SENDR*) : (* routine to pass register value to lower level *);
      7 (* LIFTR*) : (* routine to return register value to higher level *);
      8 (* TO   *) : (* routine to advance input pointer and establish
                        next node to be executed *)
      9 (* JUMP *) : (* routine to establish next node to be executed *);
     10 (* GETR *) : (* routine to get the value of a register *);
     11 (*  *   *) : (* routine to get the value of the star register *);
     12 (* GETF *) : (* routine to retrieve feature from the lexicon *);
     13 (*APPEND*) : (* routine to add a data item onto a register *);
     14 (* BUILD*) : (* routine to combine the values in various registers
                        in order to build a new structure *)
end; (* case *)

end;  (* command procedure *)
```

Each command routine would pull parameters that it needs from the grammar and call the command routine as needed. For example if the CAT command determines that the category being sought is true, then the actions for that arc will be executed. The terminal action for that arc will cause the return from the CAT routine with the location counter set to point to the next node to be executed.

Using the same grammar presented earlier, let us trace the execution of the interpreter as it analyzes the sentence,

The class took a test.

The grammar starts at the first arc set, S/. The first arc within that arc set begins with PUSH. The token PUSH is found in the command table, giving us the index 2. Then the command procedure is called with the index 2, and the routine for PUSH will be selected. PUSH expects an ATN name as the item following the command, in this case NP/; that ATN will be called to determine whether that particular type of phrase exists in the sentence. Therefore the PUSH routine would save the current input pointer and would find the location of the ATN from the ATN table. It would transfer control to NP/ which would check for a noun phrase and return the structure found. In this example, the NP/ ATN would build the noun phrase,

(NP (DET "The") (N "class"))

and return that as the value of the call. On return, since the phrase type was found, the actions for that arc would be performed by calling the command found in the grammar list. For this arc, the actions are two SETRs, to set the type register to declarative and to set the noun phrase register to the value returned by the NP ATN. Then the terminal action TO would return the value of the Q1 node to the interpreter. The interpreter would then proceed to the Q1 node and the whole thing would continue with the next arc set at Q1. The input would be tested for a verb phrase by calling the VP/ ATN. If a verb phrase was found and returned, then the final step of the interpreter would be to call the POP routine to build the sentence structure from the parts constructed during processing. That would complete the analysis of the sentence.

Major Exercise: Write a program to implement the two-phase sentence analyzer presented in this section. Test it with several different grammars and a variety of sentence types. Include appropriate error checking in order to catch invalid sentences.

ATN's were originally developed to replace transformations as a method for sentence analysis. As such, they are a definite improvement. One inherent drawback is that the grammars, and thus the programs to interpret the grammars, can become quite complex and unwieldy. Figure 5.8, taken from one of Woods' articles on ATN's, is an illustration in network format of the

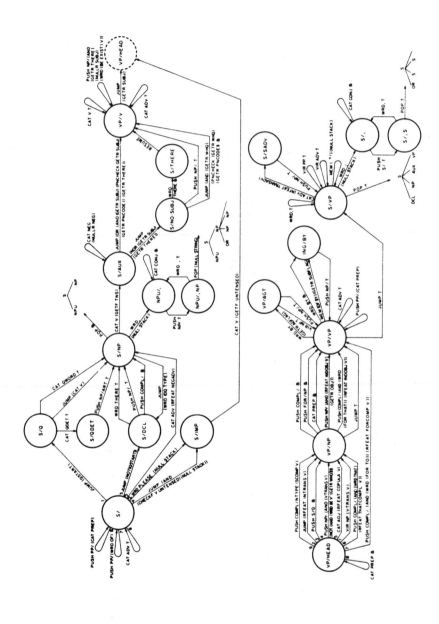

Figure 5.8   A Transition Network Grammar (From William Woods, "An Experimental Parsing System for Transition Network Grammars," in *Natural Language Processing*, edited by Randall Rustin, © 1973, Algorithmics Press. All rights reserved.)

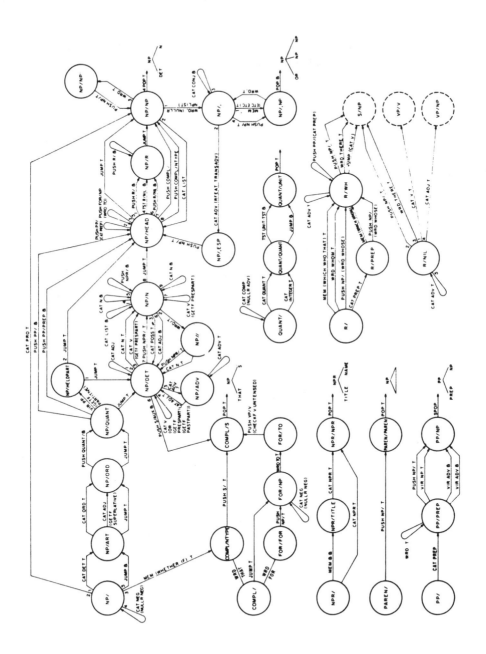

complexity of the grammar needed to handle even moderately complicated sentence input. The complexity involved cannot be eliminated or reduced without severely restricting the sentence structures accepted. Alternate approaches to sentence analysis use the same representational scheme, i.e., networks, but substitute different techniques for representing structure and knowledge. The following chapters will elaborate on some of these other methods.

Chapter 6

Case Grammar

Case grammar, developed by Charles J. Fillmore, describes language from a more semantically oriented perspective than the transformational grammars of Chomsky. [1] Fillmore's intention was to expand the theories of transformational generative grammar by providing more than a description of the structural relationships within a sentence; he included as well, notions about the *functional relationships* among the various phrases within a sentence, the part of syntax that conveys meaning. As explained in Chapter 1, in case grammar the verbal elements of the sentence are the major source of the structure: the main verb in the proposition is the focus around which the other phrases, or cases, revolve, and the auxiliary verbs contain much of the information about modality. Case grammar is much more consistent with the theories of the generative semanticists in representing the deep structure of a sentence as a semantic representation, rather than providing only syntactic information.

To review some concepts of language mentioned in Chapter 1, remember that declarative sentences can generally be divided into a subject and a predicate —comparable to the NP + VP structure of generative grammar. The subject of the sentence is the element which the verb describes. The verb can be intransitive or transitive.

> The girl ran.   INTRANSITIVE
>
> The boy threw the ball.   TRANSITIVE

Only transitive verbs have direct objects (*The ball* in the sentence above). Some transitive verbs, such as *give* and *tell*, have two objects.

> He told his son a bedtime story.

(*He*—subject, *told*—verb, *his son*—indirect object, *a bedtime story*—direct object)

These sentence parts are referred to as *surface cases,* and do not correlate directly with *deep cases,* in Fillmore's sense of the term. The subject is in the nominative case, and the two objects are in the objective case. However, if we change the sentence into its passive form,

His son was told a bedtime story by him.

the subject is now *his son,* there is no indirect object, and *him* (the objective form of *he*) is part of a prepositional phrase. Thus, the surface cases correspond to different lexical items even though the meaning of the sentence is essentially the same. According to case grammar, however, the deep cases have not changed. In both sentences, *he* (or *him*) is the agent, the teller of the story; *his son* is the goal, the receiver of the story; and *a bedtime story* is the object, the thing told.

Definition of Case Grammar

Let us recall the description of case grammar given in Chapter 1, starting with the rewrite rules:

S → M + P

M → tense, aspect, . . . <all the modes>

P → V + C1 . . . Cn

V → run, break, put, . . . <all verbs in the vocabulary>

Ci → K + NP

K → (PREP)

A sentence S is made up of the modality M and the proposition P, where the modality is a series of terms which describe aspects of the sentence as a whole. The proposition P is defined as a verb V and some number of cases, where each case is a Kasus K and a noun phrase NP. The Kasus, which may be null, is the preposition which introduces the noun phrase and defines its relationship with the verb.

NP must be more adequately defined. Robert F. Simmons discussed a method for handling noun phrases in case grammar in his chapter, "Semantic Networks: Their Computation and Use for Understanding English Sentences," in the book, *Computer Models of Thought and Language.* [2] His definition was as follows,

NP → (PREP) + (DET) + (ADJ|N)* + N + (S|NP)

in which the usual abbreviations apply: the parentheses indicate optional elements, the asterisk (*) indicates that the element can be repeated, and the vertical bar (|) means alternation (either S or NP). Using the earlier rule for Ci, the preposition was included as K, which could be null, so the optional preposition would not be needed in the rule given above. However, the preposition will remain in the NP definition, rather than being handled separately.

Notice that, if the preposition is included, the NP here has the same form as a prepositional phrase (PREP + NP) in the grammars described earlier. This rule for NP allows for an optional preposition, an optional determiner, zero to several adjectives and/or noun modifiers for the primary noun in the phrase, and an optional postpositional modifier (S | NP). Examples of noun modifiers are fire truck, fire house door, ice tray, and house cat. Examples of the postpositional modifier are

```
1. the boy who went home
   DET N    . . . S . . .
```

(where S is an embedded sentence transformed from

```
    the boy went home
    the boy [the boy went home])
```

```
2. the church in the meadow
   DET   N        DET N
             PREP  NP
```

Translating these rules into data structures starts with the sentence:

```
type casesentence = record
                modality : (* definition of modality *)
                proposition : record
                                 verb : word;
                                 cases:(* all the appropriate cases *)
                              end; (* proposition record *)
               end; (* casesentence record *)
```

Word will be defined as a string:

```
type word = string;
```

Modality

If we use Simmons' list of modes to define modetype [3],

```
modetype = (tense, aspect, form, mood, essence, modal, manner, time);
```

then modality can be defined as:

```
modality : array[tense..time] of mode;
```

For now, mode will be defined as a string. (Modetype is a user-defined scalar type, which has the advantages of allowing the user to name the elements and to define an explicit order. Thus the modetype names can be compared [e.g., tense < aspect] and can be used as array variable subscript names. If m is a simple variable of modetype, then

```
for m := tense to time do <statement>
```

would index through all the values of modality.)

The modality of a sentence is defined by the combination of the various modes listed above. Each mode individually identifies one aspect of the verb phrase of a sentence. The possible values Simmons attributed to the modes are as follows:

Tense—present, past, future

Aspect—perfect, imperfect

Form—simple, emphatic, progressive

Mood—declarative, interrogative, imperative

Essence—positive, negative, indeterminate

Modal—may, can, must

Manner—adverbial

Time—adverbial

Tense indicates the basic time orientation of the sentence.

The dog runs.	PRESENT
The dog ran.	PAST
The dog will run.	FUTURE

Aspect adds to the value of *tense* by telling whether the action is continuing:

The girl has sung.   PERFECT

or completed:

The girl had sung.   IMPERFECT

The mode *form* provides more information about the verb phrase by showing whether it is simple:

The dog runs.

or emphatic:

The dog does run.

or progressive:

The dog is running.

The *mood* of a sentence relates to the order of the elements of the sentence; declarative sentences are usually of the form NP + VP in usual order. The examples above are all declarative. Interrogative sentences, questions, are often partly inverted: AUX + NP + VP:

Is the dog running?

or have a tag sentence to indicate the question:

The dog is running, isn't he?

Imperative sentences, commands, usually begin with the verb and have a subject which is understood to be the person spoken to—*you*:

Hurry! Catch the bus!

The *essence* of the verb phrase shows whether it is positive:

The dog is running.

or negative:

The dog is not running.

or indeterminate:

The dog may be running.

The modals are the *helping* verbs, *may, can,* and *must*, which provide additional meaning to the verb phrase. The presence of one of these verbs, or an alternate form of one of them, indicates the value of the mode Modal. The last two modes, *manner* and *time*, are indicated by the adverbial parts of a sentence.

He caught the bus at the last minute.   TIME
The driver closed the doors quickly.   MANNER

The modes all provide additional information about the verb phrase in a sentence; since the verbal elements are the focus of the sentence in case grammar, determining the modality establishes a large part of the overall meaning.

Exercise: Make a list of sentences with varying modalities. Use as many different modes in different combinations as you can think of. What kinds of sentences do not fit the pattern of description provided by modality.

List of Cases

A list of the specific cases will be used to describe the **cases** array. Several lists of cases have been developed. Chapter 1 included Fillmore's original list: agentive, instrumental, dative, factitive, locative, and objective. Simmons used a more concise list developed by Celce-Murcia: Causalactant, Theme, Locus, Source, and Goal. Borrowing Mitchell Marcus' short list of cases, which he borrowed from Stockwell, Schacter, and Partee [4], **casetype** can be declared as:

```
type casetype = (neutral, dative, locative, instrumental, agent);
```

In this list, the cases are defined as follows:

Agent—the instigator of the action, an animate being

Instrumental—the thing used to perform the action, an inanimate object

Locative—the location of the action and other cases

Dative—the recipient of the action, like Goal in Fillmore's later set of cases

Neutral—the thing being acted upon, combining the objective and the factitive of Fillmore

Using this set of cases, the `cases` array can now be declared as:

```
type cases =  array[neutral..agent] of Ci;
```

(As we shall see later, the ordering implicit in the `casetype` definition will be useful for handling the cases.)

Next the element Ci must be defined. The original rule,

Ci → K + NP

has two parts; however, as discussed earlier, the preposition is part of the noun phrase. The format then is as follows:

```
type Ci =  record
              NP :  record
                      (* description of noun phrase *)
                    end; (* NP record *)
            end; (* Ci record *)
```

Initially, let us simplify our definition of NP:

NP → (PREP) (DET) (ADJ) (NMOD) N

where NMOD will distinguish the modifier noun from the main noun in the phrase. Thus there are three optional elements and one required element. Only one occurrence of ADJ will be handled for now, and discussion of the postpositional modifier will be postponed. Thus an adequate definition of NP would be:

```
type NP =  record
              PREP,DET,ADJ,NMOD,N :  word;
            end; (* NP record *)
```

Word will be a string of sixteen characters:

```
type word = string[16];
```

For the optional elements; `PREP`, `DET`, `ADJ`, and `NMOD`; a null string will indicate that that particular element is not included in the specific sentence.

Exercise: Write a program to produce noun phrases by selecting words randomly for the appropriate constituent types from word lists containing determiners, adjectives, noun modifiers, and nouns. Include probabilities for the occurrence of the optional elements. For example, determiners are optional, but occur much more frequently than noun modifiers. How many of the noun phrases make any sense at all? How could the noun phrases be improved?

So far, our definition of the `casesentence` is:

```
type casetype = (neutral,dative,locative, instrumental,agent);
     modetype = (tense,aspect,form, mood,essence,modal, manner,time);
     mode = string;
     word = string[16];

     Ci = record
             NP : record
                    PREP,DET,ADJ,NMOD,N :  word;
                  end; (* NP record *)
          end; (* Ci record *)


     casesentence = record
                      modality : array[tense..time] of mode;
                      proposition : record
                                       verb : word;
                                       cases : array[neutral..agent] of Ci;
                                    end; (* proposition record *)
                   end; (* casesentence record *)
```

Examples of Cases

The particular cases found in any sentence depend on the verb in that sentence. For example, the verb *put* requires the *neutral* and *locative* cases and optionally has an *agent* as well. Valid examples of the verb would be

John put the vase on the table.

The vase was put on the table by John.

The vase was put on the table.

(John—AGENT, the vase—NEUTRAL, on the table—LOCATIVE)

But not,

*John put the vase.	NO LOCATIVE
*The vase was put.	NO LOCATIVE
*John put on the table.	NO NEUTRAL

The verb, *put on*, would be either a separate entry in the lexicon or a different sense of the word, *put*, as in the sentence,

Mary put on the sweater.

The verb *give* has three cases also: the *neutral* and *dative* are required, *agent* is optional.

John gave the vase to Sue.

John gave Sue the vase.

The vase was given to Sue by John.

The vase was given to Sue.

Sue was given the vase by John.

([by] John—AGENT, the vase—NEUTRAL, [to] Sue—DATIVE)

but not:

*Sue was given by John.   NO NEUTRAL

However if Sue were the *neutral*, the thing being given, this sentence would be grammatical.

*John gave the vase.   NO DATIVE

*The vase was given by John.   NO DATIVE

Either of these last two sentences could be considered grammatical under some circumstances, particularly if the context provided some of the information. For instance, if the question,

Who gave you all these wedding presents?

has just been asked, then the *dative* case is already known—*you*—and would not have to be included. This is an example of the phenomenon known as *ellipsis*—not including some part of a sentence which is normally required because it can be inferred from the context.

Case Frames

Each verb then must have a *case frame* to specify which cases are required or allowed with it. For each case there are three possibilities: it is required with this particular verb, it is optional, or it is not allowed. Thus, a three state data type can be declared to handle this situation:

```
type caseinclusion = (non,opt,req);
```

In the definition for caseinclusion, the sequence chosen produces the implicit ordering:

```
non < opt < req
```

(non—not allowed, opt—optional, req—required) Thus the general form for a case frame will be:

```
type caseframe = array[neutral..agent] of caseinclusion;
```

How are the case frames to be matched to each verb? The most direct way would be to include an identifier of a particular case frame with the verb in the dictionary. Since case frames are often shared by several verbs, the case frames could be stored as an ordered list, and an index to the ordered list would identify the specific case frame associated with a particular verb. This number would be included in our definition of a proposition:

```
type proposition = record
                        verb : word;
                        cframeid : integer;
                        cases : array[neutral..agent] of Ci;
                end; (* proposition record *)
```

The entire declaration of casesentence is:

```
type casetype = (neutral, dative, locative, instrumental, agent);
     modetype = (tense, aspect, form, mood, essence, modal, manner, time);
     mode = string;
     word = string[16];

     Ci = record
             NP : record
                     PREP, DET, ADJ, NMOD, N :  word;
                  end; (* NP record *)
          end; (* Ci record *)

     casesentence = record
                        modality : array[tense..time] of mode;
                        proposition : record
                                        verb : word;
                                        cframeid :  integer;
                                        cases :  array[neutral..agent] of Ci;
                                     end; (* proposition record *)
                    end; (* casesentence record *)

     caseinc = (non, opt, req);

     caseframe = array[neutral..agent] of caseinc;
```

Exercise: Write a program to create deep structure representations of sentences generated using case grammar. Randomly select a verb, and find its case frame. Then using appropriate probabilities for the optional cases and randomly selected noun phrases (as produced by earlier exercise), write out "sentences" as shown below. (This example is taken from an actual student program, which used a larger set of cases, including source and goal.)

```
VERB: push
     Case frame:   Neutral-required
                   Locative-optional
                   Source-optional
                   Goal-optional
                   Agent-required
```

```
AGENT:   druid
NEUTRAL: beast
SOURCE:  from dolphin
GOAL:    to owl
```

Exercise: Modify the program above to apply semantic restrictions on the noun phrases which can be used for a particular case. In other words, make sure that the noun phrase for the agent is an animate, preferably human, being. Consult the section in Chapter 4 on semantic markers, if necessary.

DETERMINING CASE STRUCTURE OF A SENTENCE

The process of mapping the cases indicated in a case frame onto the actual surface elements of a sentence must be elaborated. There are two ways of mapping: first, in generation of sentences, the concepts which need to be represented are mapped onto the case frame, and second, in analysis of sentences, the cases in the case frame are mapped onto the phrases found in the input sentence. We will consider sentence generation first.

Sentence Generation

In PARSIFAL, the parsing system developed by Mitchell Marcus, the problem of mapping between the actual sentence and the case frame is handled by applying three rules developed by Stockwell, Schacter, and Partee. [5] Each case frame is defined as an ordered subset of the entire set of cases:

(neutral, dative, locative, instrument, agent)

In a particular case frame, each case can be optional, obligatory or disallowed and must be marked appropriately. For example, using the scheme described earlier in the chapter in which each position for a case can have one of three values, the case frame might be as follows:

Neutral—req

Dative—non

Locative—opt

Instrument—opt

Agent—opt

In this example, *neutral* is required, *dative* is not allowed, and the other three cases are optional.

The three rules show how the case frame is applied and why the implied order of the cases is important.

Rule 1. How to create the subject: If the rightmost case in the case frame is obligatory, it must be the subject. If it is optional, it can be ignored and the rule reapplied to the remaining cases.

Rule 2. How to create the objects: Starting from the left of the case frame, each case, whether obligatory or optional, is made an object until all the appropriate object positions have been filled. Objects have no prepositions.

Rule 3. Prepositional phrases: Each of the remaining cases is added to the sentence marked by a preposition to indicate its case. Each case has a default, a given preposition (or set of prepositions); however, if the verb requires some preposition other than the default, that information would be stored with the verb in its lexical entry.

The specific prepositions which can identify a particular case are:

Agent—BY

Instrument—WITH, BY

Dative—TO

Locative—ON, IN, UNDER, BESIDE, . . .

The neutral case has no preposition and thus will be either an object of the sentence, or the subject if there is no agent. Although the preposition BY occurs for two different cases, it cannot identify two cases in the same sentence:

The window was broken by John.

The window was broken by a hammer.

*The window was broken by John by a hammer.

If the agent is used with the preposition *by*, the instrument must use the preposition *with*.

The window was broken by John with a hammer.

Assume the following information is known about a sentence to be generated:

```
VERB:  put

    Case Frame:  Neutral-required
                 Dative-not allowed
                 Locative-required
                 Instrumental-optional
                 Agent-optional

NOUN PHRASES:

    (The zookeeper-human, animate, . . . )

    (The cage-physical location, . . . )

    (The food-physical object, . . . )
```

Since the only animate noun is **the zookeeper**, it must be the agent and will therefore be the subject of the sentence. The only physical location is **the cage** and will thus be the locative case with an appropriate preposition. The remaining noun phrase, **the food**, must be the neutral since that is a required case. Since neutral can only be the subject or an object and a subject has already been chosen, then the neutral phrase must be an object. The only remaining problem is what preposition to combine with the locative. There is not really enough information specified here to decide; however, additional information in the lexicon about cages would indicate that putting something in the cage would probably be more functional than **under, on,** etc. Thus, if all the elements are combined as indicated, the resulting sentence would be:

The zookeeper put the food in the cage.

The example would not have worked out as nicely if the phrases had been:

```
(The zookeeper . . . )
(The cage . . . )
(The zoo director . . . )
```

This set could produce either of these two sentences:

The zookeeper put the zoo director in the cage.
The zoo director put the zookeeper in the cage.

Exercise: Extend the program from the earlier exercise to generate actual sentences, rather than merely the deep structure representation. The example in the earlier exercise should be something like:

The druid pushes the beast from the dolphin to the owl.

Sentence Analysis

Sentence analysis is somewhat different from generation in terms of the set of problems encountered in mapping between the case frame for the verb in the sentence and the other elements found. In analyzing a sentence, the prepositional phrases can be a starting point for identifying some of the case slots. For example in the sentence,

John broke the window with a hammer.

the prepositional phrase, *with a hammer*, can be identified as instrumental with the preposition as the case indicator. But the two noun phrases, *John*, and *the window* have not been identified. Additional rules are required.

Once all the prepositional phrases have been classified, how are the subject and object determined? In the sentences,

The hammer broke the window.

John broke the window.

there are no prepositions at all. These examples illustrate the fact that sometimes the classification of cases may require semantic knowledge about the words in the sentences. Since agents must be animate and instruments inanimate, the case for the subject position in the latter sentence can be determined by accessing the semantic part of a lexical entry for each word. But the decision cannot be made on a purely syntactic basis.

The rules described for generating sentences must be applied for analysis, but in a different order. First, in order to know what cases to look for in the sentence, the verb must be found. The lexical entry for the verb will provide the case frame index to obtain the case frame. The case frame will indicate which cases are required and which are optional. If we next find the prepositions and their associated noun phrases, a preliminary match can be made between the prepositional phrases found and the appropriate cases. When all the prepositional phrases are accounted for, Rules 1 and 2 are applied to find the subject and the object. Recall that in an active sentence, if the agent occurs, it must be the subject. Therefore if the noun phrase preceding the verb in an active, declarative sentence is animate, it can be assumed to be the agent/subject. Then an unmarked noun phrase following the verb will be an object. If two unmarked noun phrases follow the verb, the first one is the dative case, the indirect object, and the second one is the neutral, the direct object. If only one occurs, then it is the neutral. If no agent is found, i.e., the subject noun phrase is not animate, then the instrument can be the subject, in an active sentence. Passive sentences have different rules, which are applied in a similar fashion. Knowing whether the sentence is active or passive can be tricky, but the general scheme is to examine the verb phrase. If the verb is only one word and not a form of *to be*, the sentence is active; if the verb includes a form of *be* followed by the past participle, the sentence is passive.

John broke the window.   ACTIVE

The window was broken by John. PASSIVE

Exercise: Develop the rules for finding the cases in a passive sentence.

The rules described do not really handle all situations. For example, in the sentence,

The hammer broke the window.

it is easy to determine that one of the noun phrases is the neutral case, and one is the instrumental. But which one is which? Nothing in the rules can distinguish. In this situation additional semantic information is required about the objects being discussed in order to make a reasonable decision, and the semantic information needed must include more than semantic features. In other words, knowing that the hammer and the window are both inanimate physical objects does not help determine the cases. Only if the lexical entries for the two nouns in the noun phrases provide the information that a window is usually made of glass or some other easily breakable material and that hammers are hard, durable objects used for hitting other objects, can the inference be drawn that probably the hammer did the breaking and the window got broken. Another similar problem occurs when perfectly acceptable sentences violate the case categories, such as,

> The boy opened the door with his sister.

If the sister is being used as the instrument for opening the door, then an animate object is serving the role of an inanimate object. The problems of the additional semantic information required will be considered further in later chapters.

Major Exercise: Write a program to input sentences with appropriate lexical data provided for each word, and analyze them using the case grammar. Use only the prepositions which identify a particular case. Test your program with the various sentences which illustrate different aspects of case grammar in this chapter and in Chapter 1. What kinds of sentences cause problems in analysis? Can you classify the problems? Would additional semantic information eliminate the analysis problems? What kind?

EXTENDING THE DEFINITION OF NP

Now that the initial problems of synthesis and analysis using case grammar have been presented, let us consider the difficulties encountered with a more elaborate (and more realistic) definition for NP. Modifying the earlier definition, the new rule is:

> NP→(PREP) (DET) ADJ* N* N (S|NP)*

The following noun phrases are defined by the new rule:

> the tall red fire house doors
>
> a dog in the park
>
> the girl who won the first prize

Several considerations arise:

> How can the repeated elements be handled?
>
> How can the postpositional modifier be handled?
>
> What is involved in the recursive part of the definition (S and NP)?

All of the optionally repeated adjectives could just be concatenated together to form the adjective element, if we continue to use a string representation. However, because of the complications presented by the postpositional modifier, a different representation will be more workable. As in Chapter 5, graphs will be more flexible and better suited to the recursive nature of the definition.

Graph Representation of Noun Phrases

As explained before, a graph consists of a set of nodes connected by arcs, also called edges. The arcs are directed; thus the structure produced is a digraph. Figure 6.1 illustrates the digraph which represents the noun phrase definition, without the S as a postpositional modifier.

NP→(PREP) (DET) ADJ* N* N NP*

The graph is much simpler than those used with RTNs and ATNs. Each node contains only the constituent type, and the arcs merely indicate the paths which can be taken and what the probability is that a particular arc will be taken. The noun is the terminal node.

The data structure required to store this representation includes both node and arc definitions.

```
type probability = real;
     nodeptr  = ^node;
     contype = string[4];
     arc = record
                tail, head :  nodeptr;
                rel : probability
            end; (* arc record *)
     node = record
                info :   contype;
                ptr1,ptr2 :   arc
            end; (* node record *)
```

Each node consists of the constituent type information and two pointers, defined as arc. Each arc has a pointer back to this node, a pointer to the next node and the probability figure for that arc. Notice that the graph in Figure 6.1 has an arc from PREP to DET. Following the arc from PREP to DET if PREP was reached from N, rather than as the entry to the graph, involves recursion, in that the whole graph is being started again. Thus the recursive NP part of the definition has been dealt with by the declaration of the data structure. But the recursion on the sentence itself must be delayed until the definition of the structure for a sentence is complete.

Building the graph for a particular phrase definition can be done in two ways: either by assigning the specific values for each arc and building the graph a node at a time or by creating a data file to define the graph, thereby allowing for modifications to the structure without changing the program. Both will be left as exercises for the reader.

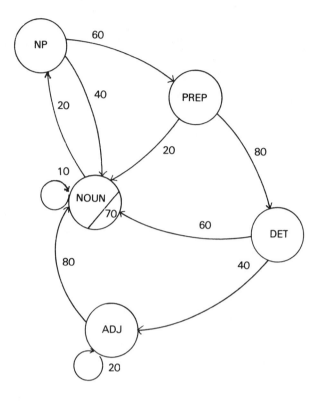

Figure 6.1   Graph Representation of the Noun Phrase Definition: NP →
(PREP)(DET)(ADJ)*N NP* Numbers on arcs indicate probability that arc will be
taken. 70% probability Noun node will be terminal.

Exercise: Write a program to build a graph by reading in a data file consisting
of triplets. Each triplet will define an arc, giving the head and tail nodes and
the relation on the arc. Each node will be identified by the constituent type it
represents. Initially assume that the nodes must be assigned in order from the
start node of the graph. Test the graph by printing the constituent type for
each node encountered on a traversal through the graph.

Exercise: How can the program above be modified to ensure that the graph
is connected, i.e., that all the arcs point to a node and that all nodes except the
terminal nodes have non-null arcs?

Exercise: Modify the program above to include probabilities that a particular arc will be taken and also that if a node is reached, the constituent will be generated. In other words, at the DET node, the probabilities for taking the arc to ADJ versus the arc to N might be 40 percent to 60 percent. If the arc to ADJ is taken, the probability that the adjective will be generated might be 50 percent. Test the program by randomly selecting appropriate words for each node reached.

Noun Phrase Generation

Generating noun phrases using the graph described above is quite simple. The start node is pointed to as the beginning of the graph, and the path taken through the graph must be determined by deciding at each node, which arc to choose. When a terminal node is reached, the determination must be made whether the noun phrase is complete, i.e., whether or not to terminate. Theoretically, traversing the graph could be endless, since the terminal node N points to the PREP node which starts all over again. In practical terms, an end would probably be reached eventually. If one were randomly generating noun phrases, the probabilities would most likely cause a termination before many repetitions had occurred. If meaningful noun phrases are being created, the graph would use up all the information to be put into the noun phrase and have nothing left to deal with.

Exercise: Write a program to generate noun phrases using the graph built by the earlier exercise. An interesting approach to testing the program is to allow changes during execution to the various probabilities for taking arcs and generating a word at a node.

Exercise: Another approach to defining the graph used for representing a noun phrase would be to include an arc from a node to every other node that could immediately follow it. This method would eliminate the probability check at each node of whether the element represented by that node was to be generated. Design a graph to handle this other approach. What are the relative advantages of the two methods?

Noun Phrase Analysis

Using the graph for analysis is as easy as for synthesis. Starting from the PREP node, if a PREP occurred in the first position, it would be recognized; a PREP in any other position would be an error (except following a N node where the preposition would indicate the phrase to be restarting the graph). If the first word were not a PREP, then the program would search each of the paths for the word type found. As an example, consider the phrase,

four red balls

(assuming that *four* is classified as an adjective). The PREP node would not be successful, so a check would be made to see if the word is a N, the only type on the other arc. If not, then the program would check for a determiner. Since that would not be found either, the path to the determiner would be taken to test for the next set of possibilities. There the next word would still not be a noun. However at that node, the test for an ADJ would be successful. The arc would be taken to the ADJ node, the word, *four*, dealt with and removed from the input string. The same procedure would continue for each additional word until the input string is used up and the terminal node is reached. In this graph it would be possible to have the pointer to the terminal node N always be the first of the two pointers. Then when the test is made at the first node for a noun, a flag could be set if the current word is not a noun. At each successive node until the word class is found, the test for the noun would not have to be repeated. When the word class was determined, the flag would be reset and reused.

Exercise: Write a program to input strings of word class identifiers, such as DET ADJ ADJ N, and determine whether they constitute a valid noun phrase.

Exercise: Modify the program above to input actual noun phrases and get the word class from the lexicon, in order to determine whether they are valid.

REPRESENTING A SENTENCE IN CASE GRAMMAR GRAPH FORMAT

Representing an entire sentence as a graph which includes all aspects of case grammar is complicated by the fact that several different kinds of nodes are required. Figure 6.2 shows the graph needed to represent a sentence, according to the grammar:

SENT → MODL + PROP

MODL → tense, aspect, form, mood, essence, modal, manner, time

PROP → VERB + Case Frame + CARG*

CARG → Case Relation + NP|SENT

NP → (PREP) (DET) ADJ* N* N (SENT|NP)

The start node is SENT, for sentence, which links to MODL, the modality, and PROP, the proposition. MODL includes an array for all the modes. PROP holds VERB and its case frame, and points to CARG, the case argument. The CARG node, which will be repeated for each case specified by the case frame,

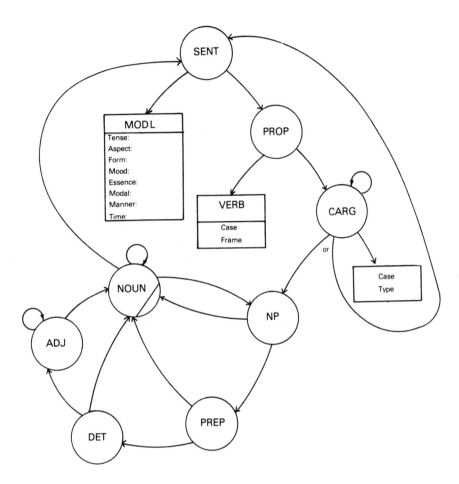

Figure 6.2   Case Grammar Graph

includes the case relation CASEREL and a pointer to NP, the noun phrase or to SENT, a sentence, for the case. Notice that the part of the graph pointed to by NP is similar to the noun phrase graph discussed earlier, but with several minor changes. One important difference is the link from NOUN to SENT. This link provides for the recursive definition of the postpositional modifier as (SENT|NP).

First the different types of nodes must be determined. The most general situation is for a node to have two pointers and some information about a word; this type applies to all the nodes in the noun phrase part of the graph except NOUN, which needs three pointers. In addition the nodes SENT and NP require two pointers, but no information. Thus the definition which would apply to all these cases is:

```
type word = string[16];
     idstr = string[4];

     gennode = record
                   nodeid : idstr;
                   info :  word;
                   ptr1,ptr2,ptr3  :  arc
               end; (* nodedef record *)
```

The field `nodeid` is needed to distinguish among the different nodes represented by this one definition. The unused pointers can be set to nil when they are not needed, and `info` set to the null string for the SENT node. `word` is currently defined as a string with a maximum length of 16 characters which would hold the actual word for that node. `Word` can be modified to include other parts of the lexical entry, such as semantic information, if required.

The next type of node to be defined is MODL, which includes the array of modes. It can be defined as MODALITY was earlier:

```
type modlnode = array[tense..time] of mode;
```

where the particular modalities which index the modes are:

```
type modality = (tense, aspect, form, mood, essence, modal, manner, time)
```

`Mode` is still defined as a string. The third type of node is PROP, which holds the verb and the case frame:

```
type propnode = record
                    verb : word;
                    caseframe : array[neutral..agent] of caseinclusion;
                    cargptr : arc
                end;  (* propnode record *)
```

The last type of node required is that for CARG, the case argument, which has the case relation, a pointer to the case data in NP or SENT, and a pointer to the next CARG node, if any. The last CARG node will have a null `cargptr`. Thus the CARG nodes will be kept as a linked list with `propnode` pointing to the head of the list. `Cargnode` is declared as:

```
type cargnode = record
                    caserel : casetype;
                    caseptr :  arc;
                    nextcarg :  arc
                end; (* cargnode record *)
```

Having four different node definitions would require a different type declaration for the pointer to each different kind of node, which would complicate the graph needlessly. An easier solution is to use a variant record definition which will allow any of these possibilities for **node** and yet require only one node pointer.

```
type node = record
       case kind : nodetype of
         gennode : (gnode = record
                                nodeid : idstr;
                                info :  word;
                                ptr1,ptr2,ptr3 :  arc
                            end (* nodedef record *));

         modlnode: (mnode = array[tense..time] of mode);

         propnode: (pnode = record
                                verb : word;
                                caseframe : array[neutral..agent] of
                                                 caseinclusion;
                                cargptr :  arc
                            end (* propnode record *));

         cargnode: (cnode = record
                                caserel : casetype;
                                caseptr :  arc;
                                nextcarg :  arc
                            end (* cargnode record *))

       end;  (* node record *)
```

With all the types included, the definition of the case grammar graph is as follows:

```
type probability = real;
     modality = (tense, aspect, form, mood, essence, modal, manner, time);
     casetype = (neutral, dative, locative, instrumental, agent);
     caseinclusion = (non, opt, req);

     nodeptr = ^node;
     nodetype = (gennode,modlnode,propnode,cargnode);
     word = string[16];
     idstr = string[4];
     mode = string;

     arc = record
              tail, head : nodeptr;
              rel     : probability
           end;  (* arc record *)
```

```
node = record
      case kind : nodetype of
      gennode : (gnode : record
                               nodeid : idstr;
                               info :  word;
                               ptrl,ptr2,ptr3 :  arc
                          end (* gnode record *));

      modlnode: (mnode : array[tense..time] of mode);

      propnode: (pnode : record
                               verb : word;
                               caseframe : array[neutral..agent] of
                                                  caseinclusion;
                               cargptr :  arc
                          end (* pnode record *));

      cargnode: (cnode : record
                               caserel : casetype;
                               caseptr : arc;
                               nextcarg : arc
                          end  (* cnode record *))
      end;  (* node record *)
```

In order to create the proper type of node at each point as the graph is being built, the routine to build the graph will call the `makenode` function with the node type as a parameter:

```
function makenode (kind : nodetype) : nodeptr;

var p : nodeptr;

begin (* makenode *)
    case kind of
        gennode : new(p,gennode);

        modlnode: new(p,modlnode);

        propnode: new(p,propnode);

        cargnode: new(p,cargnode)
    end (* case *);
    makenode := p

end; (* makenode *)
```

When the `makenode` function returns the node pointer, then the appropriate information can be placed into the node.

The diagram in Figure 6.2 is the potential structure for a sentence described by case grammar, the general case. The graph built to represent an actual sentence will include only the parts that occur in that sentence. Some nodes are required: SENT, MODL, PROP. CARG will be repeated for each case occurring in the sentence. The NP part of the graph will include only nodes which represent elements in the actual sentence.

The specific graph will be built during either synthesis or analysis as the parts of the sentence are discovered. During synthesis the nodes are created from information supplied to indicate what the structure of the sentence is to be. For example, a list of modes would be provided:

Tense: past

Aspect: perfect

Form: simple

Mood: declarative

Essence: positive

Modal: can

Manner: nil

Time: yesterday

These various facts about the sentence are stored until the surface structure is to be generated from the graph.

The verb and its case frame is placed into the PROP node, along with a pointer to the first case argument to be included. The case frame will guide the choice of case arguments in the same way that it did in the earlier representational scheme. Each CARG node will indicate which case it handles, a pointer to the noun phrase or sentence graph for that case, and a pointer to the next CARG node. The NP graph will operate essentially as it did alone, with the addition of the link back to SENT for representing the postpositional modifier. If the CARG node points to SENT, then the case is represented by an entire sentence. For example,

The building was struck by lightning *where the new tower had been added.*   LOCATIVE

The dog running in the park caught the Frisbee.   AGENT

Exercise: Write a program module to build a case grammar graph to represent a particular sentence. Input the modality information and the verb and other words interactively in response to specific requests. (For example, print out a prompt, *What is the tense?* and store the value entered.) Determine the case frame from the lexicon.

After the deep structure is built in the graph, creating the surface structure would follow much the same direction as the earlier schemes. The decision of which case would take what surface position, such as subject or object, is made by following the rules given before. The modes primarily affect the verb phrase. In the list of modes given above, for example, if the verb were *run*, the surface structure would include:

<subject> could run ... yesterday.

Developing the algorithm for generating the surface representation of a sentence from the case grammar graph will be left as an exercise for the reader.

Major Exercise: Using the graph building module developed in the earlier exercise, write a program to output the surface representation for a sentence represented in a case grammar graph.

Case grammar graphs seem particularly useful for holding the structural aspects of a sentence during the analysis process, since they are flexible and can be built a piece at a time. Thus, as the parts of a sentence are interpreted, the nodes of the graph are filled in, and the modes are inserted as they are determined. There is no implicit order to the case arguments in a sentence so the nodes are added to the list as they are found. In fact, if the case relation initially chosen proves to be wrong, changing it is simple—only `caserel` in the CARG node needs to be changed—and does not require any pointers to be shuffled or any elements to be moved. Since a case argument may be a sentence as well as a noun phrase, a sentence initially considered the main clause might become a subordinate clause if the analysis determined that were appropriate. This change would be made by putting a pointer to the sentence structure in the CARG node for the main clause.

Example of Sentence Analysis

This process of analysis can best be understood by following an example. The sentence to be analyzed is:

The young athlete will be running in Los Angeles next week.

The first word, *The*, indicates the beginning of a noun phrase. A routine to build the NP graph would be called and would find *The young athlete*, and place it in the graph. Since no case is yet known, the NP graph would be held temporarily with no classification. When the word, *will*, is encountered, a verb or verb phrase is expected. The word, *will*, establishes the mode *tense* to be future. The next word, *be*, will become the main verb until the word following that is examined. Since the word, *running*, is also a verb, it becomes the main verb, *run*, and the mode *form* is seen to be progressive. The word, *be*, is not needed since it has served the purpose of determining the form of the verb phrase. The case frame for the verb, *run*, is retrieved from the lexicon, with the following values:

```
Verb: run

Case frame:  Neutral-required
             Dative-not allowed
             Locative-optional
             Instrumental-not allowed
             Agent-required
```

This verb falls into a special category, known as reflexive-deletion, since the neutral may refer to the same entity as the agent. For example, in the sentence,

John ran to school.

John is the neutral as well as the agent:

John ran [John] to school.

The situation in which the neutral is not the same as the agent, such as,

John ran the machine.

would be like any other verb with separate agent and neutral cases.

The case frame expects at least two and perhaps three cases: agent, neutral, and maybe locative. Since the noun phrase already saved, *The young athlete*, is animate, it can be assigned the agent case as the subject of the sentence, the noun phrase preceding the verb phrase.

Following the verb phrase, the sentence contains the noun phrase, *in Los Angeles*. The lexical information about the proper noun, *Los Angeles*, would indicate that it is a place name, and the preposition, *in*, refers to location, so the **casetype** for this NP would be locative. (Proper nouns are not explicitly described by the grammar, but can be handled as a special instance of a regular noun.) The last phrase of the sentence, *next week*, is a bit more difficult to handle. The neutral case has still not been found, but the neutral case for the verb, *run*, would have to be in a certain category, such as a physical object or an organization:

John ran the machine.

Elizabeth ran the corporation.

The noun, *week*, would not fit into that category. Therefore since *run* is a reflexive-deletion category, *The young athlete* can be assumed to be the neutral as well as the agent. All the cases have been filled so the phrase, *next week*, has another role in the sentence; it is a phrase indicating time and will be assigned to the mode *time*. All parts of the sentence have been accounted for. Figure 6.3 shows the graph for the sentence.

The analysis would not necessarily proceed as described above. Several alternative approaches are possible. The noun phrase found before the verb was encountered could have been tentatively classified as the agent case, since the agent will be the subject and will precede the verb, if the sentence has an agent. The lexical entry for *week* would contain information that the word was time-related, so the decision to make it a mode rather than a case could have been based on that information rather than only considering that possibility after the word, *week*, had been determined not to be a candidate for the neutral case. There are other alternatives, as well.

The difficulty that arose with the mode *time* above illustrates that various problems do occur in determining modality. Both the modes, *time* and *manner*,

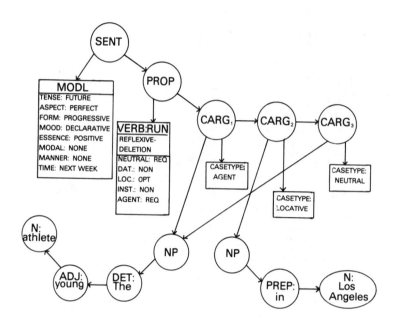

Figure 6.3   Case Grammar Graph for Sentence, "The young athlete will be running in Los Angles next week."

can look like cases, and in complex sentences, may be dependent clauses themselves.

He won the race by expending extra effort.   MANNER

The cruise ended when the ship sank.   TIME

According to the case grammar, the only way to describe a clause is to classify it as a sentence. But the grammar does not really handle modality adequately. Additional considerations must be added to the case grammar procedures to deal with more complicated sentence types.

Major Exercise: Write a program to input sentences and analyze them using the methods for handling case grammar developed in this section. Print out the analysis. Test the program using various sentences from this chapter and Chapter 1. What kinds of sentences are handled by this method that were not adequately dealt with by the previous method? (See earlier Major Exercise.) What kinds of sentences are still not adequately handled?

Answering Questions with Case Grammar Graphs

One application for which case grammar graphs can be used is answering questions about the information stored in the graphs. Assume that a system has been designed to input and analyze sentences, storing the information obtained from the sentences in graphs of the sort described above. Questions could then be input to the system about that information, such as,

Who broke the window?

and

Did someone give Sue a vase?

There are many different kinds of questions which might be asked, but the simplest is the question which can be answered *yes* or *no*. One reason this type is simple is that the only response required is one word, either *yes* or *no*. However, determining which answer is appropriate is not quite so trivial.

Let us assume that the system for answering questions has input the following sentences and created graphs for each one:

John broke the window with a hammer.

Elizabeth runs the corporation.

The dog is running in the park.

John ran a machine.

The young athlete will run in Los Angeles next week.

John gave Sue the vase.

A scheme for accessing any one of the graphs is needed; it could be provided by a vector with pointers to each of the graphs or a linked list of pointers to them. In either case the list would be scanned to locate the information related to the question asked. For example, if the question asked were,

Did John break the window?

the first step would be to locate a graph with the verb *break*. Then the case arguments for the question would be matched to the case arguments for the sentence. In this situation the case arguments would match exactly, and the answer to the question would be *yes*.

If the question were,

Did someone give Sue a vase?

a slightly more complicated process is involved. The case arguments for the question are:

Agent: someone

Neutral: a vase

Dative: Sue

However the case arguments for the sentence are:

Agent: John

Neutral: the vase

Dative: Sue

The system would need to be able to infer from the information available whether the case arguments match. If it could determine that *John* was a *someone* and that *the vase* was an instance of *a vase*, then the case arguments would match and the answer to the question would be *yes*. If the inferences could not be drawn or if the case arguments did not match, then the question would have to be answered negatively.

Other sorts of questions could also be answered with the information in the graphs. For example,

Who broke the window?

Who runs the corporation?

Where is the dog running?

Where will the young athlete run?

What did John give Sue?

When will the young athlete run?

In all except the last of these sentences the question can be answered by finding the one case argument in the sentence that fills the slot in the question. The exception—the when-question—can be answered by examining the *time* modality. Who-questions must be answered with an animate case argument; where-questions are answered by determining the locative case. The procedure for answering these questions would be as follows:

1. Find the verb and the case arguments for the question, including the empty slot (the thing being asked about).

2. Repeat step 3 for each graph with the same verb as the question until a match is found. If no graph has the same verb or no match is found, stop since the answer is not available.

3. If the case arguments for the sentence match the case arguments for the question, except for the empty slot, then do steps 4 and 5.

4. Find the case argument in the graph that fills the empty slot.

5. Generate the answer to the question from the case argument found.

Let us follow an example through the procedure: Assuming that the same sentences have been input and analyzed, and the question input is:

Who ran the machine?

The question would be analyzed into the following structure:

```
Verb: run

Case arguments:
    Agent: --
    Neutral: the machine
```

(Modality is not necessary for this example so it will be ignored.) The first step would be to locate a graph with the verb *run*. Since there are several, one by one they must be checked to see whether the case arguments match. The Neutral is known for the question; therefore the sentence with a Neutral of *the machine* will be a match. The first graph with the verb *run* has *the corporation* for the Neutral case argument, so we will proceed to another graph. The next graph would have *the dog* as Neutral since it is an instance of the reflexive-deletion usage of the verb. Finally the third graph with the verb *run* will have *the machine* as the Neutral case argument. The next step is to find the case which matches the slot to be filled. The Agent is missing in the question, and the answer must be a person because of the word *who*. The Agent case in the graph is filled by the word, *John*, which refers to a person. Therefore the answer can be formulated,

John ran the machine.

or simply,

John.

Each of the other questions listed above can be answered in a similar fashion except

When will the young athlete run?

The answer to this question can be found in the mode *time* rather than in a case argument. How-questions would usually be answered by the mode *manner*. Even with these various questions which can be handled by the case grammar techniques, there are many other types of questions which require more inferencing than is possible from the information in the graphs. Some other kinds of questions could be dealt with, if necessary, such as,

How many sentences involved running?

But questions like the following require more complex representations or more information than is stated:

> What caused the window to break?
>
> Did Sue like the vase John gave her?
>
> Where did John get the vase?

Major Exercise: Extend the earlier major exercise to answer *YES/NO* questions about the sentences input.

Major Exercise: Extend the major exercise above to answer other types of questions about the sentences input. What kinds of sentences cannot be answered from the information available? What would be required for them to be answered—more semantic information? more cases? what?

ANOTHER SET OF DEEP CASES

The chapter began with an almost intuitive definition of deep cases, giving examples comparing deep cases to surface cases. It is now appropriate to examine another approach to deep cases. Fillmore's cases should be familiar by now. The smaller set used by Marcus has been discussed extensively. Another important system of cases was developed by Marianne Celce-Murcia and used by Robert F. Simmons in his work on case grammar. [6]

Celce-Murcia's system assumes a parser capable of recognizing constituents of a sentence, such as noun phrases, prepositional phrases, finite verbs and verb phrases, and adverbs and adverb phrases, from the surface representation of that sentence. The noun phrase preceding the verb or verb phrase is the *surface subject*; one noun phrase following the verb is the *surface object*. More than one object would require subscripts: *surface object[1]* and *surface object[2]*. These elements along with other marked or unmarked noun phrases each have a particular functional relationship with the verb in the sentence. These functional relations are the deep cases in her system. (The terms, *marked*, and *unmarked*, refer to whether or not surface indications of the function of the phrase occur in the sentence. For example a preposition can *mark* a noun phrase as being one case or another. Inflections can also serve that function, as in the sentence, *She gave him the book. She* is the nominative and thus is a surface subject; *him* is objective and thus is a surface object.)

The elementary functional relations are:

Theme

Causal Actant

Locus

Source

Goal

The *theme* corresponds to the objective in Fillmore's set of cases and to the neutral in Stockwell, Schachter, and Partee's set. It is the entity—person, thing, fact, event, etc.—about which some statement is being made. It is usually required.

The *casual actant* is the entity—person, object, force, etc.—which causes the action or change of state described by the verb. It corresponds to both the agent and the instrumental in the other systems.

Locus essentially expresses the location of the theme in the sentence, although locus is used in several different ways:

The cat crawled under the table.
 (under the table—locus, the cat—causal actant)

Mary wore the sweater.
 (Mary—locus, the sweater—theme)

The last two functional relations—*source* and *goal*—which were included in Fillmore's later set of cases, generally provide directional information and are frequently marked by prepositions.

John put the ball into the box.
 (the box—goal)

Mary took the box from John.
 (John—source)

Sam moved from Detroit to Atlanta.
 (Detroit—source, Atlanta—goal)

Celce-Murcia's system requires a method for distinguishing between different kinds of causal actants:

John broke the window with a hammer.

In this sentence the theme is *the window*; both *John* and *the hammer* are causal actants. These are referred to as CA direct (John) and CA indirect (a hammer), or as CA1 and CA2. Notice that CA1 corresponds to agent, and CA2 to instrument, and are distinguished by the former being animate and the latter, inanimate. Sometimes there are two causal actants.

John played ping-pong with Mary.
 (John—causal actant, Mary—co-causal actant)

The functional relation locus includes the dative as well as the locative from the other systems. Some interesting points arise while considering examples of locus:

Tom has a new car.
(Tom—locus, a new car—theme)

New York has skyscrapers.
(New York—locus, skyscrapers—theme)

Tom knows the answer.
(Tom—locus, the answer—theme)

*The garden knows the answer.
(The garden—locus, the answer—theme)

The first two sentences with the verb, *has*, are both okay, but in the second two, the verb, *knows*, does not allow for both animate and inanimate subjects. Some verbs require only an animate locus, particularly verbs involving mental activity: *know, think, feel,* etc. The physical locus, or location, does not work the same way with these verbs. Physical locus can still be included, if it is marked:

Tom thought of the answer in the shower.
(Tom—mental locus, the answer—theme, the shower—physical locus)

One way to deal with these dual purpose functional relations is to have a primary and a secondary version of each. The primary relation must be animate; the secondary is inanimate. This duality works for both causal actant and locus. The primary causal actant is CA1; the secondary causal actant is CA2. With locus the distinction made includes the early example,

Mary wore the sweater.

as well as the mental locus and physical locus. Thus, the primary locus would include Mary in the sentence above and Tom in the previous examples.

Paradigms for Deep Case Recognition

One particularly significant feature of Celce-Murcia's system is the set of paradigms developed to assist in mapping between the input sentence and the case frame for a specific verb. For instance, with the verbs called Intransitive, **the theme is required and is the surface subject, the causal actant is not** allowed, and the other functional relations will be marked, if they are present. Some verbs in this category are *die, fly, go, call, come,* etc.

Fish swim in the ocean.

Transitive verbs require both the theme and the causal actant; in an active sentence the causal actant is the surface subject, the theme is the surface object. Other cases are marked. There are many examples of this type: *kill, make, spill, write,* etc.

The carpenter made a cabinet.

The paradigm called *ergative* requires the theme, which is the surface object if a causal actant is present. The causal actant is the surface subject, if it is present; if not, the theme is the surface subject. Some examples of ergative verbs are *open, move, begin, replace, melt,* etc.

There are three types of transfer verbs. Two-way transfer verbs have theme, causal actant, source, and goal, all required. In these the causal actant is the surface subject, the theme is the surface object, and the other cases are marked. Examples include *carry, bring, take,* etc.

> John carried the beer from the van to the campsite.
> (John—CA1, the beer—theme, the van—source, the campsite—goal)

The second type of transfer verb has the source as the surface subject:

> John sent the book to Mary.
> (John—source, the book—theme, Mary—goal)

> Jane sold the car to Bob.
> (Jane—source, the car—theme, Bob—goal)

The third type is the reverse of the second; the goal is the surface subject:

> Mary got the book from John.
> (Mary—goal, the book—theme, John—source)

> Bob bought the car from Jane.
> (Bob—goal, the car—theme, Jane—source)

Another set of verbs similar to the transfer paradigm includes verbs like *put* and *take*, which are in opposition to each other. With *put*, the causal actant (surface subject) transfers the theme (surface object) to a goal; with *take*, the causal actant (surface subject) transfers the theme (surface object) from a source. In each of these situations the non-subject case—goal or source—is marked.

> Ann put the book on the shelf.
> (Ann—CA, the book—theme, on the shelf—goal (marked))

> Jeff pulled the rabbit out of the hat.
> (Jeff—CA, the rabbit—theme, out of the hat—source (marked))

Verbs such as *have* need another paradigm, which requires a locus as surface subject and the theme as object:

> Eddie owns a plane.
> (Eddie—locus, a plane—theme)

The converse of verbs of that sort are those like *occupy* which place the theme in the surface subject position and the locus in the object position:

> The dog inhabits the house.
> (the dog—theme, the house—locus)

A set of verbs to which Celce-Murcia does not assign a paradigm are related to mental activities: *know, think, remember, decide, want,* etc. These have a primary locus (animate) as the surface subject and require a theme (which is frequently a dependent clause).

> Terry remembered the incident.
> (Terry—primary locus, the incident—theme)
> Jane thought she knew the man.
> (Jane—primary locus, she knew the man—clause functioning as theme)

Using this system of functional relations together with the paradigms, a rather explicit set of rules and strategies can be developed for analyzing an input sentence.

1. The surface structure is parsed into labelled constituents.
2. Each noun phrase not marked by a preposition is identified by its surface role: subject or object.
3. The form of the verb is determined: active or passive.
4. The case frame and any other relevant information for the verb are retrieved from the lexicon.
5. The heuristic for the particular paradigm is found.
6. The heuristic is applied to the surface structure to find the appropriate deep structure.

At that point the process is complete; the sentence has been analyzed.

Celce-Murcia's system of case relations is important for computational linguistics because it is fairly complete. In addition to defining the functional relations and describing the individual paradigms, she presents a strategy for the analysis procedure. The system emphasizes the fact that any workable system must operate at several levels. The surface level must be dealt with and used as a source of as much information as possible. The focus of the deep case relations is the function that each case performs in relation to all the other elements of the sentence.

Major Exercise: Write a sentence analysis program using the Celce-Murcia cases, paradigms, and strategy. Test the program with a variety of sentence structures, and compare the results to those of the earlier analysis program. In what ways is this system better?

CONCLUSION

Case systems have been important in the development of natural language processing. Although the theories of case grammar were originally developed in a strictly linguistic setting, computational linguists have used case systems frequently. Many of the important systems implemented over the years have been based on these notions. In addition case grammars have served as the foundation for more recent theories, such as functional representation and conceptual dependency.

Chapter 7

Semantic
Networks

During the 1960's cognitive psychologists worked on developing an understanding of the functions of the human brain, including memory. The problems of storing knowledge for later recall of specific facts as well as for categorizing and organizing that knowledge led researchers in Artificial Intelligence to develop a type of structure known as a *semantic network* for representing memory. Semantic networks are graphs much like the graphs used to represent case structures in Chapter 6. These networks are made up of nodes which generally represent a word-meaning and links between the nodes which reflect the relationships among the nodes. As the word *semantic* implies, most of these structures are used to represent meaning, sometimes independently of natural language text. In other words, semantic networks may be built as a pre-existing memory structure against which text input can be matched and to which text input can add knowledge.

One early contribution to the development of semantic networks was made by M. Ross Quillian, who sought to create a *semantic memory* built of nodes interconnected by *associative* links. [1] Each node stood for a word concept and was considered the *head* of a *plane*. (See Figure 7.1.) Each sense of a word had a different plane. The links within the plane from the head to other elements form the structure of the information known about that word concept. For example these links could indicate a class of which this word concept was a subclass, the modifiers of the category, disjunction and/or conjunction, and subject/object relations. Links could also point from inside the plane to another plane to express the definitions of the words used in the plane to describe the head. If the link from the word concept points directly into a group of other nodes which define that word concept, the node is called a *type* node. If the link points to another node which is then further defined, the node is called a *token* node, or simply token. Only one type node can exist

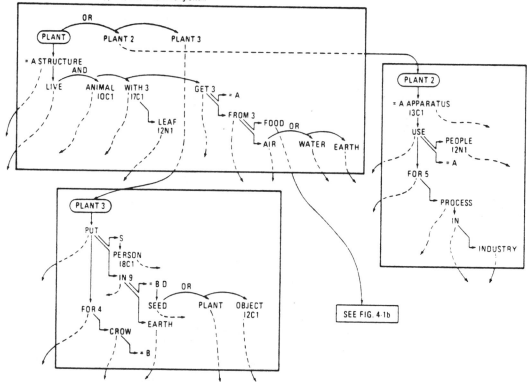

PLANT.   1.   Living structure which is not an animal, frequently
              with leaves, getting its food from air, water, earth.

         2.   Apparatus used for any process in industry.

         3.   Put (seed, plant, etc.) in earth for growth.

Figure 7.1   Quillians' Planes (Reprinted by permission of the author M. R. Quillian from "Semantic Memory," *Semantic Information Processing,* ed. Marvin Minksy, Cambridge, Massachusetts: MIT Press, **1975.**)

for a word concept, but there may be many tokens providing elaboration of the definition.

One important contribution of Quillian's work was the combination of the superclass/subclass taxonomic hierarchy and the description of properties provided by attribute/value pairs. The definition of a word according to the class it falls into is sometimes referred to as an **IS–A** relation, and identifying a word concept as representing a part of another concept is often called a **PART-OF** relation. For example, the sentence

The professor is a tennis player.

[(The professor) **IS–A** (tennis player)]

classifies the concept denoted by the noun phrase *The professor* as being one of the items in the class of things identified as *tennis players*. The phrase,

The ball bearings in the wheel

would provide the relation that *ball bearings* are **PART-OF** a wheel. Attribute/value pairs describe the properties of a concept, and as we shall see in later examples of semantic networks, are an extension of Katz and Fodor's ideas of semantic features.

Robert F. Simmons used semantic networks to represent sentences defined by case grammar. He said,

> A semantic network purports to represent concepts expressed by natural-language words and phrases as nodes connected to other such concepts by a particular set of arcs called semantic relations. Primitive concepts in this system of semantic networks are word-sense meanings. Primitive semantic relations are those that the verb of a sentence has with its subject, object, and prepositional phrase arguments in addition to those that underlie common lexical, classificational and modificational relations. [2]

Simmons' definition of semantic networks certainly applies to the discussion of case grammar graphs as described in Chapter 6. However the only semantic relations considered in the previous chapter were deep case relations and modality relations. The deep case relations are only one type of relation possible between nodes. And other word classes besides verbs can be considered in relation to various parts of a sentence.

Some of the various kinds of relations between nodes are as follows:

1. Deep case relations: **CA1, CA2, THEME, SOURCE, GOAL, LOCUS**
2. Modality relations: **TIME, MANNER, MOOD, ASPECT**, etc.
3. Logical connectives: **OR, NOT, AND, BUT, IMPLY**, etc.
4. Attributive relations: **MODIFIER, POSSESSIVE, HASPART, ASSOC, SIZE, SHAPE**, etc.
5. Quantitative relations: **ORDINAL, DET, COUNT**
6. Token relations: **TOK**
7. Set relations: **SUPERSET, SUBSET, EQUIVALENT, PARTOF**, etc.

The deep case and modality relations are relations between the verbal elements of a sentence and the other parts of the sentence, as discussed in Chapter 6. The other relations apply to different kinds of sentence parts. The logical connectives can be applied at various levels; between noun phrases these relations could indicate coordination of the noun phrases. For example,

The dog ran down the street and into the park. (coordination of two NP's used as locus)

Either John or Sam took the money. (coordination of two NP's used as agent)

At the clausal level the logical connectives bind clauses together to form compound and complex sentences. For example,

The moon shone brightly, and the wind whistled through the trees.	COMPOUND
The program did not work because the logic was faulty.	COMPLEX
The band played and the people danced while the rain fell outside.	COMPOUND-COMPLEX

The attributive and quantitative relations apply more to nouns than to verbal elements, in the sense that the two concepts describe entities rather than actions. Thus these two types of relations function to relate nouns to their modifiers in much the same way that deep case relations relate the verbal elements to the case arguments in a sentence. For example, in the noun phrase,

John's three large red blocks

the attributive relations, **possessive**, **color** and **size**, and the quantitative relation **count** would function together to describe and distinguish the blocks. See Figure 7.2 for a diagram of these relations.

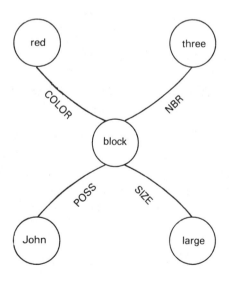

Figure 7.2   Diagram of Relations in Phrase, "John's three large red blocks"

The token relation is used to connect the specific value for a node to that node; in other words, the particular word described by that node falls in the tok relation to that node.

The set relations can provide additional information about the interrelations among elements in a sentence. In the sentence,

One of the ships in the harbor is flying an Italian flag.

the phrase, *One of the ships in the harbor*, indicates one instance of the set of elements which comprise *the ships in the harbor*. An example of the set relation subset is,

All the second grade girls are Brownies.

Thus the set made up of *All the second grade girls* is a subset of the set, *Brownies*.

Functional Relation of Sentences with *Be* Verbs

Case grammar does not handle the verb *to be*, since the primary function of the verb is to express the relationship between two noun phrases, as in,

The doctor is a pediatrician.

or between a noun phrase and its modifier,

The professor is bald.

rather than expressing some relationship between the verb and each noun phrase. In these instances the relationship between the two noun phrases, *the doctor* and *a pediatrician*, and the relationship between the noun phrase, *the professor* and the predicate adjective, *bald*, are expressed in terms of set relation and attributive relation, respectively, rather than by a deep case relation. Thus, the elements of sentences with *be* as the main verb are better described by functional relations other than deep cases. This notion is another example of the IS-A relation used in other semantic network systems.

Data Structures for Semantic Networks

Modifying the data structure used to represent the case grammar graph to allow for all of these relational types is not a difficult matter. The earlier representation provides the information needed for syntactic recognition of the elements of the sentence at the parsing stage. However, the semantic network which is currently being developed is almost totally semantic, although it can be argued that the semantic level is still quite close to the syntactic level of the graph in Chapter 6. The noun phrase section of the semantic network has to show the relations among the various parts of the noun phrase rather than simply the order in which the word classes occur. Thus the NP node will point to the noun, and each relevant node will be connected to the noun by an arc which indicates the particular relationship. Since sentences as a whole can be connected in various ways as the clauses in compound and complex sentences, an arc between two or more sentences must be added. Recall that both the NP node and SENT node in the last version of the case grammar graph were instances of the gennode, defined as

```
type gennode = record
               nodeid : idstr;
               info   : word;
               ptr1,ptr2,ptr3 : arc
           end; (* gennode record *)
```

In this definition nodeid identifies the type of node being represented, SENT, NP, etc. Info holds the actual value, the word or phrase which the node describes. The three pointers are defined as arcs. In the semantic network one of the relations is tok, which is the actual value for the node, but holding the value of the nodes in info is more straightforward. Nodes can have varying numbers of relations and therefore varying numbers of arcs required. An appropriate solution would be to use a linked list to structure the relations associated with a particular node. Therefore the three pointers will be replaced by a single element rel, which will be the head of a linked list of all the relations associated with this node. The definition of arc will be changed to reflect the requirements of the semantic network. An arc will be defined as:

```
type arc = record
           reltype : relation;
           pointer : nodeptr;
           nextarc :  arcptr
       end; (* arc record *)
```

Relation is defined as,

```
type relation = (CA1, CA2, THEME, . . . , TIME, MANNER, . . . , OR,
                 NOT, AND, . . . , POSSESSIVE, SIZE, SHAPE, . . . , etc.);
```

Nextarc will point to the arc which follows in the list. If the relation is the last one of the list, nextarc will be nil. The gennode definition will now be:

```
type gennode = record
               nodeid : idstr;
               info :   word;
               rel :   arc
           end; (* gennode *)
```

By this definition the noun phrase, *John's three large red blocks*, shown in Figure 7.2 would be represented as diagrammed in Figure 7.3.

Several functions which will be useful for manipulating semantic networks are:

Makenode—to create a node, assign the node type, and store the value for the node in info, returning a pointer to the new node

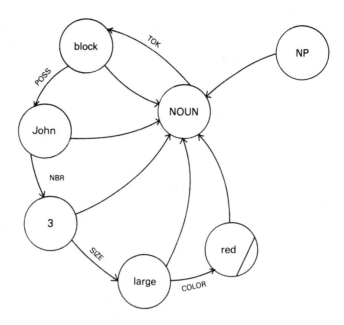

Figure 7.3   Semantic Network Representation of "John's three large red blocks."

Makearc—to create an arc, assign the relation type and set up the pointers, returning the pointer to the new node

Addrel—using makenode and makearc to add a relation to an existing node (may be a procedure rather than a function)

Findrel—to locate an arc with a particular relation on it and return the value of the node it points to

---

Exercise: Write the functions and / or procedures makenode, makearc, addrel, and findrel for manipulating semantic networks.

Obviously in order to build semantic networks from input sentences, additional information is required for each word input besides the word class. Thus when the sentence,

John's three large red blocks fell on the floor.

is read in, the lexical phase of input would signal that *John's* was the POSS of John, that *three* was a COUNT, and so on. Thus the relations would be identified before the network has to be built. One method for attaching the relation information to the word would be to expand the definition of word to include the relation as well as the string of characters. The definition would be:

```
type word = record
               wordstr : string[16];
               rel     : relation
            end;  (* word record *)
```

(If more than one relation were needed for each word, the definition could be expanded.)

Major Exercise: Write a program to input sentences and store them in semantic networks. A more complex lexicon is required for this program, since the lexical phase must be able to provide the relational data for each word. Output a sketch of the network to test the program.

Answering Questions from Semantic Networks

The kinds of questions which can be answered based on the information stored in the semantic network which was described above are more extensive than with case grammar graphs. The primary reason is that more information is being stored explicitly. For example, with case grammar, the phrase,

three large red blocks

would be stored as three adjectives preceding a noun. Therefore no questions could be answered based on that information (unless you want to ask a question like, "How many adjectives modify the noun?"). However, if the adjectives have been classified by adding the relation which each has with the noun, then questions can be answered, such as,

How many large red blocks? . . .

What color were the three large blocks? . . .

and so forth.

In addition more elaborate inferences are now possible, especially with the logical connectives. For example, if a sentence has been input saying,

If John broke the window, then he owes Jane money.

This sentence would be stored as two sentences:

s1: John broke the window.

and

s2: He (John) owes Jane money.

with the logical connective IMPLIES:

s1 IMPLIES s2

Therefore if another sentence is input:

John broke the window.

then the system can infer that John owes Jane money. If the input sentence had been:

John does not owe Jane money.

then the inference drawn would be that John did not break the window. In other words, if the two sentences,

If John broke the window, then he owes Jane money.

John does not owe Jane money.

have been input and stored in a semantic network, when the question,

Did John break the window?

is input, the response would be:

No, John did not break the window.

Thus, using semantic networks allows for more complicated questions to be answered.

Major Exercise: Write a program to input sentences and store the information in semantic networks of the kind described above. Then input and answer questions about the information stored.

Partitioned Semantic Networks

Another type of semantic network was developed by Gary Hendrix and used in the SRI Speech Understanding System for storing knowledge. [3] According to Hendrix,

> In its simplest form, a semantic network consists of a collection of nodes interconnected by an accompanying set of arcs. Each node represents an object (a physical object, situation, event, set, and others), and each arc represents an instance of a binary relation. Typical of the binary relations used in networks are set membership and *deep case relations*. A deep case relation is a relationship between a situation (or other gestalt concept) and a participant in the situation. For example, there is an OBJ case relationship between an owning situation and the object that is owned. [4]

Since the deep case relations function much as they did in the other systems already considered, let us examine the set membership relations first. Various nodes are defined in this system according to the objects which make up a set. There can be at the highest level a set called *universal*, which would be a superset of all other sets in the domain. Each of the other sets would be a subset of *universal*, and this relation would be designated with an S arc (S for subset of the set). One particular member of a set would be related to that set by an E arc (E for element of the set). Figure 7.4 shows an example of this sort of semantic network. Each node connected to the one above it by an S arc is a subset of the node above it; each node connected by an E arc is an element of the set represented by the node above it. The arcs identified by AGT, OBJ, START-TIME, and END-TIME are case relations. The node B is an element of all SITUATIONS of BUILDING (the event, not the structure), which relate the node GENERAL.DYNAMICS, the node HENRY.L.STIMSON and the start and end time nodes. The overall relationship expressed by this semantic network is that General Dynamics is the corporation which built the submarine *Henry L. Stimson* over the period of time defined by the start time T1 and the end time T2.

These semantic networks provide for a hierarchy among the concepts represented by the various nodes. There are, in addition to the S(ubset) and

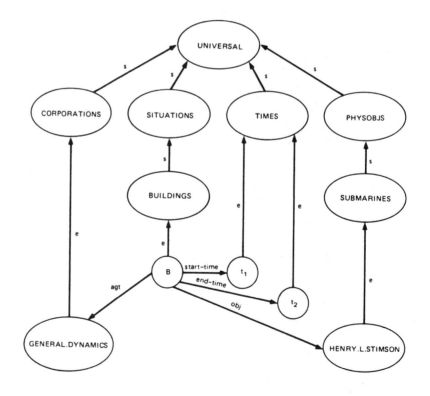

Figure 7.4   An Example Semantic Network (From Walker, p. 127)

E(lement) arcs, two more arc types: DS and DE arcs. DS arcs indicate that the subsets of a given parent set are DISJOINT, that they have no elements in common. DE arcs indicate that the elements of a given set are DISTINCT; in other words, they are not references to the same object. An example of the use of DS and DE arcs is given in Figure 7.5. Here there are three kinds of SHIPS: CARRIERS, SUBMARINES, and P.SHIPS. Because of the DS arcs, CARRIERS and SUBMARINES are mutually exclusive, but P.SHIPS can be either CARRIERS or SUBMARINES. P.SHIPS are subdivided into NUKES and DIESELS. The node NUKE.SUBS indicates that there is an intersection of the sets SUBMARINES and NUKES, which has as two of its elements the distinct objects WHALE and HENRY.L.STIMSON. The node X which has an E arc, not a DE arc, could refer to either WHALE or HENRY.L.STIMSON or to some other nuclear submarine not specified here.

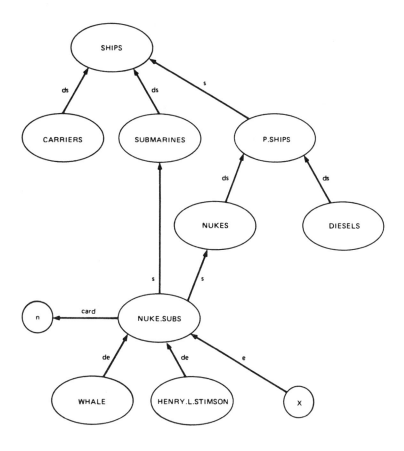

Figure 7.5   The Use of DS and DE Arcs (From Walker, p. 131)

Notice that by including set membership information in the semantic network, the kinds of questions that can be answered from the available information has increased from what was possible using the schemes discussed in Chapter 6. For example, in the semantic network shown in Figure 7.5, the question, "Is the Whale a carrier?" can be answered,

No, it is a nuclear submarine.

Other sorts of questions that can be handled should be fairly obvious to the reader.

Exercise: Make a list of questions that can answered from the semantic networks shown in Figures 7.4 and 7.5.

Partitions

There is an additional organizational scheme for Hendrix's semantic networks, which allows for nodes to be grouped according to some commonality. Thus, every node and arc of a network is assigned to one or more *spaces*. Each *space* contains all the associated nodes and arcs, and becomes a higher order structural element, which can be dealt with in somewhat the same way that nodes and arcs can. Nodes, arcs, and spaces are completely cross-indexed, so that one may determine all the spaces in which a node or arc lies, as well as all the nodes and arcs in a particular space. Hendrix also defines *vistas*, which are groupings of spaces. Vistas provide more information about the hierarchy in that they show the relationships among spaces. For example, in Figure 7.6 the spaces are shown by the blocks drawn around the nodes and identified by the name in the upper right corner of each block. The heavy lines connecting the spaces indicate the vistas, or the view that can be seen from a particular space. For example, the space S has a view of all the other spaces, whereas the space V has a view of only the space called *background*. The network in Figure 7.6 represents the knowledge that a corporation C was the agent in the building of an object, submarine S. Notice that in addition to the set membership information, deep case information is also provided which shows the syntactic relationships of the objects.

Another structure built into these semantic networks is the *supernode*. A supernode is a space which has all the characteristics of a node; in other words, it can be connected by an arc to a node or another space and can have specific information saved about it. Supernodes are used when a relation is true only about the entire set of nodes and arcs represented by a space. For instance, a belief that a person has is made up of a number of concepts and only the entire set of concepts can be said to be true or false. In partitioned semantic network form, that belief would be a space represented by various nodes and arcs, and the entire structure which represents the belief can be considered true or false.

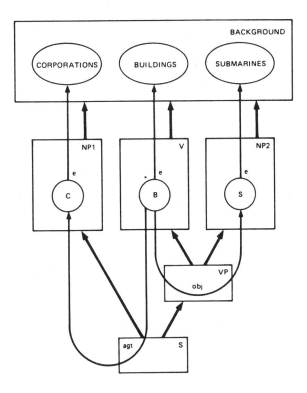

Figure 7.6   Use of VISTA in Syntax Encoding (From Walker, p. 135)

These higher-order structures, spaces and supernodes, were included in the networks to allow an efficient means for representing logical constructs and quantification. The primary logical connectives are *conjunction, disjunction,* and *negation.* From these three all the more complex connectives can be developed.

Conjunction is the relation between some number of *terms* or *conjuncts* such that if all of the conjuncts are true, then the entire proposition is true. This relation is generally expressed by the English word *and.* Thus, if P, Q, and S are all true, then the proposition,

P *and* Q *and* S

is also true. If X and Y are true, but Z is false, then the proposition,

X *and* Y *and* Z

is false. With partitioned semantic networks the concept of conjunction is expressed by placing the nodes for the terms in the same space. Thus the concept of a space is essentially the same as the concept of conjunction. See Figure 7.7 for an example.

Disjunction is the relation between some number of *terms* or *disjuncts* such that if any one of the disjuncts is true, then the entire proposition is true. The English word *or* is generally used for this relation. Thus if X and Y are true and Z is false, then the proposition,

X *or* Y *or* Z

is true. Only if all three terms were false would the proposition be false. The concept of disjunction is represented in partitioned semantic networks by showing that the nodes for the terms are elements of the set *disjunction*. See Figure 7.8 for an example.

The relation negation is used to reverse the truth of a proposition, the concept expressed by the word *not* in English. The concept of negation is expressed by representing the node (or supernode) to be negated as an element of the set *negations*. Figure 7.9 shows an example of the negation relation.

The logical connective *implication* can be defined as a combination of the primary connectives. The proposition

P *implies* Q

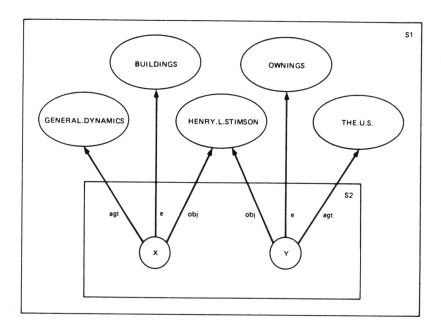

Figure 7.7   The Conjunction, "The Henry L. Stimson was built by General Dynamics and the Henry L. Stimson is owned by the U.S." (From Walker, p. 139)

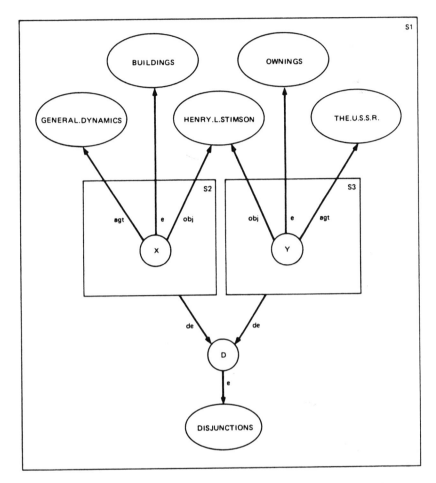

Figure 7.8 The Disjunction, "Either the Henry L. Stimson was built by General Dynamics or the Henry L. Stimson is owned by the U.S.S.R." (From Walker, p. 141)

can be expressed as

not P *or* Q

In other words, either the term P is not true or the term Q is true. Figure 7.10 shows how this example of implication could be represented with the relations negation and disjunction. The relation *implication* is often expressed by statements of the form:

if P *then* Q

where P is called the *antecedent* and Q is the *consequent*. This relation is represented as shown in Figure 7.11, by identifying the antecedent and the

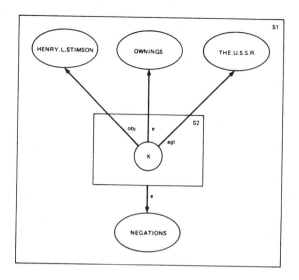

Figure 7.9   The U.S.S.R. does not own the Henry L. Stimson (From Walker, p. 143)

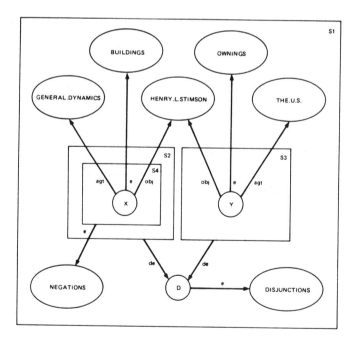

Figure 7.10   Either General Dynamics didn't build the Henry L. Stimson or the U.S. owns it. (From Walker, p. 144)

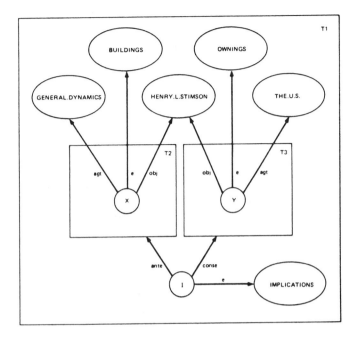

Figure 7.11 If General Dynamics built the Henry L. Stimson, then the U.S. owns it. (From Walker, p. 145)

consequent nodes or spaces and showing that together they constitute an implication.

IMPLEMENTATION OF PARTITIONED SEMANTIC NETWORKS

The basic elements of partitioned semantic networks—nodes and arcs—are similar to those of the previously discussed semantic network. The primary differences in the two systems have to do with the larger structures of Hendrix's system: spaces and supernodes.

The data structure for representing a space must refer to all the nodes and all the arcs within that space. Also each node and each arc must contain a reference to all the spaces within which it lies. Therefore the node and arc definitions will include identification of each space to which the item belongs. A node then contains the information identifying the node, a pointer to the first of any arcs associated with that node, and a pointer to the first space within which it lies. This definition can be implemented as:

```
type arcptr = ^arc;
     pnodeptr = ^pnode;
```

```
spaceptr = record
              sptr : ^space;
              nextsptr : ^spaceptr
        end; (* spaceptr record *)
pnode = record
           info : word;
           arcs : arcptr;
           space  : spaceptr
        end;  (* pnode record *)
```

As before, info is defined as word, which will be a string of characters and a list of characteristics for that word. The field arcs will contain a pointer to the first arc leaving this node; if there is more than one arc associated with this node, then arcs is the head of a linked list of nodes. The field spaces will function the same way as arcs, in that it will serve as the head of a linked list of space nodes; if the node only has one space associated with it, then the linked list only has one element.

Arc and space must be defined now. Arc will have a field to identify the relation represented by the arc, pointers to the head and tail nodes of the arc, a pointer to the rest of the arcs associated with the tail node, and a pointer to the list of spaces within which the arc lies. The relations possible are the set membership relations: S, E, DS, DE; the deep case relations: AGT, OBJ, etc.; and the logical relations: ANTE and CONS.

```
type  reltype = (S, E, DS, DE, AGT, OBJ, . . . , ANTE, CONS);
      arc = record
               relation  : reltype;
               head, tail : pnodeptr;
               nextarc    : arcptr;
               spaces     : spaceptr
            end;  (* arc record *)
```

The definition for space will contain the name of the space spaceid, and pointers to the lists of nodes and arcs which fall in that space.

```
type space = record
                spaceid : string;
                pnodes  : pnodeptr;
                arcs    : arcptr
             end;  (* space record *)
```

To pull all the spaces together, there must also be a list of all the spaces:

```
type spacevector = array[1..maxspaces] of space;
```

As each space is created, it will be added to the space vector. The decision of whether the space vector should be kept in order is dependent on the situation in which it is being used. If there are only a few spaces, having them in order does not help much; however, if there are many spaces, ordering the vector can reduce search time considerably by allowing for a binary search instead of a linear search. The space vector could also be represented as a linked list, which would allow for easier insertions and deletions; however, a linked list demands sequential access which is generally slower if the list is at all long.

The concept of a supernode should not be represented as a different data structure because a supernode is just a space with certain characteristics of a regular node. The method for handling a supernode will be to add a variant part to the definition of a space, so that if the flag **super** is true, i.e., if the space is a supernode, it will contain a section for the **pnode** characteristics. This new definition for **space** is

```
type space = record
                 spaceid : string;
                 pnodes  : pnodeptr;
                 arcs    : arcptr;
                 super   : Boolean;
                 case super of
                      true : (snode : pnode)
             end;  (* space record *)
```

Now a space considered a supernode would include a node definition. This approach may seem wasteful in that parts of the **snode** section are already represented in the regular **space** definition, but the advantage of using this definition is that if **snode** is defined as a **pnode**, then a **pnodeptr** can point to an **snode**. Thus the supernode can be linked by arcs to other supernodes or to nodes without a different pointer type being established.

The whole definition then for partitioned semantic networks is as follows:

```
type arcptr = ^arc;
     spaceptr = record
                     sptr : ^space;
                     nextsptr : ^spaceptr
                 end; (* spaceptr record *)
     pnodeptr = ^pnode;
     reltype  = (S, E, DS, DE, AGT, OBJ, . . . , ANTE, CONS);

     pnode = record
                 info   : word;
                 arcs   : arcptr;
                 spaces : spaceptr
             end;  (* pnode record *)

     arc   = record
                 relation   : reltype;
                 head, tail : pnodeptr;
                 nextarc    : arcptr;
                 spaces     : spaceptr
             end;  (* arc record *)

     space = record
                 spaceid : string;
                 pnodes  : pnodeptr;
                 arcs    : arcptr;
                 super   : Boolean;
```

```
                    case super of
                        true : (snode : pnode)
                end;  (* space record *)

        spacevector = array [1..maxspaces] of space;
```

Exercise: Write a program to build partitioned semantic networks such as those in the examples in this chapter. Develop a scheme for inputting the information for representing nodes, arcs, spaces, etc.

Exercise: The concept of vistas requires that the connections between nodes and spaces be directed in such a way that from a particular point one can "see" all the nodes and spaces at higher levels in the network. Design a method for ensuring that the concept of a vista is valid for partitioned semantic networks.

Major Exercise: Develop a system for inputting declarative sentences to be stored as partitioned semantic networks and questions to be answered from the information stored.

PROCEDURAL SEMANTIC NETWORKS

A semantic network representation has been developed by Hector Levesque and John Mylopoulos, which adds another dimension to semantic networks. [5] In their system there are three aspects to the representation of semantic networks: classes, relations, and programs. Classes group objects which have properties in common, much as other systems define groups of objects. There are four basic operations which can be performed on classes:

1. an instance of a class can be created
2. an instance of a class can be destroyed
3. all instances of a class can be fetched
4. a test can be made to determine whether an object is an instance of a class

Relations establish the connections between classes, by mapping from one class (the *domain*) to another (the *range*). A relation can be thought of as a class in which the objects are assertions about the relationships between other classes. There are also four basic operations on relations:

1. a given relation exists between two objects
2. a given relation does not exist between two objects
3. all objects connected by a given relation can be fetched
4. a test can be made to determine whether two objects are connected by a given relation

The third aspect of the representation, *programs*, sets this system apart from those discussed previously. Essentially a program is considered a "class whose instances are called *processes* and correspond to program activations." [6] This aspect of the structure of semantic networks allows for procedural interpretation of classes and their relations. For example when an instance of a particular class is encountered, a certain procedure can be activated to operate on that class or perform whatever action is necessary under the circumstances. The developers of this system argue that it is not only adequately descriptive to handle most situations, but it also has the advantage of being quite modular and therefore easily modifiable.

The organization of the semantic networks is considered an *abstraction mechanism*, in the sense that making assertions about the relationships among classes allows the details of lower-level classes to be hidden. There are two main abstraction mechanisms: the *is-a* hierarchy and the *part-of* hierarchy. An *is-a* hierarchy is generated by dividing classes into subclasses, thereby expressing a simple universal quantification. An *is-a* hierarchy of objects would be partially defined by the sentence,

A sophomore is a student.

Notice that the previous sentence expresses the same idea as the universal quantification proposition,

All sophomores are students.

Figure 7.12 illustrates the taxonomy into which this information falls. Notice that the top of the hierarchy is a class called *object*, into which all objects fall. Relations can also be organized in an *is-a* hierarchy, as shown in Figure 7.13. The top node then is an *assertion*. In addition to having classes organized into a taxonomy, an advantage of the *is-a* hierarchy is *inheritance of properties*.

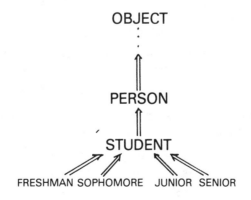

Figure 7.12   Taxonomy of IS-A Hierarchy

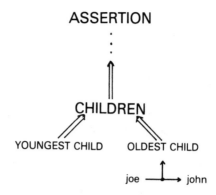

Figure 7.13   Relations in IS-A Hierarchy

Anything which is true of a class will also be true of its subclasses. For example, the statement,

All students must pay tuition before September 15.

also applies to the class of all sophomores, but not, of course, to the class of all persons.

The second abstraction mechanism allows for the creation of a *part-of* hierarchy, which expresses existential quantification. This mechanism creates functional units out of classes of objects which are interrelated in some way. For example, if the classes <pupil> and <lesson> are described as being *part-of* the unit called *grade*, then there is an instance *john* of the class *student* to whom a particular score called *mark*, with a numerical value of 78, has been assigned as *grade23* which is an instance of the lesson for *course CSC374*. Figure 7.14 illustrates this scheme. The parts of a unit are called *slots*—in this example, <pupil> and <lesson>. Slots are considered placeholders and often start out with a *default* value which is used if no other value is found to fill the slot. Slots may also have *dependencies*, which are restrictions on the ways in which slots can be associated with other classes. Because of the dependencies, a particular structure may have several different procedures to be activated depending upon the particular circumstances. Examples of possible procedural interpretations include:

1. When creating an instance of the class, the relations satisfied by the dependencies are tested and if they are not satisfied, the instantiation fails (prerequisite).

2. When creating an instance of the class, these relations are simply asserted of the given slot fillers (side-effect).

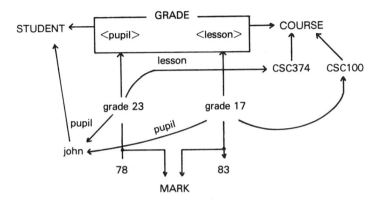

Figure 7.14   PART-OF Hierarchy

3. When creating an instance of the class with some of the structure provided, the relations can be accessed to infer the rest of the structure (slot filling).

4. The testing operation of the class can use the structure to recognize as an instance any object satisfying the dependencies (pattern matching). [7]

In addition to the normal classes, this system of semantic networks also includes *metaclasses*, which allow for a distinction to be made between generic and specific classes; for example, the properties of *students* differ from the properties of *collections of students*. In a course we can calculate a property called *average-grade* which is based on the grades of all students on one particular lesson. This property would apply to the class of all students in that course, but would not apply to any one student since the property *average-grade* is undefined on one grade for one lesson. This distinction between normal classes and metaclasses has been overlooked in many versions of semantic networks.

Exercise: Design a scheme for representing semantic network nodes to identify classes including *is-a* hierarchies and relations including *part-of* hierarchies.

Programs

Levesque and Mylopoulos do not have the only system of semantic networks which allows procedural knowledge, but it is one of the few that includes a notation for including the procedures as part of the network itself, rather than as a hook to some piece of code in the host language, such as LISP. The advantage of including programs as part of the network is that the programs can themselves be treated as declarative knowledge—i.e., as data. The most primitive programs in their system are the four operations allowed on classes and the four allowed on relations. Program modules can be one of two types (as in Pascal): *procedures*, which perform some operations, or *functions*, which return a value to be tested or stored. Levesque and Mylopoulos decompose the program modules as follows:

1. Determine the acceptability of the proposed action by considering the conditions that must be true before the action can be performed. For example, to assert that a relation holds between two objects requires that the objects be instances of the domain and range respectively. If any of these conditions are false, the action is refused and a failure occurs.

2. Assuming the initial conditions are satisfied, the action itself must be performed. This can involve primitive actions such as storing results in a table, or more complex actions that pass the buck to other classes and relations. These actions may themselves fail.

3. Given that the action is successful, there may be additional inferences to be drawn as a result of this success, requiring further actions.

4. If the action is unsuccessful, however, in view of the fact that the initial conditions were satisfied, there may be steps that can be taken to remedy the situation at this level, rather than relinquishing control and allowing the procedure itself to fail. [8]

The programs then can be defined in the semantic network as consisting of the following four parts:

1. PREREQUISITE, a logical expression that must be true before the body can be executed;

2. BODY, an action for procedures or an expression for functions;

3. EFFECT, an action performed after a successful completion of the body;

4. COMPLAINT, an action or expression to be used after unsuccessful completion of the body. [9]

Implementation Problems

One requirement for implementing procedural semantic networks as defined by Levesque and Mylopoulos is a programming language in which procedures and functions can be treated as data. Most common programming languages including Pascal do not have that capability; LISP does and is commonly used for implementing semantic networks. However the limitation in programming languages such as Pascal can be reduced in some respects. In

Chapter 8 a method is described for storing a code to identify the particular procedure which is to be executed in a case statement. Other schemes include using assembly language routines to call stored procedures dynamically or to define a monitor to oversee the execution of all procedures including procedure names stored as data.

Major Exercise: Add program capability to the system designed in the previous exercise.

EXTENDED SEMANTIC NETWORKS

The semantic network representation developed by Lenhart K. Schubert, Nicholas J. Cercone, and Randolph G. Goebel differs in several ways from those discussed previously. [10] It uses a variation of the traditional logical notation of predicate calculus to encode natural language propositions, which allows fairly straightforward representation of logical operations, time, and quantification, as well as identification of concepts and their interrelationships. In addition the *extended semantic network* representation, as it is called, imposes a second order organizational scheme on the knowledge stored through the mechanism known as *topic hierarchies.*

Representation of Propositions and Concepts

The system represents n-ary relationships, in which any number of arguments are related by one or more predicates. An argument corresponds, more or less, to a noun phrase, and the predicate expresses some relationship among the arguments. Arguments can be a class (man, elephant) or an individual (John, Dumbo), an adjectival value (pretty, happy, gray), a time or location indicator (Thursday, in Dallas). Predicates can also be of several types: logical connectors, modal operators, or verbs.

The notation for this representation is an infix form of predicate calculus which is more English-like than the usual form in that the predicate is placed following the first argument rather than before all the arguments. Compare this form:

```
[argl pred arg2 arg3 ...]
```

with the traditional form:

```
pred (argl arg2 arg3 ...)
```

A specific example makes the advantage clear:

```
[[John happy] because [John knows [Mary loves John]]]
```

rather than

```
because (happy (John), knows (John, loves (Mary, John)))
```

Thus propositions are expressed by applying a predicate to a tuple of arguments. If a function is applied to a tuple of arguments, then a concept is produced as its value. The concept may be individual or generic. Figure 7.15 shows several examples of the application of functions.

Arguments in a proposition may be joined by logical connectives, such as negation, conjunction, disjunction, implication, and equivalence. Some examples of such connections follow:

```
Conjunction
    John, Jim, and Joe love Mary.
    [[John loves Mary] and [Jim loves Mary] and [Joe loves Mary]]

Negation
    Mary does not love John.
    [[Mary loves John] NOT]
```

(The **NOT** follows the propositional content to correspond with the general form of having the predicate follow the first argument.)

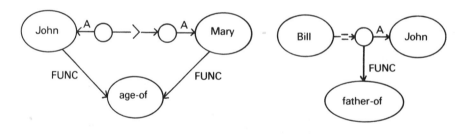

(a) "John is older than Mary"
    [(age-of John) > (age-of Mary)]

(b) "Bill is the father of John"
    [Bill = (father-of John)]

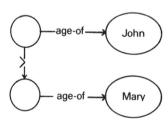

(c) "John is older than Mary"
    [Age1 age-of John] [Age1 > Age2],
    [Age2 age-of Mary]

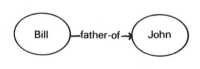

(d) "Bill is the father of John"
    [Bill father-of John]

Figure 7-15

Causation

John left Town because Mary does not love him.

[[John left Town]] because [[Mary loves John] NOT]]

Implication

If Mary is not at home, then she is at the supermarket.

[[[Mary is-at Home] NOT] ==> [Mary is-at Supermarket]]]

Equivalence

John is only happy when he is with Mary.

[[John happy] <==> [John near Mary]]

(<==> means "if and only if")

Modal operators can join individuals, concepts or propositions. For example the modal *believes* requires an individual as its first argument and a proposition as its second:

John believes Mary does not love him.

[John believes [[Mary loves John] NOT]]

Combining a logical connective with a modal operator can handle sentences which are a problem for some other systems, such as:

John mistakenly believes that Mary does not love him.

[[John believes [[Mary loves John] NOT]] and [Mary loves John]]

Other modal verbs include *think, feel, know, remember,* and so on. Other modal operators are the necessity operator,

9 is necessarily greater than 8.

the causal operator:

John left town because Mary does not love him.

and the counterfactual conditional:

If it snowed in New Orleans for Christmas, the streetcars would not run on St. Charles Avenue that day.

If John Lennon were still alive, the Beatles would sing together again.

These examples of modal operators bring up some complex problems beyond the scope of this book.

Representation of Time and Events [11]

The method of representing knowledge in extended semantic networks involves definition of particular *states*, or conditions which hold at a particular time. The state-based representation allows more complex concepts to be stored than possible with other techniques.

Every predicate includes a time argument, represented by either one or two values. An instant of time requires one value; an interval requires two.

Time relations allow representation of a complex sequence of states. Thus events are defined as a sequences of states over a period of time. For example, the statement,

Mary went to Atlanta.

could be restated as:

The physical location of Mary was some place other than Atlanta at time T1.

During the time interval T1 to T2 Mary caused her location to be changed from some place other than Atlanta to Atlanta.

At time T2 the physical location of Mary was Atlanta.

T1 and T2 occurred before NOW.

Other concepts often regarded as primitive can be broken down into a sequence of states to provide more explicit meaning. (See Chapter 8 on Conceptual Dependency Theory for further discussion of primitives.) For example, in the sentence

John stubbed his toe while walking down the sidewalk.

if *walking* is considered primitive and thus indivisible, then *stubbing a toe* must also be primitive and the relationship between the two would not be easily represented. However if *walking* is considered to be a sequence of states involving moving one foot forward while being supported by the other leg and so on, then *stubbing a toe* can be a concurrent event which involves bringing the toe of the foot being moved forward into contact with an unmovable object with a force great enough to cause pain.

One advantage of representing events as a sequence of states is that the level of decomposition is flexible. In the previous example the concept *walking* needs to be broken down further to explain the relationship with *stubbing a toe*, but in the sentence,

Terry and Susan watched the sunset as they walked along the beach.

the important information has nothing to do with Terry's and Susan's feet. Therefore the concept *walking* would not need to be decomposed. However, the context could be changed in the next sentence:

Susan stepped on a shell and cut her foot.

which would probably disrupt the implied romance of the previous sentence.

Quantification

Propositions which make an assertion about all members of a class or some members of a class are said to be *quantified*. The statement,

All men are mortal.

is an example of the universal quantifier, whereas the statement,

Some men are bald.

illustrates existential quantification. These can be written in predicate calculus notation as:

```
(Ax)[x man] ==> [x mortal]
```

```
[For all x, where x is a man, x is mortal.]
```

and

```
(Ex)[x man] ==> [x bald]
```

```
[There exists an x, where x is a man, such that x is bald.]
```

Schubert and Cercone also use Skolem functions to represent existentially quantified variables which are functionally dependent on universally quantified variables. To cite some of their examples,

```
(Ax)(Ey)[y bigger-than x]    <in predicate calculus form>
```

becomes

```
[(yx) bigger-than x]        <Skolemized>
```

(The first can be read *for all x, there exists a y, such that y is bigger than x.* The second applies the Skolem function y of the existentially quantified variable to the universally quantified variable x, making up the first term of the assertion. The predicate remains in the second position.)

```
There is a man who likes all women.
```

```
[Man1 man], (Ax)[[x woman] ==> [Man1 likes x]]
```

(Here Man1 is a constant used to represent a particular man in the class of men.)

```
Every man likes some woman.
```

```
(Ax)(Ey)[[x man] ==> [[y woman] & [x likes y]]]
```

(For all x there exists a y, such that if x is a man, then if y is a woman then x likes y.)

```
No one likes John.
```

```
[(Ex)[[x person] & [x likes John]]NOT]
```

(The negation operator is placed to indicate the scope, that the negation applies to the entire proposition.)

```
John believes that everyone likes him.
```

```
[John believes (Ax)[[x person] ==> [x likes John]]]
```

These examples illustrate some of the types of information which can be accurately recorded with extended semantic networks.

Uncertain or Vague Information

Unfortunately for natural language processing, many statements in natural language are not as clear-cut as the examples given above. The kind of statement which causes particular problems is one in which the credibility of the assertion is not clear; it is not immediately obvious whether the statement is true or false. For example,

John doubts that Mary is happy.

The statement provides no information about the true value of whether Mary is or is not happy; what is asserted is that John has only a slight belief that Mary is happy, but he does not totally disbelieve it either. Doubt falls somewhere on a scale between belief and disbelief. In extended semantic networks this notion can be represented with the propositional function D (for degree of belief) which is given a value (between 0 and 1) to indicate the position on the scale between belief and disbelief. Thus the sentence would be represented as:

```
[(D John [Mary happy]) = .3]
```

Similarly credibility is defined as a propositional function C to be applied to propositions. For example the sentence

John probably loves Mary.

becomes,

```
[(C [John loves Mary]) = .8]
```

This method for representing uncertain information is similar to fuzzy logic, in which varying values are given to situations in which the truth value is not known. L. A. Zadeh has developed the concept of applying fuzzy logic to natural language representation thoroughly in "PRUF— A Meaning Representation Language for Natural Language." [12]

Major Exercise: Design a system to represent propositions and concepts as described in this section. Include all the capabilities: logical operations, representation of time and events, quantification, and doubt and credibility.

Topic Hierarchies

Another unique feature of extended semantic networks is the technique of imposing a second order organizational strategy on the networks. This scheme defines topic hierarchies. A *topic* is "a predicate over proposition-concept pairs." [13] Topic predicates are connected into subtopic/supertopic relationships known as *topic hierarchies*. Topic hierarchies are made up of slots representing the various subtopics. Every topic hierarchy includes the two slots *specialization* and *generalization* to link that particular structure into the overall knowledge representation. Specialization defines subconcept relationships as well as instances of this particular topic; generalization assigns the type or superconcept for the topic. Figure 7.16 shows a topic hierarchy for physical objects. The topic hierarchy as a whole is a kind of template for all the information that can be known about a topic. For a particular instance of acquiring knowledge, a *topic access skeleton* is developed to fill in the specific information known in this instance. Thus as assertions are made, the topic access skeleton is built in the form allowed by the topic hierarchy. As additional assertions are

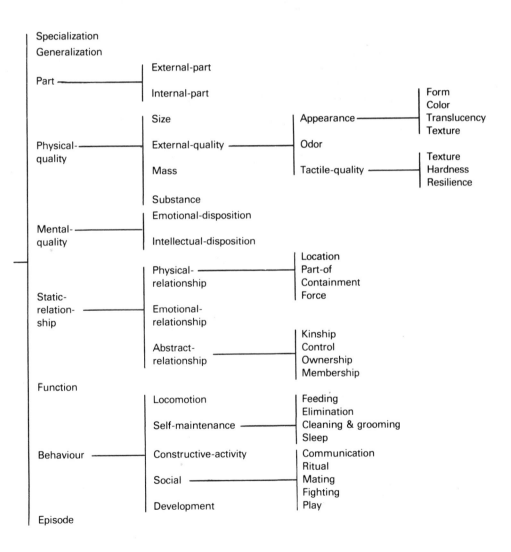

made, the relevant slots of the topic access skeleton are filled in. When questions are asked about the information stored, the topic access skeleton is referenced to find the appropriate answer.

The advantage of imposing topic hierarchies on the knowledge base represented by extended semantic networks is that the information can be accessed more readily because of the additional organizational scheme. Essentially the number of propositions scanned is determined by the number of topics within a hierarchy. "In a full access skeleton with N propositions distributed somewhat uniformly over the K terminal topics of a topic hierarchy, the number of propositions scanned is reduced by a factor of 1/K. In a sample hierarchy with K=40, this would represent a significant reduction." [14] For example if an access skeleton had 1000 propositions over the 40 terminal topics in a topic hierarchy, the reduction would be 1000*1/40 or 25 propositions to be scanned (in the worst case) rather than 1000.

Major Exercise: Add the capability of representing topic hierarchies to the system designed in the previous exercise.

Conceptual Dependency Theory

Conceptual dependency theory was developed originally by Roger Schank in the late sixties and early seventies; it grew out of the same linguistic environment that case grammar did, as a reaction to Chomsky's theories and the work of the other transformational generativists. [1] This theory is similar to case grammar in that the representation of the meaning of a sentence revolves around the action of the sentence and includes some number of cases to relate the other parts of the sentence to the action. But there are significant differences between case grammar and conceptual dependency theory. Perhaps the most important difference is that the action of the sentence is not represented by the verb, but rather by the interrelationship of a set of primitive acts, each of which is a concept involved in the meaning of the verb. In other words, the action is represented by the *concepts* in the verb, rather than by the lexical item, the word itself.

A major axiom of conceptual dependency theory is that any two sentences with the same meaning will have the same internal representation, whether or not they contain the same words in the same order. As we discussed with earlier systems, the active and passive forms of a sentence are considered to have the same meaning expressed in a different form. In some systems these two forms would have different representations, although each can be transformed into the other. In conceptual dependency theory, as in generative semantics, the two sentences would have the same representation. For example, in each of the two sentences,

John broke the window.

and

The window was broken by John.

the action is represented by the concepts which make up the verb *break*, John is the person doing the action, and the window is the object of the action. Thus the representation would be same for either sentence.

Showing another example of the use of conceptual dependency theory, the two sentences,

John gave the vase to Mary.

and

Mary received the vase from John.

have essentially the same meaning, although they are not identical because of the shift of emphasis. However the same basic concepts are being conveyed. In case grammar (and all the other systems discussed so far) these two sentences would be stored internally in completely different forms. In conceptual dependency theory the difference would be apparent only in the internal representation of the person doing the action. Let us consider this example in more detail. The event described by the sentence,

John gave the vase to Mary.

includes the actor *John* performing an action, which is the transfer of the possession of an object *the vase* to a recipient *Mary*. In the other sentence,

Mary received the vase from John.

the actor is *Mary*, but the action is still transfer of the possession of the object *the vase*, and *John* now assumes the role of the donor. In fact each sentence includes implicit information as well as information stated explicitly, that John is the donor and Mary is the recipient. Thus the only difference is the actor.

Conceptual dependency theory specifies that the transfer of the possession of an object is the primitive act **ATRANS**. **ATRANS** involves a change in some abstract relationship between a physical object and an animate being. In these two sentences the ownership of the object is being changed from one person to another. The representation of the event must include certain information: an **event** includes an **actor**, an **action**, an **object**, and a **direction** (which describes both donor [**from**] and recipient [**to**]). In the first sentence above, the representation would be:

```
EVENT1
   ACTOR:    John
   ACTION:   ATRANS
   OBJECT:   the vase
   DIRECTION: FROM:  John
              TO:    Mary
```

The second sentence would be:

```
EVENT2
    ACTOR:   Mary
    ACTION:  ATRANS
    OBJECT:  the vase
    DIRECTION:  FROM:  John
                TO:  Mary
```

Thus EVENT1 and EVENT2 each show the basic meaning of the respective sentences while maintaining the difference in emphasis provided by the differing actors.

Not all sentences represent actions. For example, in the sentence,

John is in Chicago.

the meaning includes the location of John, but no action. Other examples of sentences of this type are:

The table is 72 inches long.

My cat is an Abyssinian.

In each of these sentences a situation, rather than an event, is being described; there is no action in these sentences. Representing the information here requires a different structure; in each there is an object which is in a particular state. The value of the state provides specific information. The kinds of information, called *states*, include physical attributes, such as color, size, weight; relationships between objects, such as ownership, control, possession; and a number of descriptive attributes which apply to animate beings, such as anger, health, consciousness. Figure 8.1 contains some possible values for various states. Storing the information in a stative sentence requires identifying the object being described, the particular state involved, and the value of the state. For example, the sentences above would be described as:

```
SITUATION1
    OBJECT:  John
    STATE:   location
    VALUE:   Chicago

SITUATION2
    OBJECT:  The table
    STATE:   length
    VALUE:   72 inches

SITUATION3
    OBJECT:  My cat
    STATE:   breed
    VALUE:   Abyssinian
```

HEALTH:	goes from -10 to +10.		
	Examples:	dead	-10
		gravely ill	-9
		sick	-9 to -1
		all right	0
		tip top	+7
		perfect health	+10
FEAR:	goes from -10 to 0.		
	Examples:	terrified	-9
		scared	-5
		anxious	-2
		calm	0
ANGER:	goes from -10 to 0.		
	Examples:	furious	-9
		enraged	-8
		angry	-5
		irked	-3
		upset	-2
		calm	0
MENTAL STATE:	goes from -10 to +10.		
	Examples:	catatonic	-9
		depressed	-5
		upset	-3
		sad	-2
		OK	0
		pleased	+2
		happy	+5
		ecstatic	+10
PHYSICAL STATE:	goes from -10 to +10.		
	Examples:	dead	-10
		harmed	-9
		injured	-5
		broken	-5
		harmed	-1 to -7
		hurt	-1 to -7
		OK	+10
CONSCIOUSNESS:	goes to 0 to +10.		
	Examples:	unconscious	0
		asleep	5
		awake	10
HUNGER:	goes from -10 to +10.		
	Examples:	starving	-8
		ravenous	-6
		hungry	-3
		no appetite	0
		satisfied	+3
		full	+5
		stuffed	+8
DISGUST:	goes from -10 to 0.		
	Examples:	nauseated	-8
		revolted	-7
		disgusted	-7
		bothered	-2
SURPRISE:	goes from 0 to +10.		
	Examples:	surprised	+5
		amazed	+7
		astounded	+9

STATES WITH MORE USUAL ABSOLUTE VALUES	STATES WHICH ARE RELATIONSHIPS BETWEEN OBJECTS
LENGTH (sometimes called SIZE)	CONTROL
COLOR	PART (Inalienable Possession)
LIGHT INTENSITY	POSS (Possession)
MASS	OWNERSHIP
SPEED	CONTAIN
	PROXIMITY
	LOCATION (special form of PROXIMITY)
	PHYS. CONTACT (special form of PROXIMITY)

Figure 8.1 Sample State Values

To formalize conceptual dependency theory somewhat, let us consider the various aspects of the theory in turn. The information in a sentence is represented by an internal structure known as a *conceptualization*. Within these structures there are various roles to be played: actor, action, object, direction, instrument, and state. The concepts which can play the various roles are

PP's: picture producers, physical objects, including animate beings

ACT's: actions which are done to objects by actors

LOC's: location, such as the physical location in which the action occurred

T's: time, may be either a specific time or a range from some start time to a finish time

PA's: attributes of PP's, defined by **STATE(VALUE)**. PP's are described by a collection of **PA**'s. (See Figure 8.1 for a list of states and various values.)

These concepts are combined by a number of rules, which are selected to match the particular **ACT** involved. These rules are called *conceptual syntax rules*.

(1) PP ⟺ ACT   Some PP's can ACT.

(2) PP ⟺ PA   PP's have attributes.

(3) ACT ←O— PP   ACT's have objects.

(4) ACT ←D—⌐ → LOC   ACT's have directions.
           ⌐ < LOC

(5) ACT ← R —⌐ → PP   ACT's have recipients.
           ⌐ < pp

(6) ACT ←—I—— ⇕   ACT's have conceptualizations as instruments.

(7) PP   PP's can be described by
  ↑   conceptualizations in which they occur.
 ⟺

(8) T   Conceptualizations have times.
 ↓
⟺

(9) LOC   Conceptualizations have locations.
 ⇓
⟺

(10) PP ⟺ PP   One PP may be equivalent to another.

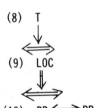

There are other rules that will be presented when they are needed. These rules describe the relationships among the other aspects of the theory: the roles, the concepts and the conceptualizations. The three roles—object, direction, and instrumental—work much like the cases of case grammar and are sometimes referred to as *conceptual cases*. The particular combination of conceptual cases in each conceptualization depends on the ACT; each act has its own set of cases like a case frame.

Conceptualizations can also have tenses. The tenses are:

(null)	present
p	past
f	future
/	negation
ts	start of a transition
tf	finish of a transition
c	conditional
k	continuous
?	question

The tenses function much as modalities do in case grammar, describing the entire conceptualization.

The Primitive Acts

There are only a small number of primitive acts, which in combination are used to represent the meaning of all actions. The eleven ACT's include five which describe physical actions performed by people, MOVE, PROPEL, INGEST, EXPEL, and GRASP; two which specify state changes, ATRANS and PTRANS; two used for communication, SPEAK and ATTEND; and two mental ACT's, MTRANS and MBUILD. In addition there is a dummy act DO which can stand in as an unknown. These will be explained in turn.

MOVE is any action which involves movement of a part of a person's body. Only humans can move. The human is the actor; the part of the body moved is the object. The only cases expected are the direction and the object. In fact, the instrumental case is not allowed; thus, MOVE is somewhat more basic than the other acts since many of them are described in terms of MOVE. The sentence,

John moves his hand to his mouth.

would be represented as:

PROPEL is an action performed by a person which causes some object to change location. The person is the actor; the cases expected are direction, object, and instrumental. For example,

John throws the ball to Mary.

would be

$$John \Longleftrightarrow PROPEL \leftarrow O - the\ ball \quad D - \begin{bmatrix} \rightarrow Mary \\ \leftarrow John \end{bmatrix}$$

INGEST involves the action of taking something into a person's body and is used primarily to describe eating and drinking. The cases needed are the object ingested and the direction. Instrumental can also be included as PTRANS.

John eats the sandwich.

would be

$$John \Longleftrightarrow INGEST \leftarrow O - the\ sandwich - D - \begin{bmatrix} \rightarrow inside\ (John) \\ \leftarrow \end{bmatrix}$$

In addition to the basic information provided here, this sentence also implies quite a bit more. Normally one eats a sandwich by moving the food to the mouth. Thus this information can be added to the representation above to serve as the instrumental case:

(PTRANS will be explained fully later, but basically it means to transfer an object physically from one location to another.)

The act GRASP is used to refer to the action of a person taking hold of an object. Thus in order for John to move the sandwich to his mouth, he must grasp it with his hand. GRASP requires the objective and directional cases, and can include the instrumental, which would be expressed by MOVE.

$$John \Longleftrightarrow GRASP \leftarrow O - the\ sandwich \leftarrow D - \begin{bmatrix} \rightarrow his\ hand \\ \leftarrow \end{bmatrix}$$

EXPEL can be considered the opposite of INGEST, in that it conveys the notion of something moving from inside the body of an animate being to the outside of the body. Many bodily functions are expressed by this act. It also expects the object, direction, and instrumental (usually PROPEL or MOVE).

The two acts, **ATRANS** and **PTRANS**, specify the transfer of some object, but differ in the type of transfer involved. **PTRANS** is essentially a physical transfer, changing the location of a physical object. This act requires three of the cases: *objective, direction, and instrumental*. An example of **PTRANS** was given above as the instrumental case for the sentence,

John eats the sandwich.

In that example the instrumental case for **PTRANS** is not included, but can be inferred to be

John moves his hand to his mouth while he is grasping the sandwich.

As discussed earlier, **ATRANS** represents some change in an abstract relationship between an object and an animate being, as in giving something to someone. No physical transfer or movement of the object is necessary. If the object **ATRANS**ed is a house, one would assume that it would remain in the same place, but if the object is small, it could be expected to be physically transferred. The physical object holds the objective case, and the animate being involved is in the *to* part of the *direction* case.

The two acts, **SPEAK** and **ATTEND**, relate to communication of information between a human and the rest of the world. **SPEAK** means to produce a sound; thus any verbal communication emanating from a person is represented by **SPEAK**, including singing, yelling, and so on. **SPEAK** requires the *objective* case and the *direction* case, with the *from* part being the person producing the sound. For example,

Sam recited a poem.

would be

$$Sam \Longleftrightarrow SPEAK \longleftarrow 0\longrightarrow a\ poem \longleftarrow D \longrightarrow \begin{array}{c} \nearrow \\ \diagdown Sam \end{array}$$

Perhaps additional information should be included to indicate the difference between recitation and normal speech, but for now this diagram will suffice.

ATTEND works the other way; it indicates that a person is receiving information from some external source. Thus the person **ATTEND**ing is the *to* part of the *direction* case. **ATTEND** is used for reading and hearing. In the sentence,

Mary reads the newspaper.

part of the representation would be:

$$Mary \overset{K}{\Longleftrightarrow} ATTEND \longleftarrow 0\longrightarrow eye \longleftarrow D \longrightarrow \begin{array}{c} \nearrow the\ newspaper \\ \diagdown \end{array}$$

The k above the arrows indicates the tense—that the act is continuous. Both SPEAK and ATTEND are frequently used as instrumentals themselves. In addition to the notion of ATTEND, the act of reading involves doing something with the information being read. For this concept, the mental acts are needed.

In order to understand the mental acts, a description of the mind in conceptual dependency theory is required. The mind is the information processing part of an animate object and is made up of the conscious processor (CP), the intermediate memory (IM), and the long term memory (LTM). The CP handles immediate information and performs the processing; the IM holds information, but is used primarily for expressions such as, *on one's mind*. LTM is the main storage area of the mind into which information is placed for *remembering* and from which information is retrieved while *recalling*. Information stored in the mind is said to be mentally located in one of the parts—MLOC (LTM (Mary)). The two mental acts are MTRANS and MBUILD. As with the other TRANS acts, MTRANS involves a transfer, in this instance, a transfer of information—a mental transfer involving the brain. MBUILD involves combining mental information and is used for concepts such as *thinking* or *considering*. Both of these acts normally have the objective, recipient, and instrumental cases. If a person knows something, as in,

Mary knows John is sick.

the knowledge is located in the LTM:

$$\begin{array}{c} \text{John} \\ \Updownarrow \Longleftrightarrow \text{MLOC (LTM (Mary))} \\ \text{HEALTH}(-5) \end{array}$$

In other words, John can be described by the state in which his health is -5 on a scale of -10 to $+10$, and this information is (mentally) located in the long term memory of Mary. If Mary remembers something, it will be represented by a transfer of information:

Mary remembered that John was sick last week.

$$\text{Mary} \Longleftrightarrow P \Longrightarrow \text{MTRANS} \longleftarrow O - \begin{array}{c} \text{John} \\ \Updownarrow \\ \text{HEALTH}(-5) \end{array} \Longleftrightarrow T \text{ (week } (-1)) \longleftarrow R \begin{array}{c} \rightarrow \text{CP (Mary)} \\ \\ \langle \text{LTM (Mary)} \end{array}$$

Thus at time (week (-1)), a week ago, John's health was -5, and Mary mentally retrieved that information from her long term memory. (Notice the p indicating past tense above the arrows.)

The sentence,

John decided to leave the house.

will illustrate the use of MBUILD:

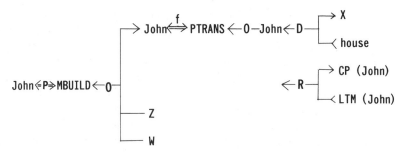

MBUILD combines information received from inputs Z and W and outputs the decision to physically transfer himself away from the house. In this example the inputs are not explicitly stated. If the verb were *consider*, the input would be what was being considered and the output would not be stated (unless the decision is included).

The dummy act **DO** is used when the particular action involving the sentence is not known. For example in the sentence,

John made Mary angry.

we do not know what John did, but whatever it was, it caused Mary's state of anger to increase:

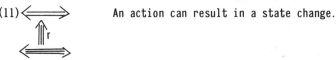

Causation

This particular example introduces another aspect of conceptual dependency theory, that of causation. This sentence could be restated as,

John did something that caused Mary to become angry.

Notice the r in the example above. The symbols in this diagram indicate the main conceptualization—John did something—caused another conceptualization —the state of Mary's anger changed. This particular causation is known as *result causation*; the other types of causation are *enabling, initiation,* and *reason.* With result causation an action results in a state change. Schank designed rules for the various types of causation situations, which he referred to as *causal syntax* rules, since they present the causal relationships among conceptualizations and states. The rule for result causation is

$$(11) \Longleftrightarrow \qquad \text{An action can result in a state change.}$$
$$\Uparrow r$$
$$\Longleftarrow$$

Enabling causation, indicated by an E next to the arrow in the diagram, provides information that a state enabled an action to occur. For example,

John ate the sandwich because it was on the table.

The state of the sandwich being located on the table enabled John to eat it. The rule for enabling causation is

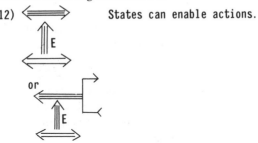

(12)   States can enable actions.

A state can also disable an action, by preventing it:

John could not eat the sandwich because it was spoiled.

The rule for disabling causation is the same as enabling except that a dE is substituted for the E.

The initiation causation occurs when a mental state is initiated by a state or an act:

Sam became frightened because the movie was scary.

Sam became frightened because John yelled at him.

The rule for initiation causation is

(13)   States or acts can initiate changes in mental state.

The fourth type of causation provides a reason for an action:

Sam left the movie because he was afraid.

The rule for reason causation is

(14)   Mental acts can be reasons for physical actions.

Inferences in Conceptual Dependency Theory

One of the most significant aspects of conceptual dependency theory is the built-in capability for inference. A lot of information can be inferred from the representations of the sort described above. For example, if we have represented the sentence,

John went from Chicago to New York.

then we can infer that John is no longer located in Chicago and he may be in New York. (The information that he actually arrived in New York is not available.) If we know that

John gave Mary the vase.

we can determine that Mary now has the vase and John does not. We might also infer that John wanted to do something to please Mary since giving people things is one way to please them.

Exercise: Think of all the inferences that can reasonably be drawn from each of the primitive acts. How many are certain? How many are speculative? How does one tell the difference? When does one stop inferencing (since one can infer the world from a single sentence)?

Inferences can usually be drawn about the instrumental case of a conceptualization from the primitive act in it. Notice that in several of the examples above the instrumental case is required, but was not included in the example. The reason is that it can often be inferred. If the information is not stated explicitly in the sentence, it would still be added to the representation. One obvious example occurs with verbs involving eating and drinking. These verbs imply that the food or drink being ingested must go into the mouth; thus it must be moved to the mouth, probably by the person who is actor of the act INGEST. One normally moves food to one's mouth with one's hand directly or indirectly with a utensil held in the hand. If any of these assumptions is not the case, then that information would be noteworthy and would probably be included in the sentence explicitly:

John ate his sandwich with his feet.

John drank the soup from the bowl.

Each of the primitive acts has one or more particular acts which serve as the instrumental case. These are:

Primitive Act	Instrumental
INGEST	PTRANS
PROPEL	MOVE, PROPEL or GRASP
GRASP	MOVE
EXPEL	PROPEL or MOVE
PTRANS	MOVE or PROPEL
MOVE	none
ATRANS	PTRANS, MTRANS or MOVE
MTRANS	SPEAK or ATTEND
MBUILD	MTRANS
SPEAK	MOVE (one's tongue)
ATTEND	none

Notice that **MOVE** is the ultimate instrumental for all the physical acts, and **MTRANS** is the basis for **MBUILD**. The two communication acts, **SPEAK** and **ATTEND** are the instrumentals for **MTRANS**. **SPEAK** also has **MOVE** as an instrumental whereas **ATTEND** has no instrumental. One could argue that **ATTEND** involves the movement of sense organs, but that gets into details too fine to be concerned with. This chart can help to determine the instrumental expected, even when it does not occur explicitly in a sentence.

The causation relations provide a considerable amount of information which can be inferred since they show the relationships among the states and events represented. As with the instrumental case, the causation relations themselves must be inferred. For example, in the sentence,

John cried because Mary said she loved Bill.

it is perfectly obvious to a human observer that John is not crying because Mary talked, but rather that what Mary said caused John to think, which caused him to become sad, and being sad caused him to cry. This chain of causes must be inferred from the explicit information provided. Another example of this sort is the sentence,

Mary cried because John hit her.

This example is somewhat ambiguous in that we do not know specifically whether Mary was hurt physically or emotionally. The sentence could be mean either

Mary cried because her arm hurt after John hit her.

or

Mary cried because John hurt her feelings by hitting her.

In either case additional information can be determined, but which set of additional information must be decided from the context, if at all.

Implementing Conceptual Dependency Theory

One of the goals of conceptual dependency theory is to avoid the syntactic stage of parsing into a syntactic structure; this goal is achieved by interpreting the sentences input and storing the information directly into the conceptual structure. Thus the data is immediately available for analysis or inference or question answering. In order to make this larger jump from the raw language input to the internal storage form, the lexicon will store more information about each word than is required with some of the other systems. (Some would argue that the goal of avoiding the syntactic stage is not achieved in that the syntactic information is simply hidden in the lexicon rather than handled as a separate phase of processing.) Let us consider the structure of the conceptualizations and the lexical entries.

As discussed earlier, a conceptualization represents either an event or the state of some object. Event conceptual structures include objects and their attributes since the actor and object parts of the structure are PP's (picture producers). A stative conceptual structure includes the identification of which physical object is being described, the relevant attribute being considered, and the value of that attribute. Thus if the object to be represented is

the red ball

then the attribute is *color* and its value is *red*:

(ball (color red))

For convenience let us assume for now that all the attribute values can be mapped onto the set of integers; later other possible methods will be considered. Attributes can then be declared as:

```
type attrib = record
              state : stateid;
              stateval : integer
          end; (* attribute record *)
```

where stateid is a string. Thus an object (which is a PP in conceptual dependency theory) would be identified by its name and its atttribute.

```
type PP = record
          ppname : string;
          ppattrib :  attrib
      end; (* PP record *)
```

Since a physical object can have a number of attributes, some means must be provided to relate all of these attributes to the object. One straightforward scheme is to use a linked list of attributes. Thus the object representation will be changed to include a pointer to the attributes, which can then be chained together.

```
type attptr = ^attrib;
     attrib = record
              state : stateid;
              stateval : integer;
              nextattrib : attptr
          end; (* attrib record *)

     PP = record
          ppname : string;
          ppattrib :  attptr
      end; (* PP record *)
```

A conceptualization which represents an event includes an actor, the action, the object involved in the action, the direction of the action, and optionally the instrumental case. In addition each event happens at a particular time in a particular location, and therefore the representation will include a time and a location. Thus an event conceptual structure will be represented in general as:

```
type eventconc = record
                 loc : (* location information *)

                 time : (* time information *)

                 actor : PP;  (* with human attribute *)

                 action : (* the act and its associated tenses *)

                 object : PP;

                 direction : (* including TO and FROM *)

                 instrumental : (*a link to another conceptualization *)
             end; (* eventconc record *)
```

Location can be represented by physical coordinates within a space, by proper name such as *in Chicago*, or by a general description such as *in the room at the end of the hall*. For our purposes using a string for a proper name or a general description will suffice.

Time can also be represented in various ways—in absolute value: month, day, year, hour, minute, second; relative to the present time, such as *week* (−1), meaning last week; or relative to some other time, such as *the Friday after Mardi Gras*. Once again, time will be stored as string data for convenience, although in some applications other schemes would be more appropriate.

Exercise: Develop a structure to store time and location in any of the formats mentioned above. Are there other ways to represent these types of information?

The actor and object parts of an event representation are defined as PP's, as described earlier. The action part will contain the specific act—one of the primitive acts—as well as tense information associated with the act. More than one tense may be associated with an act; for example, an act might be in the past, continuing from a starting point to an ending point. Therefore the tense information needs to be stored in a linked list format with each node containing one tense. Thus the basic structure for action will be:

```
type acttype = (MOVE, ATTEND, SPEAK, GRASP, PROPEL; PTRANS,
                INGEST, EXPEL, MTRANS, ATRANS, MBUILD, DO);

     tensetype = (present, past, future, negation, start, end,
                  conditional, continuous, interrogative, timeless);
```

```
tenseptr = ^tense;

tense = record
            tenseinfo : tensetype;
            nexttense : tenseptr
        end; (* tense record *)

action = record
            act : acttype;
            acttense : tenseptr
        end; (* action record *)
```

Direction will differ somewhat depending on which act it is associated with. For example, with the physical actions—GRASP, MOVE, PROPEL, PTRANS, INGEST, EXPEL—direction must indicate the origin of the action and the destination of the action, both of which are physical locations. With ATRANS, however, the action requires knowing the donor of the object and the recipient of the object being ATRANSed, which are human PP's. Thus a variant record is required to store the differing information for direction. The variation is based on the act type. Thus the structure needed within the *concept* record will be:

```
case acttype of

    MOVE, ATTEND, SPEAK,
    GRASP, PROPEL, PTRANS,
    INGEST, EXPEL            : (FROM, TO :  loc);

    ATRANS, MTRANS, MBUILD  : (DONOR, RECIP : PP)

end;  (* case *)
```

The final part of an event to be considered is the instrumental case, which is essentially a connector to another conceptual structure, either state or event. A stative conceptual structure is a simple form of an event structure since the object can be described either alone as having particular attributes or as the thing being acted on by a primitive act. Therefore one record declaration will suffice to describe both state and event structures, and that record will be dynamic and accessed through a pointer. Thus the instrumental case points to another concept, as follows:

```
type concptr = ^concept;

    concept = record
                .
                .
                instrument : concptr;
                .
                .
              end; (* concept record *)
```

Thus the entire structure for a concept would be:

```
type acttype = (MOVE, ATTEND, SPEAK, GRASP, PROPEL; PTRANS,
                INGEST, EXPEL, MTRANS, ATRANS, MBUILD, DO);

tensetype = (null, past, future, negation, start, stop,
             conditional, continuous, interrogative, timeless);

tenseptr = ^tense;

tense = record
          tenseinfo : tensetype;
          nexttense : tenseptr
        end; (* tense record *)

attptr = ^attrib;

attrib = record
           state :   stateid;
           stateval :  integer;
           nextattrib :  attptr
         end; (* attrib record *)

PP = record
       ppname : string;
       ppattrib :  attptr
     end; (* PP record *)

concptr = ^concept;

concept = record
            loc, time : string;

            object : PP;

            case conctype : (active, stative) of

              active :

                (actor : PP;

                 action : record
                            act : acttype;
                            acttense : tenseptr
                          end; (* action *)

                 instrument = concptr;

                 case acttype of

                   MOVE, ATTEND, SPEAK,
                   GRASP, PROPEL, PTRANS,
                   INGEST, EXPEL          : (from, to :  loc);

                   ATRANS, MTRANS, MBUILD  : (donor, recip : PP))

          end; (* concept record *)
```

With this declaration for a conceptualization, called concept, either type of conceptual structure—stative or active—can be referenced by the concept pointer concptr. The common information for the two types includes the time, the location, and the object, which includes the PP and its attributes. The rest of the information will be included for an event structure. Creating a concept requires a function makeconc to call the new procedure to have space allocated for the structure and to initialize the parts appropriately.

Exercise: Write the function makeconc to create each of the various types of conceptual structures : stative, active with physical primitive act, or active with the abstract primitive act.

Algorithm for Conceptual Analysis

Let us now consider the structure of the lexicon and the type of processing to be done on the conceptual structures. These two issues are interdependent. In general each entry for a word in the lexicon will contain appropriate information to identify how that word correlates with the conceptual structure being built. The processing scheme described here is based on the conceptual analyzer described by Lawrence Birnbaum and Mallory Selfridge in *Inside Computer Understanding*. [2] The overall algorithm for analyzing natural language input will be as follows:

```
For each lexical item in the input stream do

   1. Get the lexical item.

   2. Find the information in the lexicon relating to that item.

   3. Perform the appropriate actions specified by the lexical data.
```

Essentially the actions in step 3 will build the conceptual structure to represent the input sentence. The kind of information in the lexicon for a particular word depends on the function of that word. Since a verb determines the primitive act for a conceptual structure, the entry for a verb will be rather involved. An article, on the other hand, does not affect the overall structure very much, and it will, therefore, have a fairly simple entry in the lexicon. Whatever the complexity of the entry, the general form is the same. Each lexical item has one or more *requests*, indicating the actions to be taken and the conditions under which the actions are to be done. Each request is made up of a test and an action part. When these requests are found for a lexical item, they will be stored temporarily on the request list, called the RLIST. Step 3 will consider the requests found on the RLIST and perform the tests and the appropriate actions. Another structure is needed to hold lexical items and parts of the conceptual structure as it is being built. This list is called the CLIST, or concept list, and it serves as short term memory. Referring to these data structures, the algorithm can be more explicitly defined.

```
For each lexical item in the input stream do

   1. Get the next lexical item (word or phrase).
```

2. Fetch the requests associated with this item in the lexicon and store them on the RLIST.

3. Consider the requests on the RLIST, testing the conditions and performing the appropriate actions, using the CLIST as short term memory.

Let us consider the kinds of tests and actions that might occur in a request. If the lexical item input is the verb *throw*, then the primitive act for that word will be PROPEL. Knowing the primitive act provides the overall structure for the conceptualization, since the various parts of the conceptual structure are determined by the specific act. Thus for the act PROPEL, the parts required are actor, object, and direction. A structure then can be established with the various parts having null values:

```
(PROPEL (ACTOR NIL)
        (OBJECT NIL)
        (DIRECTION (FROM NIL)
                   (TO NIL)))
```

(For the moment we are ignoring the other aspects of a conceptual structure, such as time, location, and instrumental.) Finding a verb which identifies a particular primitive act means that the framework for the conceptual structure can be added to the CLIST. Therefore there must be a request which adds the structure to the CLIST. One request in the lexical entry for the verb *throw* will be as follows:

```
REQUEST:
    TEST:   T (* True, since this action must always be done *)
    ACTION:   Add the following structure to the CLIST:
              (PROPEL (ACTOR NIL)
                      (OBJECT NIL)
                      (DIRECTION (FROM NIL)
                                 (TO NIL))
```

If the lexical item were a noun rather than a verb, the request would be different. Generally a noun structure will be added to the CLIST, but no other action will be triggered by the noun. Thus if the lexical item were *ball*, the request would be:

```
REQUEST:
    TEST: T
    ACTION:   Add the following structure to the CLIST:
              (PP (PPNAME "ball") (CLASS PHYSICAL-OBJECT) (TYPE BALL))
```

It should be obvious that some additional requests are needed to fit this type of structure into the final conceptualization. In fact, when a verb is found, there will usually be several requests rather than just the one to add the framework of the conceptual structure to the CLIST. For example, for the verb *throw*, the requests needed in addition to the one shown above, are:

REQUEST:
    TEST: Is there a human PP on the CLIST preceding the conceptual
           structure?
    ACTION: Place it in the ACTOR slot of the conceptual structure.

REQUEST:
    TEST: Is there a physical object PP on the CLIST following the
           conceptual structure?
    ACTION: Place it in the OBJECT slot of the conceptual structure.

Additional requests would be needed to identify and save the TO and FROM parts of the *direction* substructure, as well.

Example of Sentence Analysis with Conceptual Dependency Structures

Following the analysis through an entire sentence will clarify the process. The sentence to be input is:

The cat ate a cricket.

When the first word *the* is encountered, the lexical entry found is the request:

REQUEST:
    TEST: Has a new structure been added to the CLIST?
    ACTION: Mark it with a definite reference.

In step 2 this request is added to the RLIST. In step 3 the test is made, but no action is taken since this is the first request and there are no structures on the CLIST.

The next word *cat* produces the following request to be added to the RLIST:

REQUEST:
    TEST: T
    ACTION: Add the following structure to the CLIST:
          (PP (PPNAME "cat") (CLASS PHYSICAL-OBJECT) (TYPE ANIMATE))

This request is added to the RLIST in step 2. Then in step 3, the true test causes the structure for *cat* to be added to the CLIST. When that request is completed, it is deleted from the RLIST, and the next request on the RLIST is considered. The test, *Has a new structure been added to the CLIST?* is now true, so that structure is marked with a definite reference:

    (PP (PPNAME "cat") (CLASS PHYSICAL-OBJECT) (TYPE ANIMATE)
      (REF DEFINITE))

There are now no requests left on the RLIST, since each request is removed when its action has been taken. The next word input is *ate* which will have the following requests:

```
REQUEST:
   TEST: T
   ACTION: Add the following structure to the CLIST:
           (INGEST (ACTOR NIL)
                   (OBJECT NIL)
                   (TENSE PAST))
```

```
REQUEST:
   TEST:  Is there an animate PP preceding the INGEST structure on the
          CLIST?
   ACTION:  Place it in the ACTOR slot of the INGEST structure.
```

```
REQUEST:
   TEST:  Is there a physical object (presumably edible) following the
          INGEST structure on the CLIST?
   ACTION:  Place it in the OBJECT slot of the INGEST structure.
```

All three of these requests are added to the RLIST in step 2; then in step 3, the first request is done, since the test is true. Thus the INGEST structure is added to the CLIST following the *cat* structure. The next request also tests true, since the *cat* structure is animate. Therefore the *cat* structure is placed in the ACTOR slot of the INGEST structure. The last request is false since nothing follows the INGEST structure on the CLIST.

The next word *a* is handled much as the article *the* was, with the following request added to the RLIST:

```
REQUEST:
   TEST:  Has a new structure been added to the CLIST?
   ACTION: Mark it as an indefinite reference.
```

This request will not be acted on until the next structure is added to the CLIST, which is produced from the lexical entry for the word *cricket*:

```
REQUEST:
   TEST: T
   ACTION:  Add the following structure to the CLIST:
            (PP (PPNAME "cricket") (CLASS PHYSICAL-OBJECT)
               (TYPE ANIMATE))
```

After this structure is added to the CLIST, then the next request on the RLIST is true and the *cricket* structure is marked indefinite. Since all the input has been read and processed, the analysis is complete. The RLIST is empty, and the CLIST contains only the conceptual structure:

```
(INGEST (ACTOR (PP (PPNAME "cat") (CLASS PHYSICAL-OBJECT)
                   (TYPE ANIMATE) (REF DEFINITE)))
        (OBJECT (PP (PPNAME "cricket") (CLASS PHYSICAL-OBJECT)
                    (TYPE ANIMATE) (REF INDEFINITE)))
        (TENSE PAST))
```

Other primitive acts require different types of requests. All the physical actions expect an actor and an object, at least. As in case grammar, the actor is assumed to be an animate being, and the object is a physical object, which can be an animate being in some cases. With MOVE, the object is a part of the body of the actor. Some acts have additional restrictions on the actor: MOVE, SPEAK, and ATTEND as well as the abstract acts, MTRANS, MBUILD, and ATRANS, require the actor to be human, not merely animate. Thus for this set of acts, one request would be to test for a human PP on the CLIST preceding the conceptual structure. The physical acts expect the direction of the conceptual structure to contain physical locations for TO and FROM, whereas the abstract acts expect direction to indicate the recipient and donor, which are animate PP's. Thus the requests for the two groups would differ in the expectations: the physical acts would test for locations; the abstract acts would test for animate PP's. For example the verb *give* has ATRANS as its primitive; therefore the requests associated with this verb would be as follows:

```
REQUEST:
    TEST: T
    ACTION:  Place the following structure on the CLIST:

    (ATRANS (ACTOR NIL)
            (OBJECT NIL)
            (DIRECTION (FROM NIL)
                       (TO NIL))
```

```
REQUEST:
    TEST: Is there a human PP on the CLIST preceding the ATRANS
          structure?
    ACTION:  Put it in the ACTOR slot of the ATRANS structure and in
             the FROM part of the DIRECTION slot.
```

```
REQUEST:
    TEST: Is there a human PP on the CLIST following the ATRANS
          structure?
    ACTION: Put it in the TO part of the DIRECTION slot.
```

```
REQUEST:
    TEST: Is there a physical object on the CLIST following the ATRANS
          structure?
    ACTION:  Put it in the OBJECT slot of the ATRANS structure.
```

There would also be requests to fill the other parts of the structure—LOC, TIME—which will be considered later. Notice that the first request in the lexical entry for a verb functions in much the same way the case frame does in case grammar, in that the first request always provides the overall structure for the final conceptual structure. Thus each act has its own structure identified in the lexical entry for the particular verb found in the input.

Requests

Requests can have one of three types of tests.

1. The simplest is the test which is set to *true*; in other words, if the lexical entry is found, the action part of this request must be performed.

2. The second type of test—the type seen in the examples so far—looks for certain semantic or ordering properties of the conceptual structures on the CLIST: is there an animate PP on the CLIST? Is there a PP following (or preceding) the conceptual structure on the CLIST?

3. The third type of test looks for the occurrence of a particular word or phrase. For example, if the lexical item found is the verb *look*, it might be part of a verb phrase, such as *look around* or *look forward to*. In order to test for that occurrence, a request would be included for *look* to seek the specific word *around* or words *forward to* following the verb *look*. If the specific words are not found, then the verb would be treated as a single word.

A request can perform any of several kinds of actions.

1. A conceptual structure can be added to the CLIST.

2. A slot in a conceptual structure can be filled by some other structure.

3. A request can activate other requests, by adding them to the RLIST.

4. A request can de-activate itself or other requests, if conditions warrant it.

In many sentences the instrumental is not explicit and cannot be determined during the basic analysis cycle, but can be implicitly added after the structure is complete. Thus the final stage of conceptual analysis would be to infer the instrumental part of the structure. For example in the sentence

The cat ate the cricket.

after the structure is built, the inference can be drawn that the means by which this action was accomplished was that the actor (the cat) PTRANSed the object (the cricket) from some unspecified location to the mouth of the actor. Thus the information in the sentence has been expanded and could be stated as

The cat ate the cricket by placing the cricket in its mouth.

This inference could be taken further by inferring that the PTRANS to the mouth took place by the cat moving its mouth to the cricket rather than by the cat using a fork or spoon. This inference would be based on the knowledge that the actor in this case is an animal rather than a human and would therefore not be expected to use eating utensils. The process can go even farther in that the means by which the cat moved its head to the cricket involved movement of the neck and perhaps taking a step and so on, but the elaboration must stop somewhere. The decision of where to stop depends on the situation.

Adjectives primarily affect state information by providing specific attributes for a PP. For example, the tall man

the cold, blue lake

the mean teacher

all include adjectives which specify attributes of the noun in the phrase. Thus each adjective entry in the lexicon would need a request which identifies which state is affected and what value to include. For *cold* the request would be:

```
REQUEST:
    TEST:   Has a new PP structure been added to the CLIST?
    ACTION:   Add the following attribute to its list of attributes:
            (TEMP -5)
```

and for *blue* would be:

```
REQUEST:
    TEST: Has a new PP structure been added to the CLIST?
    ACTION:   Add the following to its list of attributes:
            (COLOR BLUE)
```

Adjectives can also be found more distant from the noun they modify. In the sentences below:

The boy is hungry.

The class is boring.

The rope is ten feet long.

the predicate adjective must be matched to the subject noun phrase, since these are really the same as,

the hungry boy

the boring class

the ten-foot long rope

The linking verb *is* (and other forms of *to be*) will not have requests like other verbs. Instead it will provide only tense information and indicate that the final structure will be stative rather than active. However if a form of the verb *to be* is used with other verb forms (as in this sentence, e.g., *is used*), then it will be overridden by the presence of the other verbs and the final structure will not be stative. Some other verbs indicate stative information besides *be* verbs; for example

The rock weighs a ton.

has the same meaning as

The weight of the rock is a ton.

Here the state is identified by the subject *weight*; the object being described, the PP, is the object of the preposition *of*, and the predicate nominative *a ton* supplies the value of the state:

```
(PP (PPNAME "rock") (WEIGHT 2000 pounds))
```

Obviously many possibilities exist among the various sentence structures which can occur in the language.

Other word classes produce different types of requests. For example many prepositions relate to physical location: *under, on, beside, toward,* etc. These prepositions would include a request to identify the item following as a location. This information can then be used to fill the **LOC** slot in the conceptual structure. Other prepositions provide information about time: *before, after, until,* etc., and thus help fill the **TIME** slot. The preposition *of,* as mentioned earlier, often relates a **PP** to an attribute:

> the top of the hill
>
> the length of the rope
>
> the function of the word

Adverbs frequently indicate location or time as well: *yesterday, later, afterwards, nearby,* etc.; but many adverbs supply other kinds of information. For example the adverb *quickly* provides the tense information that the length of time between the start time and the end time is quite small. *Very,* which is used in many contexts, functions as an intensifier, making the value of the state being described more extreme. The phrase, *very cold,* means that the state of being cold is intensified. If the value of the state *temperature* were expressed on a scale of -10 to $+10$ and -5 were used to indicate *cold,* then the adverb *very* would change the value to -8, perhaps.

Thus the requests associated with each word in the lexicon will supply the semantic information necessary to indicate how the meaning of the word can be used in a conceptual structure. If the word relates to length, then a request specifying how to establish the *length* attribute will be needed. If the word requires some other part of the sentence to complete its meaning, then the request will save the word until the other part is available. The mechanism of using requests to indicate how the semantic information is to be stored is flexible enough to handle many structures found in natural language. Whether it is able to handle all or even most aspects of natural language is debatable, and the resolution of the debate will require additional research including building an extensive lexicon.

Implementation of Requests in the Lexicon

Requests are made up of a test part and an action part. Therefore the declaration for a request would be:

```
type request = record
                   testpart : reqtest;
                   actionpart : reqaction
               end;   (* request *)
```

The RLIST is a linked list of requests defined as follows:

```
type   rlistptr = ^rlistnode;

       rlistnode = record
                       reqpart : request;
                       nextreq : rlistptr
                   end; (* rlistnode *)
```

```
var RLIST : rlistptr;
```

Additional variables that might be useful include a pointer to the end of the RLIST and a couple of temporary pointers,

```
var rlisttail, rl1, rl2 :   rlistptr;
```

The CLIST is a linked list of conceptual structure and would thus be defined as:

```
type clistptr = ^clistnode;

     clistnode = record
                     structure : concept;
                     nextstrc  : clistptr
                 end;  (* clistnode *)
```

```
var CLIST : clistptr;
    clisttail, cl1, cl2 : clistptr;
```

Exercise: Write the functions needed to create nodes for the CLIST and RLIST, and to add and delete nodes from each list.

The tests and actions can be represented either as data or as procedures. A test could be coded to indicate the particular characteristics being sought on the CLIST or in the input stream. This code would then be interpreted by a section of the analysis program and the determination made whether or not the test was true. If the procedural approach is taken, the lexical entry would contain a function or procedure call, rather than a data code, to cause the test to be performed. Similarly, the particular action to be taken when a test is true can be represented either as a data code or as a procedure call. As mentioned in Chapter 7, implementing the procedure call directly is not possible in most languages including Pascal; LISP is the obvious exception. In LISP the distinction between a function name and a data item is not significant. The method of identifying the test and action with a data code is more universal and therefore will be the one explained here.

The concept structure needed in the CLIST has already been defined, but the request structure has not. As stated earlier, every request consists of two parts: the test part and the action part. These two parts will be considered in turn. The three types of tests are:

1. Always true
2. Does the **CLIST** contain a particular structure (with possible ordering requirements)?
3. Does the input contain a particular word or phrase?

These three tests could be coded as follows:

T—always true, therefore perform the action

C—check the **CLIST** for a particular structure

M—match a particular string of characters to the input stream

In addition to the code indicating the type of test, for the two latter types additional information is required. The M test must include the string of characters (the word or phrase sought). The C test must indicate what kind of structure is needed and whether its location on the **CLIST** is significant.

The actions are varied and therefore require a more elaborate coding scheme. The four types of actions are:

1. Adding a structure to the **CLIST**
2. Placing a substructure into a slot within another structure (and removing the substructure from the **CLIST**)
3. Activating another request by placing it on the **RLIST**
4. Deactivating a request by removing it from the **RLIST**

The first action requires identification of the structure to be added to the **CLIST**. To reduce the bulk of the lexicon the actual structures could be stored in a separate file with only an index to the particular one needed in the action part of the request. The second action is generally used to insert one structure on the **CLIST** into a slot of another structure on the **CLIST**. Therefore the two structures on the **CLIST** would be indicated by the index to the structure to be inserted, the type of structure to be added to, and the slot to be filled within that structure. The third and fourth actions would have to indicate the type of request that is to be activated or deactivated.

The test part of a request can be defined as follows:

```
type testtype = ('T','M','C');
     structype = (PP, PRIMACT, ???);
     ordertype = (before, after, mostrecent, nil);

test = record
          ttype : testtype;
          word  : string;
          case ttype of
             'C' : (struc : structype;
                    order : ordertype)
        end; (* test record *)
```

The action part of a request is somewhat complicated since each type of action requires different data. Thus a variant record is needed, which in general form is as follows:

```
type reqaction = record
              case actiontype = (add, move, activate, deactivate) of
                 add : (* data for adding structure to CLIST *)
                 move : (* data for placing a substructure into a
                           slot in another structure on the CLIST *)
                 activate : (* data needed to activate a new request *
                 deactivate : (* data needed to remove a request
                                 from the RLIST *)
           end; (* reqaction record *)
```

An efficient way to store the structure forms is to create a separate file of structures (called strcfile) and only include an index to a particular structure in the lexical entry in the lexicon. This same index can be used for an add action in a request. If the index is defined as

```
type strcindex = 1..maxstrc;
```

then the add section of the variant record would simply include a data element of that type:

```
add : (strcid : strcindex)
```

The move action identifies two structures on the CLIST: the substructure to be inserted into the more major structure, as well as that more major structure. In addition move requires specification of the slot into which the substructure is to be placed. Since each of the structures is on the CLIST, a pointer to a clistnode would identify the structure. The slot would be identified by a slot type.

```
type slottype = (ACTOR, ACTION, TIME, LOC, INSTRUMENT,
                 FROM, TO, RECIP, DONOR);

   move : (mainstrc, substrc : clistptr;
           slotid : slottype);
```

The activate action will include the request to activate, thus making the definition of a request recursive:

```
activate : (newreq : request)
```

The fourth and final type of action deactivates a request which is on the RLIST. Identifying the request is tricky since the action cannot locate a specific request on the RLIST; the RLIST is created during execution of the analysis and the action has been stored as part of the lexicon. An identification code for the various kinds of requests could be added to each request; then the deactivate portion of the action would contain that code. In this scheme the request declaration would become:

```
type request = record
                testpart : reqtest;
                typereq  : reqtype;
                actionpart : reqaction
        end;  (* request *)
```

With this declaration the deactivate part would be:

```
deactivate : (oldreq : reqtype)
```

Reqtype would have to be defined to establish the different types of requests, but that will be left as a consideration for the reader.

The complete reqaction record would be declared as:

```
type strcindex = 1..maxstrc;
        slottype = (ACTOR, ACTION, TIME, LOC, INSTRUMENT,
                FROM, TO, RECIP, DONOR);

        reqaction = record
                case actiontype = (add, move, activate, deactivate) of

                add :  (strcid :   strcindex);

                move :  (mainstrc, substrc : clistptr;
                        slotid : slottype);

                activate :  (newreq :  request);

                deactivate :  (oldreq :   reqtype)

        end; (* reqaction record *)
```

The implementation of requests is influenced by the design of the RLIST and the CLIST, and vice versa. Together the lexicon, including the requests and the file of structures, and the CLIST and RLIST make up the major portions of the data set needed for analysis.

Major Exercise: Design a system to build conceptual structures using the scheme developed in this section.

IMPLEMENTING CAUSATION LINKS

Earlier in the chapter the concept of causation was described as being of several kinds: result, initiation, reason, or enablement (or disablement). In each of these types of causation the basic structure is the same: causation is a link between conceptual structures, whether they are event or state representations.

```
type causation = record
                causetype :  (result, initiation, reason,
                                enablement, disablement);
                causelink :  concptr
        end; (* causation record *)
```

Since all conceptual structures can potentially include a causation link, that link can be included in the declaration of the conceptual structure itself. If this link is included, the concept declaration becomes:

```
type acttype = (MOVE, ATTEND, SPEAK, GRASP, PROPEL; PTRANS,
                INGEST, EXPEL, MTRANS, ATRANS, MBUILD, DO);

     tensetype = (null, past, future, negation, start, stop,
                  conditional, continuous, interrogative, timeless);

     tenseptr = ^tense;

     tense = record
                 tenseinfo : tensetype;
                 nexttense : tenseptr
             end; (* tense record *)

     attrib = record
                  state :   stateid;
                  stateval :   integer;
                  nextattrib :   attptr
              end; (* attrib record *)

     attptr = ^attrib;

     PP = record
              ppname : string;
              ppstate : attptr
          end;  (* PP record *)

     concptr = ^concept;

     concept = record
                   loc, time : string;

                   object : PP;

                   causation = record
                                   causetype : (result, initiation, reason,
                                                enablement, disablement);
                                   causelink :   concptr
                               end; (* causation record *)

                   case conctype : (active, stative) of

                     active :

                        (actor : PP;

                         action : record
                                      act : acttype;
                                      acttense : tenseptr
                                  end; (* action *)

                         instrument = concptr;
```

```
case acttype of
    MOVE, ATTEND, SPEAK,
    GRASP, PROPEL, PTRANS,
    INGEST, EXPEL         : (FROM, TO :  loc);

    ATRANS, MTRANS, MBUILD : (donor, recip : PP)
```

```
end;  (* concept record *)
```

Notice that `causelink` is defined as a `concptr`, since it is a link to another conceptual structure and `concptr` is defined as

```
type concptr = ^concept;
```

Thus a sentence such as

John made Mary angry.

which could also be stated:

John did something that made Mary angry.

contains an example of result causation, in that what John did resulted in the state of Mary's anger changing. Thus the action part of the main conceptual structure would be:

```
(ACTION  (ACT DO)
         (TENSE PAST)
         (CAUSATION (CAUSELINK ^Concept)
                    (CAUSETYPE RESULT)))
```

How would the causation links be discovered? In many cases the lexical entry for words which indicate causation would include the identification of the type of causation and produce appropriate requests to handle the causation link. The word *because* is a good example of a word that triggers the search for the action caused or the state changed by the main conceptualization, but the word *because* does not identify the cause type. In the previous example

John made Mary angry.

the verb *made* is the signal that a state change has occurred. However *made* can have several different meanings, and thus several different structures. For example

John made the table from scraps of lumber.

John made his son eat his spinach.

John made up a story.

John made a face at the taste of Mary's cooking.

In the first example,

John made the table. . . .

John is the actor, and the table is the object. In the next example,

John made his son eat his spinach.

John is the actor, but there is no object; this is another sentence which can be best expressed by the dummy act **DO**:

John did something that caused his son to eat his spinach.

The sentence,

John made up a story.

could be said to contain a different verb, since *made up* expresses the action, which would be represented by **MBUILD**. However it illustrates the point that finding a single word, such as the verb *made*, does not necessarily mean the whole verb has been found. There are many examples of verbs of this sort:

look after

look out for

run over

run away

take over

take away

The lexical entries for the main verb in each of these must include the appropriate information about the possibility of these variations occurring. If other words are found which indicate that the main verb is not used alone, a different set of requests may have to be used from the set needed with only the single word verb. The last example above,

John made a face. . . .

would have **MOVE** as the primitive act since making a face involves moving a part of the body, the face, into an unusual configuration.

Conceptual dependency theory is the foundation for a theory of knowledge representation which will be discussed in Chapter 9. These theories developed by Roger Schank and his associates have had considerable influence on natural language research and will be used as the basis for the design of the natural language system presented in Chapter 10.

Chapter 9

Representation of Knowledge

Unit III as a whole describes the data structures needed to store information derived from natural language input and the algorithms required to access those structures for whatever purpose they have been developed. Thus this chapter, entitled "Representation of Knowledge", is not the first introduction to the subject. However the term *Representation of Knowledge* has a specific meaning in the area of natural language processing. It would not be applied to the output from a strictly syntactic parse, such as a phrase structure tree described in Chapter 4, or an ATN from Chapter 5 or a case frame from Chapter 6. However semantic networks discussed in Chapter 7 do in fact store knowledge, as do conceptual dependency structures in Chapter 8. Any meaning representation created by the semantic mapping from a surface structure to an internal form can be considered to represent knowledge.

Some of the early methods for storing knowledge have been mentioned—Quillian's development of a semantic memory, for example. Propositional logic and predicate calculus, as in Schubert and Cercone's extended semantic networks, have been used to store the meaning of statements. Case grammar graphs developed to hold the verb and the various noun phrases related to it also represent the content of a sentence. But representation of knowledge includes more than storing the facts from one sentence. Interpreting even one sentence often requires more than syntactical and semantic analysis—often pragmatic analysis is needed as well. *Pragmatics* involves accessing knowledge of the world, having a frame of reference, understanding the context in which a statement is made. For example, the difference in the two sentences,

Cathy wanted to play softball, but it rained.

and

Cathy wanted to play racquetball, but it rained.

illustrates the need for world knowledge. The first sentence seems quite reasonable because part of everyone's world knowledge is the fact that softball is played outside and therefore the rain would interfere. However the second sentence is not as reasonable since racquetball is played inside. Thus the clause added to the sentence, *but it rained,* must have some significance other than indicating that the racquetball game was cancelled because of the weather. Perhaps Cathy is the TV weather forecaster and had to work late revising forecasts because of the rain. Knowledge about Cathy's job would not be general world knowledge, but rather specific information about a particular person, but it would be necessary to understand the sentence in that context. When people use natural language, a great deal of information is not stated explicitly, but can be inferred from what is stated. The following illustrates the point:

> Scott cannot be in the school band because he plays the cello. So he plans to join the debate team.

Various kinds of information are needed to understand this sentence, and additional information can be learned from it. Most bands do not normally include stringed instruments (other than guitars), and school bands are frequently marching bands. Only Woody Allen would attempt to carry a cello in a marching band since a cellist sits down to play. This knowledge of bands and cellos allows us to understand the first sentence. But what is the relationship between this information and the next sentence? Playing a musical instrument and debating do not seem similar in many respects, but playing in a school band and being on the debate team are both common extracurricular activities for high school students. Since high school students are frequently encouraged to participate in extracurricular activities, choosing one when another is not an option is quite understandable. Thus from these two sentences we have learned that Scott is probably a high school student who is planning on participating in extracurricular activities (for some unexplained reason).

Let us consider what kind of knowledge needs to be represented and what sort of processing is required to understand these sentences. During parsing, the semantic information stored about each word would be retrieved from the lexicon, providing information as follows:

> *Scott*—male, human, actor of verb phrases *cannot be in, plays,* and *plans to join*
>
> *school band*—musical organization associated with a school, frequently marches in parades or during football games, usual instruments are wind, brass, percussion
>
> *cannot be in*—verb phrase indicating lack of ability to be a member of some organization

plays—verb describing action of producing music from a musical instrument (in this case a cello)

cello—musical instrument with strings found in orchestras, played by bowing while seated

plans to join—verb phrase indicating intention of future action of becoming a member of an organization

debate team—high school organization which practices and competes in debate (which is a contest of ability in formal argument, with two teams taking opposite sides of a specified question)

Actually this list only represents the particular word for this situation; determining which word sense is appropriate involves matching the meanings of the various words in order to produce a correspondence. For instance, the sense of the word *play* chosen would be *play a musical instrument* because there are several words associated with music and none involving sports as in the earlier example, *play softball*, or toys, and so on. Similarly the appropriate sense of *band* and *team* would be decided.

In addition to the words described above, other words in the sentence carry meaning because of the functions that they perform. For example the word *because* creates a particular kind of link between the clauses of the first sentence. The word *so* introduces some intended action resulting from the action of the previous statement. The definite article *the* indicates one specific school band; since most schools have only one, the conclusion which can be drawn is that *the school band* being referred to is the one at the school Scott attends. Although the story does not state that Scott is a student at a school, the assumption can be made from the content.

Knowing that the actor in the story goes to school allows us to draw conclusions about the situation because there are certain common elements involved in attending school: taking a prescribed program of classes, participating in extracurricular activities, associating with others of the same age group, and so on. This chunk of information about attending school sets up a reference for the actual statements made. For example when it is determined that Scott attends school (probably high school), then the references to the school band and the debate team focus the narration on extracurricular activities. Similar chunks of information describe other common activities—going to a restaurant, buying groceries in a supermarket, etc.

The remainder of this chapter will present some technical aspects of the various methods for storing knowledge. The points to be considered are first, some issues being debated by those studying appropriate methods for representing knowledge; next, two frequently discussed methods for representing chunks of information—frames and scripts; and finally KL-ONE, a well-developed knowledge representation language used in a variety of application areas.

ISSUES IN REPRESENTATION OF KNOWLEDGE

No consensus has yet been reached on the best method for representing knowledge, and research is continuing in order to develop more efficient ways to store information to conserve memory and processing. As Goldstein and Papert said in the article, "Artificial Intelligence, Language, and the Study of Knowledge,"

> The fundamental difficulties facing researchers in the field today are not limitations due to hardware, but rather questions about how to represent large amounts of knowledge in ways that still allow the effective use of individual facts. [1]

In general these questions can be answered in different ways under different circumstances. Some of these circumstances will be presented now.

Static Data Base vs. Active Knowledge

The earliest systems for storing knowledge used a data base designed and created independently from the access of that data base. In other words when a program which could answer questions about the information in the data base was run, the structures for storing the information were already established and could only be accessed during processing with no modification possible. The questions to be answered were analyzed and stored in some format to relate to the knowledge base, but the knowledge base remained intact. This type of system can be useful for certain applications. The LUNAR system developed by William Woods allowed questions to be asked about the lunar rocks brought back during the Apollo missions. [2] Since no more rocks are arriving from the moon, there is no reason to modify that data base. Many other examples of static data bases can be given, and such data bases certainly serve valuable purposes. However most data must be modified at some point. With a system designed with a static data base, the modification stage would be totally independent of the access stage.

With an active knowledge base more complex access is possible. In addition to the knowledge stored originally, an active knowledge base can acquire knowledge. In other words new knowledge can be added to it during processing, which might be called *learning*. It should be obvious that an active knowledge base is more complicated than a static one since the access mechanisms may have to be reorganized during processing, requiring greater flexibility of access. For example if the information is referenced through an indexing scheme, the knowledge base could grow too large for the indexes originally established and then the indexes would have to be reorganized. Thus active knowledge would require the ability to modify the structures representing the knowledge during processing.

Declarative vs. Procedural Knowledge

Generally the discussions of various representational schemes presented throughout Unit III have assumed that the knowledge is stored as data, that a statement has been made and the information derived from that statement has been saved in some form. This method of representing knowledge is called *declarative* and involves use of standard data structures and file structures. These structures generally represent objects, properties of those objects, and the relations among the objects and their properties. *Procedural* knowledge, on the other hand, is knowledge represented, not as data, but as code—a program module or procedure. Procedural knowledge would be used by executing the code rather than by matching or reading the data. As Goldstein and Papert describe it, with procedural knowledge, "an item of knowledge, a concept, or whatever, is seen as an active agent rather than as a passive manipulatable object." [3] As we shall see later in the chapter, many recent systems for representing knowledge use both declarative and procedural knowledge. Declarative knowledge is efficient and easily accessed and modified whereas procedural knowledge allows more flexibility. Thus both can be advantageous in a knowledge base.

Network vs. Non-network Structures

Another issue on which researchers hold various opinions is whether to use network or non-network structures for representing knowledge. As we saw in Chapters 6 and 7, network structures are quite flexible and frequently reflect the actual relationships among objects more accurately than any other scheme. However depending on the implementation, they may take up more storage space and require more processing than non-network structures. On the other hand non-network structures, which are often implemented as arrays or records in Pascal, do not require extra memory for pointers to link items together and are quickly accessed because the location of a particular item does not change during processing. The disadvantage of these structures derives from their advantages—they cannot be changed. Therefore the decision of whether to use network or non-network structures cannot be ultimately resolved, but depends upon the specific information being represented. This issue of network vs non-network structures will be considered further in Chapter 10.

FRAMES AND SCRIPTS

The concept of frames was first expounded by Marvin Minsky in 1975 in the article, "A Framework for Representing Knowledge," in *The Psychology of Computer Vision*. [4] Minsky presented *frames* as an approach to solving "problems arising from the construction of adequate theories for vision, for memory, for logical reasoning, and for the comprehension of language." [5] All of these various areas seemed to require some larger structure for organizing individual facts known about some aspect of the subject. Natural language researchers recognized frame theory as a solution to some of the difficulties of understanding language. As we have seen throughout Unit III, understanding language involves recognizing both structure and content, and the facts about each must be accumulated and interrelated. Minsky defined frames in several ways:

> A Frame is a collection of questions to be asked about a hypothetical situation; it specifies issues to be raised and methods to be used in dealing with them. [6]

In this sense a frame serves to guide the understanding of discourse about the situation. It contains information about what various aspects of the situation must be considered and ways of elaborating on the exact content of the discourse. In more specific terms, Minsky stated,

> A *frame* is a data-structure for representing a stereotyped situation, like being in a certain kind of living room, or going to a child's birthday party. Attached to each frame are several kinds of information. Some of this information is about how to use the frame. Some is about what one can expect to happen next. Some is about what to do if these expectations are not confirmed.
>
> We can think of a frame as a network of nodes and relations. The "top levels" of a frame are fixed, and represent things that are always true about the supposed situation. The lower levels have many *terminals*—"slots" that must be filled by specific instances or data. Each terminal can specify conditions its assignments must meet. (The assignments themselves are usually smaller "subframes".) Simple conditions are specified by markers that might require a terminal assignment to be a person, an object of sufficient value, or a pointer to a sub-frame of a certain type. More complex conditions can specify relations among the things assigned to several terminals.
>
> Collections of related frames are linked together into *frame systems*. The effects of important actions are mirrored by transformations between the frames of a system. [7]

The interrelationships among the frames in a frame system are used to establish a broader context for the discourse. Thus a frame is selected to represent a particular situation, the parts of the frames identify what kind of information needs to be found in the discourse for the situation to be understandable, and the links between one particular frame and related frames represent the additional world knowledge which the situation requires.

In a paper, "Narrative Theories as Computational Models," presented at the Modern Language Association Conference in 1980, Patricia Galloway described frames as

... generalized structures containing slots which are filled in when the frame is mapped onto a specific occurrence. They are learned by repeated exposure to the kinds of entities that they represent, and they may be altered, expanded, or split off on the basis of new experience. In machine terms the frame is a data structure whose variables are bound to actual instances from the input text at run time, thus providing context for and further knowledge about those items. [8]

Thus a frame is a structure to hold information about a situation or an object; the structure contains slots temporarily filled with default values which can be replaced with actual values found in the input. If an actual value is not found, then the default value remains. Frames can also be used to deduce more knowledge about the situation than is stated in the input text.

There are various types of frames. Minsky provides the following list:

Surface Syntactic Frames: Mainly verb cases. Prepositional and word-order indicator conventions.

Surface Semantic Frames: Deep syntactic frames perhaps. Action-centered meanings of words. Qualifiers and relations concerning participants, instruments, trajectories and strategies, goals, consequences and side-effects.

Thematic Frames: Topics, activities, portraits, setting. Outstanding problems and strategies commonly connected with topic.

Narrative Frames: Stories, explanations, and arguments. Conventions about foci, protagonists, plots, development, etc., with the purpose of causing the listener to construct a new Thematic Frame in his own mind. [9]

Surface syntactic frames correspond to case frames described in Chapter 6. Frame theory developed originally out of considerations of case grammar, which attempted to structure the syntactic aspects of a sentence around the primary verb. Surface semantic frames are like conceptualizations in conceptual dependency theory discussed in Chapter 8, in which the action of the sentence supplies the focus for the organization of concepts involved. The collection of questions which make up a surface semantic frame would be:

What caused it? (agent)

What was the purpose? (intention)

What are the consequences? (side effects)

Who does it affect? (recipient)

How is it done? (instrument) [10]

The ideas for thematic and narrative frames were Minsky's contribution to frame theory; these ideas developed into what are now usually referred to as frames and scripts. Although Minsky identified four types of frames in 1975, later researchers have generally acknowledged his third type, thematic frames, to be *frames*, and the fourth type, narrative frames, to be *scripts*. (There are other aspects to narrative frames dealt with by plans and themes, but those will not be discussed in this book. These terminological problems are not settled at this point, but for the sake of clarity, the term *frame* will refer to generally static situations, and *script* will refer to dynamic situations. This point will be discussed further in the next paragraph.) Thematic frames provide a structure for a variety of things—objects, people, settings, events, and so on. This grouping has been subdivided by other researchers since Minsky's formulation of the notion. Narrative frames deal with situations which extend over some interval of time, such as stories, logical arguments, and so on.

Thematic and narrative frames are somewhat similar to static and event schemas described by Philip J. Hayes, [11] although the subtypes within each are divided up differently. Hayes chose the term *schema* to refer to any "precomputed chunk of knowledge," in order to avoid the confusion in terminology mentioned before. A *static schema* is a structure for organizing various aspects of a description of an object or person or location. It describes the topic in whatever manner is appropriate. Physical objects for example have size, appearance, structure, and so on, whereas persons have age, family, and jobs as well as size and appearance. A location is a particular setting, such as my aunt's living room or the inside of Greg's car. An *event schema* describes a dynamic situation—an event or activity—by identifying the participants and their actions. The participants can be described with static schemas and their actions by a sequence of states, as suggested by Schubert and Cercone, or by interrelationships among conceptualizations as Schank prefers. In addition event schemas, like narrative frames, can include plot and justification, as well as simply identification of a sequence of actions.

Galloway classifies frames in still another way. She recognizes the following types of frames:

> *Situational frames*, which organize knowledge, including sequences of expected actions, about frequently encountered situations or activities; *state frames*, which contain information from common sense physics and psychology about generalized behavior patterns of things and people in the world; *action frames*, which organize the requirements for individual actions; and *object/person frames*, which outline the sorts of descriptive items that can be predicated of classes of objects and persons. (emphasis mine) [12]

In this scheme action frames and object/person frames serve somewhat as primitives within situational frames and state frames, respectively. If we match Hayes' classification scheme with Galloway's, the following correspondence is derived:

```
            PRIMITIVE              COMPOSITE

Static schema  ====>  Object/Person frame    State frame

Event schema   ====>    Action frame     Situational frame
```

If Minsky's first two types—surface syntactic and surface semantic frames—are considered separately, then this scheme serves as a fairly good taxonomy for frames. It does not specifically include all aspects of narrative frames, but they can be added as a special type of situational frame.

Implementation of Static Schema

Let us investigate the implementation of the first two types of frames classified above: *object/person* frames and *state* frames; *action* frames and *situational* frames will be considered later. Every frame will have some characteristics in common, no matter what type it is. All frames will have a name and a type. Each different type of frame will also have appropriate slots.

```
type frametype = objpersframe, actionframe, stateframe, sitframe;
     frame = record
                  name : string;
                  typeframe : frametype;
                  .
                  . (* slots for specific type frame *)
                  .
              end; (* frame record *)
```

Object/Person Frames

Object/person frames include a physical description: size, shape, appearance, age, location and so on. Other features distinguish objects from persons or animals; therefore variant parts of the frame allow for adaptation of the general object/person frame to the individual instance. Thus an object/person frame is defined as:

```
type opframe = record
                  name : string;
                  typeframe : objpersframe;
                  case typeframe of
                      size,
                      shape,
                      location,
                      age,
                      appearance : sometype;
                      (case typeob : (animate, inanimate) of
                            animate:
                                case typeanimate : (human, animal) of
                                      human: (family,
                                              occupation,
                                              etc : sometype);
```

```
                                        animal: (domesticity,
                                                 feedingpatterns,
                                                 etc : sometype))
                        inanimate:
                                    mass, composition, etc : sometype)
             end (* opframe record *);
```

Notice that the individual slots in the frame are simply described as being of sometype, which has not been defined. Each slot will be given a type definition, and in most cases an initial value will be assigned to serve as the default if no other information is found in the discourse.

State Frames

State frames relate information about situations which are timeless or extend over a substantial period of time, situations which cannot be called events. Being a college student is not an event, whereas graduation from college is. The distinction is time-related, but it is not necessary to be exact about the point at which the time interval is long enough to stop being an event and start being a state. The distinction will be considered intuitive. Getting married is an event; being married is a state. Writing a program is an event; being a programmer is a state. Events usually cause a change in state, as suggested by Cercone's method for representing events as sequences of states.

State frames must represent the relationships among the objects or persons involved in the state in addition to referring to their object/person frames. For example to describe a family consisting of John, the husband; Mary, the wife; and Sally and Dick, the children, the frame would include the relationships of *spouse* between John and Mary, of *sibling* between Sally and Dick, of *parent* between each of the parents and each of the children and so on. Some of the information is redundant, in that relationships are bidirectional. Thus if John is the spouse of Mary, then Mary is also the spouse of John. If Mary is the parent of Dick, then Dick is the child of Mary. The state frame for *family* has slots for the persons involved in the family and also slots for the relationships. For example, the frame might be as follows:

```
FRAME
     NAME:  FAMILY
     TYPE:  STATE
     PARTICIPANTS: John, Mary, Sally, Dick, Cindy, Kelly
     PARENT-RELATIONS:
             (MALE-PARENT: John,
              CHILD:  Sally, Dick)
             (FEMALE-PARENT: Mary,
              CHILD: Sally, Dick)
```

```
SPOUSE-RELATION: John, Mary
SIBLING-RELATION:  Sally, Dick
OTHER-RELATIVES:
        (AUNT:  Cindy,
         NIECE: Mary)
        (COUSIN: Kelly,
         COUSIN-OF:  Sally, Dick)
```

The participants are listed altogether in one slot. That slot might be an appropriate place to include references to the subframes for each person. The relations present each individual related to each other individual, which may seem redundant. However even though families have traditionally had the structure indicated here, a particular family may consist of two spouses, each with children from another marriage and a child of this marriage; for example:

```
FRAME
    NAME: FAMILY
    TYPE: STATE
    PARTICIPANTS: Tom, Susan, Jane, Harry, Amy, Howard, Alice
    SPOUSE-RELATION: Tom, Susan
    PARENT-RELATION:
            (MALE-PARENT: Tom,
             CHILD: Harry, Amy)
            (FEMALE-PARENT: Susan,
             CHILD: Jane, Amy)
            (MALE-PARENT:  Howard,
             CHILD: Jane)
            (FEMALE-PARENT: Alice,
             CHILD: Harry)
```

The basic implementation pattern for state frames requires at least the name, type, and participant slots, and at least one relation slot to be filled. The choice of data structure for a state frame is governed by the requirement for some flexibility. If Pascal had variable dimension arrays, the structure could be defined with varying numbers of entities in varying numbers of slots, depending on the type of frame. Simple relations could be expressed as a varying array of entities, whereas complex relations would need to be defined with a varying array of relation records (`relrecord`). This structure would be defined as:

```
type relrecord = record
                    relname : string;
                    case slottype : (simple, multiple) of
                        simple: (relpart : array[1..numsentity] of entity);
                        multiple: (relarray : array[1..numsrelrec]
                                             of relrecord)
                end; (* relrecord *)
```

```
sframe = record
          name : string;
          typeframe : stateframe;
          participants : array[1..numentity] of entity;
          relationslots : array[1..numrelrec] of relrecord
      end; (* sframe record *)
```

The definition of `relrecord` is recursive in that if the slot type is multiple, then there is an array of `relrecord`. At some point the slot type must be simple to halt the recursion. (Please note that this definition is not valid Pascal; Standard Pascal as currently implemented does not allow variable dimension arrays or recursive static structures such as `relrecord`.)

Another solution to defining this structure would be to make it dynamic—substituting nodes in a linked list for the elements of the variable arrays. That will be left as an exercise for the reader.

Exercise: Define a dynamic data structure for state frames as described above.

Frame Representation Language—FRL

Ira P. Goldstein and Bruce Roberts developed a knowledge based scheduling program called NUDGE in an experimental language known as FRL-0: Frame Representation Language, version 0. [13] Their program, which kept track of schedules for a number of people in an office, added some interesting features to frame theory. The *Frame Gestalt* of the scheduling program was,

> a set of generic frames, instantiated appropriately for a particular scheduling request. The generic frames are selected on the basis of clues implicit in the scheduling request; knowledge-based reasoning begins with a recognition process. Information missing in the request is then computed from defaults, constraints, and procedures—all associated with these generic frames. [14]

Their system uses six representation techniques in conjunction with frames: comments, abstraction, defaults, constraints, indirection, and procedural attachment. *Comments* from the natural language routines can be attached to values placed into the slots of a frame to identify the source of the value or to describe the reason for selecting a particular value. *Abstraction* allows inheritance of values from one level to another; as in Quillian's system, values from a generic description can be inherited by a specific instance of that generic type. For example if the meeting being scheduled is a particular type of meeting—i.e., a conference—then it will have the characteristics of a conference: relatively small with group interaction, etc. Having *default* information in slots gives them a value from the beginning, while allowing those initial values to be overridden when specific information is encountered or inferred. The fourth

```
IRA
    AKO                         $VALUE      PERSON
    (MEETING WHEN)              $PREFER     (DURING AFTERNOON)
                                              (ON FRIDAY)
    (MEETING WHERE)             $DEFAULT    NE43-819
                                $PREFER     (IN 545-TECH-SQUARE)
    (PA-MEETING WHEN)           $DEFAULT    (AT 3 PM)
                                              (AT 10 AM)
                                $PREFER     (ON TUESDAY)
```

Figure 9.1   FRL Frame Showing Preferences and Defaults

representation technique is referred to as *constraint*, which can be either a *requirement* or a *preference*. Requirements, preferences, and defaults can work together to produce compromises. If, for example, a meeting has been scheduled for a particular time, but a conflict arises, an alternative time for the meeting can perhaps be found by matching requirements, preferences, and defaults. Figure 9.1 shows a frame which illustrates preferences and defaults; Figure 9.2 illustrates requirements also. The slot labelled *AKO*, which stands for A Kind Of, identifies the type of frame.

The technique known as *indirection* connects the separate frames used to represent people and activities. For example the frame for a particular person identifies the subject as a person with a name and includes a list of the activities scheduled or requested in which that person will participate. In addition the frame for each of the activities will identify the persons involved in that activity. Thus indirection provides "a simplified kind of mapping between concepts." [15] The sixth representational technique used in NUDGE is *procedural attachment*, in which procedures to accomplish certain tasks are attached to the slots in the frame. Three types of actions could trigger execution of a procedure: *if-added, if-needed,* or *if-removed*. Figure 9.2 shows the *if-needed* and the *if-*

```
ACTIVITY
    AKO                         $VALUE      THING
    WHO                         $REQUIRE    (AKO PERSON)
                                $IF-NEEDED  (ASK)  [TYPE: REQUEST]
                                            (USE TOPIC)  [TYPE: DEDUCE]
    WHEN                        $IF-ADDED   (ADD-TO-CALENDAR)
                                $REQUIRE    (AKO INTERVAL)
```

Figure 9.2   FRL Frame Showing Requirements and IF-NEEDED and IF-ADDED Actions

added actions. *If-needed* generates one of two methods for acquiring information: *request*, or ask the user, and *deduce*, or match up slots from different frames. The most general frame in NUDGE is called *thing*, which in Figure 9.3 has two slots *AKO* and *INSTANCE*. *AKO* and *INSTANCE* serve as two-way links between a frame and its generalization. The attached procedures in *thing* in Figure 9.3 allow the database to be maintained properly. For example if *AKO* slot is filled in one frame, then an *INSTANCE* slot must be filled in its generalization, and so on.

Implementation of FRL Features

Addition of these FRL features to the data structures described earlier is fairly straightforward. A comment is just a string of natural language text which can be added to a slot. Defaults are the values initially stored in the slots of a frame and thus require no further definition. The technique of abstraction can be provided by establishing *AKO* and *INSTANCE* slots in a frame, to be filled by pointers to the appropriate superframe or subframe as needed. Constraints—which can be requirements or preferences—would be added as tests to be made on the values in the slots to determine what kind of compromises are possible. Indirection is accomplished by including pointers from one type of frame to another to link them together; in the example of the participants in an activity, the person frame for the participants would point to the activity frame, and the activity frame would point to the person frames. These five representation techniques could be included in a generic frame structure defined as follows:

```
type frametype = objpersframe, stateframe, actionframe, sitframe;

     slot = record
                slotname : string;
                comments :  string;
                constraints :  record
                                    requirements :  sometype;
                                    preferences :  sometype
                               end; (* constraints *)
                value : sometype
          end; (* slot record *)

     frame = record
                name : string;
                typeframe : frametype;
                AKO : ^frame;
                INSTANCE : ^frame;
                case frametype of
                       objpersframe : (* slots for opframe   *);
                       stateframe   : (* slots for sframe    *);
                       actionframe  : (* slots for aframe    *);
                       sitframe     : (* slots for sitframe  *)
          end; (* frame record *)
```

```
THING
    AKO                    $IF-ADDED    (ADD-INSTANCE)
                           $IF-REMOVED  (REMOVE-INSTANCE)
    INSTANCE               $IF-NEEDED   (INSTANTIATE-FRAME)
                           $IF-ADDED    (ADD-AKO)
                           $IF-REMOVED  (REMOVE-AKO)
```

Figure 9.3   General FRL Frame Showing AKO and INSTANCE Slots

The advantage of defining a generic frame structure in Pascal is that any slot in a frame can then point to any type of frame. The frame pointers for the *AKO* and *instance* slots are an example; the terminal frame in a structure will always be either an object/person frame or an action frame since those are the primitives, so in the hierarchy the type of frame being pointed to will change. For example if the highest level frame is a state frame called A, which points to B, which is a state frame pointing to C, an object/person frame, then the *instance* slot in A would point to a state frame, but the *instance* slot in B would point to an object/person frame. The same would be true going up in a hierarchy.

The notion of connecting procedures to knowledge representation structures is not original to FRL. Minsky recognized the need for procedures which could be activated when a slot was accessed, but he did not develop the concept. [16] Goldstein and Papert described the need for an *active agent* in a frame, known as a *frame-keeper*, which they refer to as an anthropomorphized computational procedure which seeks to fill the slots in his frame. [17] E. Charniak called his procedures *demons*, a term implying small forces that manipulate things without being seen. [18] Whatever they are called, these procedures are attached to a slot within a frame and are activated by some reference to that slot. The primary difficulty in implementing procedural attachment in Pascal is that the language does not allow procedure calls to be stored as data. However we shall assume that Pascal has a feature which allows representation of procedure names in the data. Let us assume that if a type is defined by an asterisk (*) followed by an identifier, then the item being defined represents a call to a procedure by that name. For example, if a slot S1 includes a variable definition V1 described as *P1, then accessing that slot would trigger a call to the procedure P1. The slot definition might look like this:

```
type  slot = record
            slotname : string;
            comments :  string;
            constraints :  record
                            requirements :  sometype;
                            preferences :  sometype
                          end; (* constraints *)
        value : sometype;
        slotproc : *procname
      end; (* slot record *)
```

FRL includes the additional feature of expressing conditions under which a procedure would be invoked, with the `if-added`, `if-needed`, and `if-removed` states. The conditional feature could be implemented by expanding the definition of `slotproc`:

```
type  condtype = (if-added, if-needed, if-removed);
      procrec = record
                      slotcond : condtype;
                      sproc : *procname;
                      nextproc : ^procrec
                end; (* procrec *)

      slot = record
                slotname : string;
                comments :  string;
                constraints :  record
                                    requirements :  sometype;
                                    preferences :  sometype
                               end; (* constraints *)
                value : sometype;
                slotproc : ^procrec
             end; (* slot record *)
```

A slot defined by this structure might look like this:

```
SLOT
      SLOTNAME:  S1
      COMMENTS:  'THIS IS A SAMPLE SLOT'
      CONSTAINTS: NONE
      VALUE:  464
      SLOTPROC:
            IF-ADDED:  *P1
            IF-REMOVED: *P2
```

These procedure names could then be stored with the slots in primary memory or auxiliary storage.

Event Schemas

Event schemas can be either situation frames or action frames. *Situation frames* are made up of *action frames*, which correspond to conceptual structures described in Chapter 8. Situational frames are more commonly called *scripts*, and are based on the interrelationships among conceptual structures. Script theory was developed by Roger Schank and Robert Abelson based on their dissatisfaction with the value of semantic memory. [19] As we have seen, "semantic memory is a memory for words that is organized in a hierarchical fashion using class membership as the basic link." [20] But Schank and Abelson argue that human memory does not consist of propositions stored according to the words in them and that memory is concept-oriented rather than word-oriented. Rather than the word-oriented semantic memory, they favor episodic memory:

> Episodic memory, on the other hand, is organized around propositions linked together by their occurrence in the same event or time span. Objects are most commonly defined by their place in a sequence of propositions describing the events associated with an object or an individual. A trip is stored in memory as a sequence of the conceptualizations describing what happened on the trip. Some of the conceptualizations will be marked as salient and some will have been forgotten altogether. [21]

Episodic memory is adequate to store both events and nominal concepts—nouns. Concrete nouns require a physical description of the object referenced as one part of their definition, but they can be more fully defined functionally by including the events in which the noun occurred. Schank and Abelson's example illustrates this point well. If one is asked, "Who was your girlfriend in 1968?" one does not scan a list of girlfriends to determine which one was current in 1968. Instead one normally thinks of 1968 and what events occurred then; in recalling these events one could consider who the participants were in the events, then select the participant who was a girlfriend.

Some episodes are like others, and Schank proposes that when we store these similar episodes, we remember them "in terms of a standardized generalized episode which we will call a script." [22] A script allows us to store an outline of an episode of a certain type, providing the capability of predicting activities not specifically referred to while organizing the actions which are specified. Scripts are made up of several parts: the props required to create the appropriate setting, the roles to be played by various participants, the conditions under which the script can begin, the results of completing the script, and the scenes which occur during the script. Figure 9.4 shows the restaurant script and its component parts. Notice that the various scenes are defined as sequences of actions which would be represented by conceptual structures as in Chapter 8.

Selection of Scripts

Scripts are selected by references in the input text which can signal that a particular situation is occurring. For example, if the input begins with the sentence,

Greg took Susan to his favorite New Orleans restaurant.

the restaurant script is a good candidate for describing the situation about to occur. The story could continue:

Script: RESTAURANT
Track: Coffee Shop
Props: Tables
      Menu
      F-Food
      Check
      Money

Roles: S-Customer
      W-Walker
      C-Cook
      M-Cashier
      O-Owner

Entry conditions: S is hungry.
                S has money.

Results: S has less money
       O has more money
       S is not hungry
       S is pleased (optional)

Scene 1 Entering

S **PTRANS** S into restaurant
S **ATTEND** eyes to tables
S **MBUILD** where to sit
S **PTRANS** S to table
S **MOVE** S to sitting position

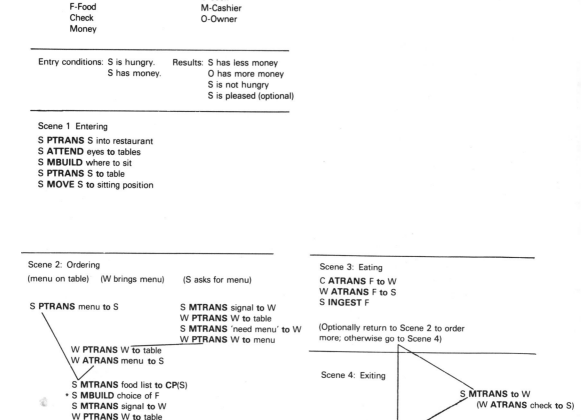

Scene 2: Ordering

(menu on table)   (W brings menu)   (S asks for menu)

S **PTRANS** menu to S

S **MTRANS** signal **to** W
W **PTRANS** W to table
S **MTRANS** 'need menu' **to** W
W **PTRANS** W to menu

W **PTRANS** W to table
W **ATRANS** menu to S

S **MTRANS** food list **to CP**(S)
* S **MBUILD** choice of F
S **MTRANS** signal **to** W
W **PTRANS** W to table
S **MTRANS** 'I want F' **to** W

W **PTRANS** W to C
W **MTRANS** (**ATRANS** F) **to** C

C **MTRANS** 'no F' **to** W
W **PTRANS** W to S
W **MTRANS** 'no F' **to** S
(go back to*) or
(go to Scene 4 at no pay path)

C **DO** (prepare F script)
to Scene 3

Scene 3: Eating

C **ATRANS** F **to** W
W **ATRANS** F **to** S
S **INGEST** F

(Optionally return to Scene 2 to order
more; otherwise go to Scene 4)

Scene 4: Exiting

S **MTRANS** to W
       (W **ATRANS** check to S)

W **MOVE** (write check)
W **PTRANS** W to S
W **ATRANS** check to S
S **ATRANS** tip **to** W
S **PTRANS** S to M
S **ATRANS** money **to** M
(no pay path): S **PTRANS** S **to** out of restaurant

Figure 9.4   Restaurant Script

> They ate seafood gumbo and barbecued ribs. Susan told the waitress
> that the food was good. Greg left a big tip.

In this story many details are left out, but anyone who knows the restaurant script can fill in the other information. For example no mention is made of ordering the food or paying the bill, but those events are assumed because of the script. In addition the big tip can be explained in the context that the atmosphere was positive: Susan said the food was good, and presumably the service was also good.

Schank and Abelson state that a script is activated when certain key concepts are found in certain contexts. The conceptualizations which call up a script are referred to as *headers*. [23] There are four kinds of headers: precondition headers, instrumental headers, locale headers, and direct headers. *Precondition* headers trigger a script by satisfying the entry conditions for that script. The sentence,

> John was hungry.

is an example of a precondition header which could trigger the restaurant script. An *instrumental* header provides information that establishes a stronger condition than a precondition header. Just because John is hungry does not mean he will necessarily go to a restaurant to eat; he might make himself a peanut butter and jelly sandwich at home. The sentence,

> John took the bus to the restaurant.

clearly establishes that the restaurant script is a strong possibility.

An even stronger predictive type of header is the *locale* header. If the time and place of the actor is such that the setting for a script is correct, then that script is even more likely. A requirement for a script which is not specified in Figure 9.4 is that the actor must be in the location of the script setting (which seems quite obvious). Compare the two sets of sentences below:

> Ben went into Toney's. He was hungry.

> Ben went into Toney's. He made a phone call.

Assuming that one knows that Toney's is an Italian restaurant on Bourbon Street, the first set of sentences would invoke the restaurant script. The second set however starts out implying that the restaurant script should be called, but since the second sentence, *He made a phone call*, is not part of that script, the intent is not quite so clear. The fourth kind of header, the *direct* header, is invoked by direct reference to one of the conceptualizations or roles in the script. For example a reference to a waitress strongly suggests the restaurant script although it might be a reference to the waitress as a person rather than as an employee, as in the sentence,

> The waitress combed her hair.

Clearly, selecting the proper script based on the input text can be tricky. In addition determining the path through a script may be involved. Notice that the restaurant script has several points at which different paths may be taken. In the ordering scene obtaining a menu can be achieved in three different ways: the menu can be on the table, the waitress may bring the menu, or the customer may have to ask the waitress to bring the menu. At other points in the script the path may be changed due to circumstances. If the customer orders food which is not available, then he can decide to choose another item or to leave without paying. These choices are referred to as interferences and distractions. *Interferences* are "states or actions which prevent the normal continuation of a script." [24] The two types of interferences are "*Obstacles*, where some enabling condition for an impending action is missing, and *errors*, where an action is completed with an unexpected and inappropriate result." In either case the actor has various options: try another course of action or leave the script. *Distractions* are "unexpected states or actions which initiate new goals for the actor, carrying him temporarily or permanently out of the script." [25] There are a number of questions which can be asked to attempt to continue a script after encountering unexpected input; answering any of these questions in the affirmative establishes a detour within the script:

a. Does it [the unexpected input] specify or imply the absence of an enablement for an impending script action? (Obstacle)

b. Does it specify or imply that a completed action was done in an unusual manner, or to an object other than the one(s) instantiated in the script? (Error)

c. Does it specify an action which can be understood as the corrective resolution of an interference? (Prescription) This question would be activated when an obstacle is inferred from or described directly in the text.

d. Does it specify or imply the repetition of a previous action? (Loop) This is activated when an error is inferred from or described directly in the text.

e. Does it specify or imply emotional expression by the actor, likely to have been caused by an interference? (Reaction)

f. Does it specify or imply that the actor will have a new goal that has nothing to do with the original script? (Distraction)

g. Does it specify or imply the motivated abandonment of the script by the main actor? (Abandonment) [26]

There are several standard patterns of these categories of detours.

```
(Obstacle) - (Prescription) - (Success)

(Error) - (Loop) - (Success)
```

```
                                           ┌(Reaction)
(Obstacle) - (Prescription) - (Failure)────┤
                                           └(Prescription) ...
```

(Obstacle) - (Prescription) - (Failure) - (Reaction) - (Distraction)

In some circumstances the detour taken will resolve the problem; in other cases it will not and the script must be terminated. The first two patterns of detours end in success, but the other two do not. The third pattern encounters an obstacle, a prescription is applied, but failure results. One possible succeeding action is reaction—an emotional response by the actor. Another action is an attempt to apply another prescription which hopefully could result in success; if not, then once again there are two possibilities. Another situation is shown in the fourth pattern where the reaction to failure results in distraction, which may lead to abandonment of the script entirely.

Scripts often overlap each other such that more than one script is active at a time. An example would be the situation described by the following sentences:

> John was eating in the dining car. The train stopped short. John's soup spilled.

This situation requires two scripts: the restaurant script and the train script. An alternative approach to complex situations is to create individual scripts for each one: the dining car script, which incorporates aspects of both the restaurant script and the train script. Further consideration of these complex situations is beyond the scope of this book.

Implementation of Scripts

Scripts consist of the various components listed earlier: the setting, the props, the roles, the conditions required to begin and the result of completing the script, as well as the events which make up the action of the script. The events of the script are represented as conceptual structures linked by causal chains, as described in Chapter 8. The parts of the conceptual structures largely make up the other components: the roles are filled by the actors of the primitive acts, the props are the objects manipulated and so on.

Scripts can thus be defined with a record containing the components mentioned, using variable length arrays for some parts:

```
type condrec = record
              condobj : PP;
              constraints : (optional, required);
              nextcond : ^condrec
          end; (* condrec *)

    scene = record
           event : concptr;
           case flow : (seq, jump, branch) of
                seq, jump : (nextevent : concptr);
```

```
                        branch : (flowcond : Boolean;
                                  tnext,fnext : concptr)
               end; (* scene record *)

      script = record
                  scriptname : string;
                  track : string;
                  props : array[0..MAXPROPS] of PP;
                  roles : array[0..MAXROLES] of PP;
                  entrycond : ^condrec;
                  results : ^condrec;
                  scenes : array[1..MAXSCENES] of scene
               end; (* script record *)
```

The values for MAXPROPS, MAXROLES, and MAXSCENES would have to be set to constants, although theoretically the arrays should be variable length. The PPs would be the definition from Chapter 8, as follows:

```
type attrib = record
                 state : stateid;  (* string *)
                 stateval : integer;  (* or some appropriate value *)
                 nextattrib : attptr
              end; (* attrib record *)

attptr = ^attrib;

PP = record
        ppname : string;
        ppstate : attptr
     end; (* PP record *)
```

A PP is an object or person with attributes. There can be multiple entry conditions and results for a script. Each condition or result can be defined as a PP in the sense that each one is an object or person with particular attributes; in other words the condition is fulfilled if the object or person named has the attributes specified. Since some conditions and results are optional, the constraints part of the condition record is added to identify whether the condition is required or optional.

The scene part of a script is a series of actions defined by the concept record from Chapter 8. Thus a scene record is defined as an event, which points to a concept and information about where to go next. If the event is followed in sequence by another event, whether it is the next one or a previous one, the nextevent field simply points to that next event. If a branch is to be taken based on some condition, then there is a flag for the condition—flowcond, which is Boolean—and two concept pointers—tnext and fnext. Since the concept record definition includes the causation link section, events within scenes can be further chained together by that means.

For a detailed description of another implementation of scripts, the reader is referred to the original source, *Inside Computer Understanding*, by Roger C. Schank and Christopher K. Riesbeck, in which the program SAM is explained. [27] SAM inputs stories, stores them as chains of conceptual structures, and paraphrases the stories or answers questions about them. The design of the data structures and program are explained thoroughly.

KL-ONE

KL-ONE is a language which is actually used rather extensively for research into problems of comprehending natural language and knowledge representation. Ronald Brachman presented the justification for KL-ONE by means of an analysis of the various types of semantic networks, in *Associative Networks*. [28] He delineated five levels of semantic networks, shown in the table below:

LEVEL	PRIMITIVES	EXAMPLES
Implementational	Atoms, pointers	Data structures
Logical	Propositions, predicates, logical operators	Hendrix, Schubert, Cercone
Epistemological	Concept types, conceptual subpieces, inheritance and structuring relations	Brachman
Conceptual	Semantic or conceptual relations (cases), primitive objects and actions	Simmons, Schank
Linguistic	Arbitrary concepts, words, expressions [29]	Szolovits et al.

The first type of network is essentially the use of net-type data structures—graphs or trees—for representing any sort of semantic information; networks of this type were described in the implementation of ATN's and case grammars, as well as some of the semantic networks. Hendrix's partitioned semantic networks and Schubert and Cercone's extended semantic networks are examples of logical semantic networks presented in Chapter 7. Each of these used logical constructs and operations to represent meaning. Simmons' semantic networks used to represent case grammar structures (in Chapter 7) and Schank's conceptual dependency structures (in Chapter 8) are conceptual networks. The final type—Linguistic Networks—were implemented in a system called OWL which included "a basic concept-structuring scheme that is used to build expressions" [30]; the primitives in OWL are principles such as specialization, attachment, and reference. Further discussion of OWL is beyond the scope of this book. [31]

The middle level of semantic networks in the chart—epistemological networks—was developed by Brachman into Structured-Inheritance Networks, which serve as a basis for KL-ONE. [32]

KL-ONE is a language for the explicit representation of conceptual information based on the idea of structured inheritance networks, . . . [and] is intended to represent general conceptual information by allowing the construction of a knowledge base of a single reasoning entity. . . . A KL-ONE network thus represents the beliefs about the world (and other possible worlds) as conceived by the system using it. [33]

KL-ONE is made up of two sublanguages: a *description language* and an *assertion language*. The description language defines the terminology for the world being modelled; it describes objects in the world by defining relationships among them. These objects are referred to as *concepts*, which are like noun phrases in systems discussed earlier. The assertion language makes statements about things in the domain of discourse using concepts. Assertions are comparable to sentences.

Description Language

Concepts are either *generic* or *individual*. Generic concepts represent classes of individuals. An individual concept is a particular object or relation, an instance of a generic concept. A concept (generic or individual) is completely defined by (1) its relation to other concepts and (2) its internal structure. The interrelationships among concepts define the taxonomy of the world. KL-ONE diagrams illustrate these relations. (Figure 9.5 gives the legend for deciphering the symbols used in KL-ONE diagrams.) The highest level concept is *thing*, as seen in Figure 9.6; *thing* subsumes all the concepts at a lower level. In addition all the characteristics of *thing* are inherited by the subconcepts. Each double arrow indicates that the lower-level concept is subsumed by the higher-level one. (The higher-level concept is called a superConcept; the lower-level one, a subConcept.)

The internal structure of a concept is made up of *roles* and the structural description of the concept. Roles "describe potential relationships between instances of the Concept and other closely associated Concepts (i.e., those of its properties, parts, etc.)." The structural description defines "the interrelations among the functional Roles". [34] Roles have names and value restrictions (V/R's) which describe potential values. There are two basic types of roles: *rolesets* and *iroles*. RoleSets identify the functional role of generic concepts; they are sets in that they can have multiple fillers, such as number restrictions. Iroles (instance roles) bind roles to individual concepts. An irole is a piece of a concept; the individual concept is the filler of the role slot in the concept. Figure 9.7 illustrates these ideas. *Arch, block,* and *square-block* are generic concepts. The *arch* concept has two rolesets, lintel and upright, whose fillers must be *Block's*. *Arch #1* is an individual concept subsumed by *Arch,* which has three iroles: *Square-block #1* and *Square-block #2,* which are fillers of the two *upright* iroles, and *Block #1,* which describes the filler of the lintel role. Figure 9.8 shows *Arch #1*.

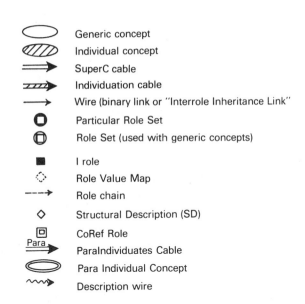

⬭ (ellipse)	Generic concept
⬭ (hatched)	Individual concept
⟹	SuperC cable
⟹ (hatched)	Individuation cable
⟶	Wire (binary link or "Interrole Inheritance Link"
O	Particular Role Set
⬤	Role Set (used with generic concepts)
■	I role
⬡ (dotted)	Role Value Map
- - -➔	Role chain
◇	Structural Description (SD)
▣	CoRef Role
Para ⟹	ParaIndividuates Cable
⬭ (oval)	Para Individual Concept
∿➔	Description wire

Figure 9.5   Legend for KL-ONE

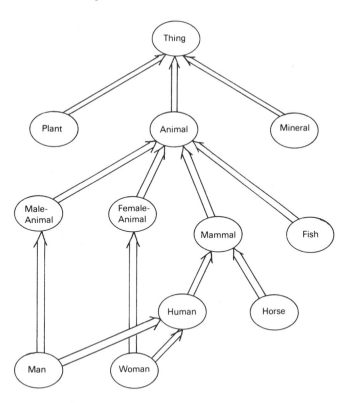

Figure 9.6   A Simple KL-ONE Network of Generic Concepts

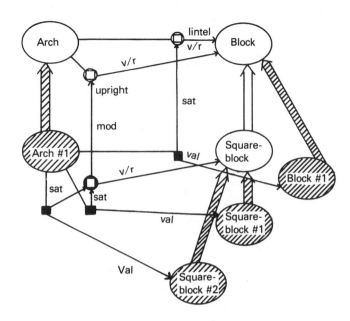

Figure 9.7   IROLES and Particular Role Sets

Arch #1

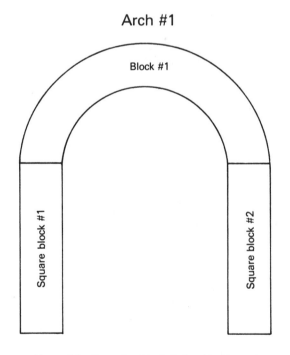

Figure 9.8   Example of Arch Defined in Figure 9.7

The relationships among roles are defined by the type of relations between superConcepts and subConcepts. Roles can be restricted as to the fillers that are allowed, and roles may be differentiated into subroles. Other relations are sometimes described as well.

RoleSetRelations (RSR's) complete the structure of a concept in KL-ONE. RSR's can be one of two types: structural descriptions (SD's) or RoleValueMaps (RVM's), which are a special case of an SD. An RVM expresses the correlation between two sets of role-fillers by establishing whether the sets are identical or that one set is included within the other. An RVM can equate fillers of two generic roles of the same concept, or roles within an individual concept and another concept. Figure 9.9 illustrates a RoleValueMap which correlates the fact that an arch has a name with the fact that an arch is dedicated to a person with a name, establishing that the name of the arch is equivalent to the last name of the dedicatee.

Structural descriptions delineate the structure of a role in the sense of defining the interrelationships among the roles of a concept. In the example of the arch, in addition to knowing that an arch includes two uprights and a lintel, a structural description provides the structural information that the two uprights support the lintel. Figure 9.10 shows the structural description of an arch (without much of the information included earlier). Structural descriptions use parameterized individual (paraIndividual) concepts to express the functional relationship among the roles of the concept. Thus the concept *support* is defined with two RoleSets, *supporter* and *supportee*. *Support#1* in the figure is a ParaIndividual Concept with corresponding Roles (known as CorefRoles) which are filled by the two uprights (as supporters) and the lintel (as supportee).

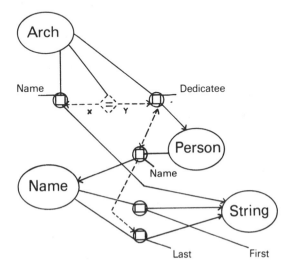

Figure 9.9   A RoleValue Map

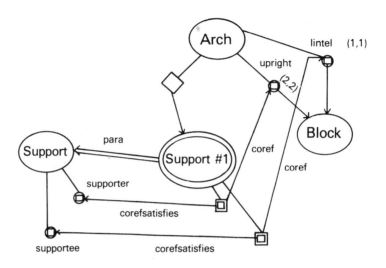

Figure 9.10   Structure Description Using Paraindividual Concept

Assertion Language

In KL-ONE concepts can be defined in the description language without any assertions being made about any individual in existence. Only by making assertions that an instance of a concept exists within a particular context is an object brought into existence. This is done by connecting the description of an object to a *nexus* within a particular *context* by means of a Description Wire.

> A Nexus is a structureless entity which serves as a locus of coreference statements; it holds together various descriptions, all of which are taken to specify the same object in the Context. Nexuses have been conveniently thought to correspond to things in the world. . . . The Description Wires are also taken to be in the Context. Contexts are . . . collections of Nexuses and Description Wires. Thus, a Context can act as a "world", which comprises a set of statements about existence and description coreference. [35]

Figure 9.11 illustrates the use of assertions; C1 asserts the existence of *the first officer of the Enterprise*, who is described to be a Vulcan whose name is Spock. C2 asserts the existence of a human whose name is Uhura who is first officer, while Spock is identified as Captain of the Enterprise. (Notice that the assertion of one context may contradict another context. No statement is being made about the truth of all contexts.)

At the time that the 1981 Workshop on KL-ONE was held, most of the emphasis in developing the language had been on the description language,

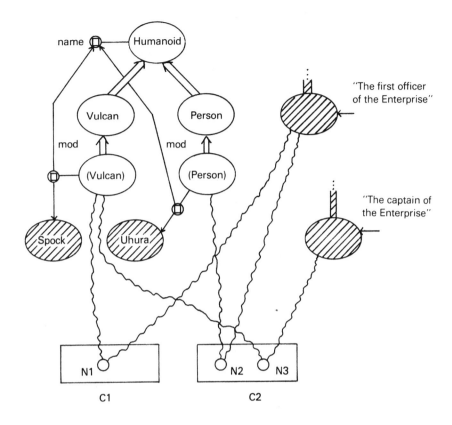

Figure 9.11   Some KL-ONE Assertions

but researchers were calling for more attention to the assertion language.
Some of the suggestions made for improving KL-ONE were to add the capability
to express disjunctions and negations (as in Partitioned Semantic Networks)
and to express logical propositions—existential and universal statements (as
in Extended Semantic Networks). Because KL-ONE is being used by a number
of researchers, changes are undoubtedly being made to the language to create
a tool which can more adequately represent knowledge in any domain. [36]

Part IV

Natural
Language
Systems

Chapter 10

Design
of Natural Language
Systems

A natural language system designed to understand and manipulate language should be capable of accepting input in natural language text, storing knowledge related to the application domain, drawing inferences from that knowledge, answering questions based on the knowledge, and generating responses. In order to understand the structure and operation of such a system, this chapter will present the design of NLS, a natural language system with these capabilities.

General Description of NLS

NLS is a knowledge based natural language understanding system. It processes natural language input and generates appropriate output. The knowledge base for this system is precompiled; in other words, a knowledge domain exists before execution begins. This knowledge base (KB) preserves both hierarchical and propositional information about the data stored. The input accepted by the system includes statements to be paraphrased, i.e., restated to assure proper understanding; statements which represent knowledge to be learned, i.e., added to the KB; and questions to be answered by accessing the KB. The system outputs appropriate responses to input, as well as paraphrases of statements and answers to questions.

The major modules of NLS include the Parser, the Understander, and the Generator. (See Figure 10.1.) The parser accepts the input string and maps it into an internal structure compatible with the KB. The generator maps from the internal structure to the output string. The understander module accesses the KB for various purposes: to obtain knowledge, to draw inferences, or to add knowledge to the KB. These three functions interact to accomplish various tasks.

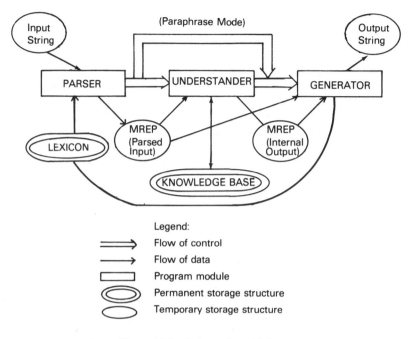

Figure 10.1   Schematic of NLS

The data sets required for NLS include the KB, the lexicon, the input and output strings, the meaning representation for the input sentence (MREP), and working data. The KB is the knowledge base which represents the memory of the system—what the system knows. The lexicon contains the vocabulary for the system—the words recognized along with syntactic and semantic information needed to parse them. The meaning representation for the input string, whether it is a statement or a question, will be produced by the parser and processed by the understander. It is a structure compatible with the KB. Additional working data structures will be needed during processing.

The Parser

The parser accepts the sentence input as a string of characters and breaks it up into lexical items. Morphological analysis is done to identify regularly inflected forms (plurals ending in -*s* or -*es*, past tense verbs ending in -*ed*, third person singular verbs ending in -*s*), and information from the lexicon is attached to each word. The goal of this phase is to convert the input string into a meaning representation of the sentence in order to allow processing. A traditional parse tree, such as the phrase markers described in Chapter 4, would not be sufficient to hold the content of the sentence; therefore a more involved structure is needed, similar to the frame structure described in Chapter 9, which will correlate to the knowledge representation to be described later.

The Generator

The generator phase of NLS produces output for the user. In some circumstances the only response required is simple acknowledgment that the input has been accepted and processed. Other times a sentence must be generated to convey information to the user. If the sentence is a declarative statement which adds knowledge to the KB, then the response could be,

I understand.

or more casually,

Okay.

If the sentence is being paraphrased or a question is being answered, then the generator will construct the output sentence from the internal structure, essentially the opposite of the parsing phase. The generator is not responsible for construction of the internal structure; that is done by the input phase for paraphrasing or the understanding phase for question answering.

The Understander

The understander is responsible for all access to the KB including any additions or modifications needed. The function that the understander is to perform depends on the type of sentence input. If the sentence is a question, it must be answered; if it is a statement, the meaning represented by the statement must be added to the KB. The simplest access would be retrieval of some information stored in the KB, determined by the type of question asked. Analysis of questions will be considered separately. Retrieval is achieved by accessing the structure of the KB. Drawing inferences from the information stored in the KB is another task for the understander. Inferencing is achieved by filling in gaps in the knowledge structure and by applying certain logical operations to assertions. Adding knowledge to the KB is more complex. If the statement merely fills in gaps in the knowledge by supplying information for an empty slot, no problems are encountered. However the new information can force modification of the structure of the existing knowledge structures if it conflicts with the current status of information stored.

The submodules within the understanding phase must interact to achieve their goals. The inferencing part needs to retrieve information, and answering questions often requires inferencing. These submodules will be implemented as coroutines—routines which operate concurrently by interfacing with each other.

The Knowledge Base

The knowledge base (KB) for NLS is made up of three primary types of data items: *entities, events* and *situations,* all of which are referred to as *packets.* Entities are objects or persons or even locations—anything which can be described or about which statements can be made. Events are actions which occur involving actors and objects, goals, sources, and instruments. Events have causes and can cause other events. Situations combine entities and events with conditions and results. All three types of data items are interconnected: entities are linked to the events and situations within which they occur, events point to entities, and situations point to both entities and events. In addition assertions can be made about entities using first order predicate calculus, and a hierarchical structure can be built by including superset/subset links within the definition of each entity. Let us examine the details of these features.

An entity is anything which can be described or about which statements can be made. In fact an entity could be an event or a situation as well as a physical object or person. Each entity has a name and a type to identify it, but entities are defined primarily by their attribute list. Attributes are any sort of information which can describe an entity, such as location, size, duration, or relationship to other entities. The specific types of attributes are not predefined, but can be added by the user as needed. Entities can be linked into a hierarchy by means of superset and subset links, like the *AKO* and *INSTANCE* slots in FRL-0. The Pascal definition of an entity is as follows:

```
type attribs = record
               attrib : string;
               attibvalue :  somevalue
               nextattrib :  ^attribs
           end; (* attribs *)

     packets = record
               thispack : ^packet;
               nextpack : ^packets
           end; (* packets *)

     asserts = record
               thisassert : ^assertion;
               nextassert : ^asserts
           end; (* asserts *)

     entity = record
               entname : string;
               enttype : (tentity, tevent, tsituation);
               superent, subent : ^packet;
               attriblist : ^attribs;
               packlist :  ^packets;
               assertlist :  ^asserts
           end; (* entity *)
```

The last two elements of **entity** are the list of packets in which this entity occurs and the list of assertions about this entity. The **superent** and **subent** links are not required since many times they will not apply, but if included, they allow inheritance of attributes. There are no intrinsic differences between generic and individual entities in NLS.

Events are quite similar to active conceptual structures defined in Chapter 8. They include an actor, an object, an action, an instrument, a source and goal, and causation. The definition is as follows:

```
type tense = record
                tensetype : (null, past, future, ...);
                nexttense : ^tense
            end;  (* tense record *)

    event = record
                actor, object : ^entity;
                action : record
                            acttype : (MOVE, ATTEND, ...);
                            acttense : ^tense
                        end;
                instrument : ^event;
                source, goal : ^entity;
                causation : record
                                causetype : (result, initiation, ...);
                                causelink : ^event
                            end
            end;  (* event record *)
```

(The tenses, actions, and types of causation are assumed to be the same as in Schank's work. The choice of primitive acts rather than actual verbs seems reasonable since work with actual verbs, as in case grammars, requires categorization of those verbs, which can be considered nearly equivalent to the use of primitives. The choice of Schank's list of primitive actions should not imply that that list is final. Further work on conceptual analysis of natural language is needed.) As with conceptual structures, the actors and objects point to entities, the action is made up of the action type which identifies the cases which apply to this event and the expected structure of the event. The instrument is a pointer to another event. The source and goal, which were distinguished as **FROM** and **TO** or **RECIPIENT** and **DONOR** in Chapter 8, are simply pointers to entities, which could be either type of data (location or person). The causation section of the event record identifies the type of causation and links to the event which caused this one.

Situations in NLS are much like scripts, in that they contain roles and props, entry conditions and results, and scenes which are made up of events. The definition is as follows:

```
type condrec = record
                    condobj : entity;
                    constraints : (optional, required);
                    nextcond : ^condrec
               end; (* condition record *)

    scene = record
                    sevent : ^event;
                    case flow : (seq, jump, branch) of
                        seq, jump : (nextevent : ^event);
                        branch : (flowcond : Boolean;
                                        tnext, fnext : ^event)
            end;   (* scene record *)

    situation = record
                    props, roles : array[0..MAX] of entity;
                    entrycond, results : ^condrec;
                    scenes : array[1..MAXSCENES] of scene
               end; (* situation record *)
```

Thus situations are based on sequences of events which can be considered in order or by branching at various turning points in the scene controlled by some condition. Props and roles point to entities defined elsewhere. The condition records used for entry conditions and results will guide the understander module during inferencing.

Packets are collections of data items, as frames are. A packet always includes an entity and can include an event or a situation as well. Thus packets are defined as:

```
type packet = record
                    pentity : ^entity;
                    case packtype : (tevent, tsituation) of
                        tevent: (pevent : ^event);
                        tsituation : (psituation : ^situation)
            end; (* packet record *);
```

Packets are used to describe more complex data elements since they combine entities with events or situations. A packet allows more flexibility when making assertions about data objects.

The knowledge base allows assertions to be made about the data objects defined. If we assume that assertions can be of the same form as propositions in Schubert and Cercone's extended semantic networks, then each assertion includes one or more operands, an operator, and a quantification factor. Assertions will be stored as binary tree structures (see Chapter 4 for description) in which the left branch is the first operand and the right branch points to the rest of the operands. Each node in the assertion tree will allow an operator and a quantification factor to apply to that assertion or subassertion. If the node is a terminal node, it will point to a packet, which could be an entity, event, or situation; a nonterminal node points to another node. Thus an assertion node is defined as:

```
type anode = record
                quant : (ALL, EXIST, NONE);
                operator : (NOT, AND, OR, IMPLIES ...);
                case leftterm : (true,false) of
                        true: (first : ^packet);
                        false : (left : ^anode)
                end; (* leftterm case *)
                case rightterm : (true,false) of
                        true: (rest : ^packet);
                        false: (right : ^anode)
            end; (* anode record *)
```

(Notice that the construction in anode is not valid Pascal; a variant record cannot be based on two different conditions to include two different variant sections.)

The KB consists then of all the packets defined so far and the various lists needed to access the information in the KB. The overall coordination of the KB is accomplished through a high-level access structure made up of lists of elements of the KB. The top-level declaration for the KB would be as follows:

```
type entities = record
                    thisentity : ^entity;
                    nextentity : ^entity
                  end; (* entities *)

     packets = record
                    thispack : ^packet;
                    nextpack : ^packets
                  end; (* packets *)

     asserts = record
                    thisassert : ^assertion;
                    nextassert : ^asserts
                  end; (* asserts *)
var KB : record
            kbentities : entities;
            kbpackets : packets;
            kbasserts : asserts
         end;  (* KB *)
```

The access structure includes a linked list of entities, which are linked individually to the packets and assertions in which they occur; a linked list of packets, which are linked back to the entities in them; and a linked list of assertions, which are linked to the entities in them. These lists should be appropriately ordered to minimize access time. Other lists could be added as needed by a particular application, such as lists of similar actions or similar logical operations.

The Meaning Representation of a Sentence

When a sentence is input—whether question or statement—it must be stored in a workable form which is compatible with the KB. That structure, MREP, is essentially an individual packet, not yet attached to the rest of the knowledge base. If the sentence is a statement which adds knowledge to the KB, then adding that information will entail finding the place for MREP in the KB, or at least the new information in the packet. Answering a question will involve first relating MREP to the KB to determine what information is known about the question being asked, and then pulling out the appropriate information to produce another packet which will be generated into an answer to the user.

The Lexicon

The lexicon for NLS contains the vocabulary which the system knows and the syntactic, semantic, and pragmatic information necessary for each lexical item to be processed by the system. Chapter 3 discussed the structure and organization of a lexicon in general; we will now consider some of the specific features of the lexicon for NLS. The primary function of the lexicon is to assist the parser in translating the input sentence into an internal meaning representation (MREP) to be processed. Thus any word used in the input must be capable of being located in the lexicon. Root forms will all be stored in the lexicon, but regularly inflected variants can be morphologically analyzed to produce the root form, saving considerable storage space. Each lexical item in the dictionary will include the *root*, the actual string of characters found in the input; syntactic information to allow identification of the structure of the sentence; and semantic and pragmatic information to facilitate creation of the internal meaning representation of the sentence.

Following the description of the lexicon developed by Cercone, [1] there are two sets of categories of lexical items: open categories and closed categories. Open categories identify the primary function of the word: *nominal, action, nominal modifier,* and *action modifier.* The vast majority of words in the vocabulary fall into these categories which essentially correspond to the standard word classes: noun, verb, adjective, and adverb. The closed categories represent those word classes which include a finite, restricted number of instances; for example, the classes containing conjunctions or determiners in a language cannot be extended. Words in open categories are sometimes called *content* words, whereas words in closed categories are known as *function* words. Figure 10.2 lists the values of the open and closed lexical categories. Each of the classes within the categories has certain features associated with it. Figure 10.3 shows the features for the various classes within the open and closed categories. These features are taken from Cercone's work, which in this respect is based on Winograd's blocks world. [2] Figure 10.4 shows the structure of each lexical entry.

OPEN CATEGORIES

N	nominal, typically either a noun or a proper noun
A	action, typically a verb
NM	nominal modifier, typically an adjective
AM	action modifier, typically an adverb

CLOSED CATEGORIES

CONJ	conjunction (and, but, or, . . .)
BIND	binder (before, if, because, . . .)
PREP	preposition (to, for, over, . . .)
PRO	pronoun (I, you, them, . . .)
DET	determiner (a, the, those, . . .)
ORD	ordinal (first, second, thirty-fifth, . . .)
NEG	negative (not)
COMP	comparative (more, greater, . . .)
OP	operator (plus, times, . . .)
QWORD	question nominal (who, why, what, . . .)
QNTFR	quantifier (some, any, none, . . .)
PRT	particle (knock 'out', fall 'over', . . .)
NUM	number (one, two, three, . . .)
INTJ	interjection (oh, . . .)

Figure 10.2   Lexical Categories

Each lexical entry contains a root and its meaning (which may consist of more than one part, as evidenced by the asterisk *). The root is the actual string of characters to be matched. The meaning consists of the identification of the applicable lexical category and the category value, as well as information that would relate this lexical item to others with the same meaning, i.e., synonyms or abbreviations. The category value would provide the syntactic data needed to identify the function of this word in the input sentence, by listing the morphological information associated with the word and the root feature which delineates the specific syntactic function of the word.

The word sense formula is used to convert the parsed sentence into a packet to be processed by the understander phase of the system. Chapter 8 discussed requests, the condition-action modules stored in the lexicon with each item, which direct the building of the conceptual structure. NLS uses the same approach to building the MREP for a sentence; the lexical item has requests associated with it which identify the type of packet to be built, including the type of information to fill in the various slots. (Review the section in Chapter 8 called *Algorithm for Conceptual Analysis*.) The RLIST (request list) and the CLIST (concept list) serve as working data structures during the parsing phase.

a. OPEN CATEGORIES

N's

NS	singular	TIME	time
NP	plural	FTIME	functional time
COLL	collective	PERS	personal
POSS	possessive	DIM	diminutive

A's

AUX	auxiliary	BE	be
WILL	future	DO	do
HAVE	have	MODAL	modality
TRANS	transitive	ITRANS	intransitive
PART	particle	IREG	irregular
PRES	present	PAST	past
INF	infinitive	TPS	third person

NM's

ADJ	adjective
COM	comparative
SUP	superlative
CLASF	classifier

AM's

Various features of adverbs will be ignored

b. CLOSED CATEGORIES

CONJ	BINDER	PREP	NUM
ORD	OP	PRT	NEG
COMP	QWORD	INTJ	

PRO's

NP	plural	COLL	collective
NS	singular	POSS	possessive
REL	relative	PERS	personal
DEM	demonstrative	DEF	definite
INDEF	indefinite	SUB	subject
OBJ	object		

DET's

DEF	definite	INDEF	indefinite
NP	plural	COLL	collective
NS	singular	DEM	demonstrative
QDET	question		

QNTFR's

NE	negative	NS	singular
NONUM	no number	NP	plural
COLL	collective		

Figure 10.3   Syntactic Features for Roots

< lexical entry >	::=	(< root > <meaning* >)
< root >	::=	root of word given meaning
< meaning >	::=	< lexical category > < category value > < synonym > < abbrev >
< lexical category >	::=	< open category > | < closed category >
< open category >	::=	N | A | NM | AM
< closed category >	::=	CONJ | PREP | ...
< category value >	::=	(< root feature list > < word sense formula* >)*
< synonym >	::=	SYN < synonym value >* | nil
< abbrev >	::=	ABB < abbrev value >* | nil
< synonym value >	::=	synonym value for root
< abbrev value >	::=	abbreviation for root
< root feature list >	::=	(< morph code > < root feature* >)*
< word sense formula >	::=	(the codes and structures needed to represent the meaning of the root and allow processing)
< morph code >	::=	-ING | -ED | ... | nil
< root feature >	::=	POSS | DEF | NP | INF | ...

Figure 10.4   Structure of Lexical Entry

Implementing NLS

Because NLS is quite involved, the implementation will be presented in the following stages:

1. **Paraphrase mode:** A sentence will be input and converted into its MREP; then the output sentence will be generated from MREP. (The understander phase is not needed.)

2. **Inference mode:** A sentence will be input and converted into its MREP; then all the possible inferences will be drawn about the sentence and the part of the KB to which it relates. The inferences will be saved as MREPs which will be passed on to the generator for output.

3. **Question-answering mode:** A question will be input and converted into its MREP. After the question is analyzed, then the KB will be accessed to determine the answer. The answer will be stored in a new MREP from which the output sentence will be generated.

4. **Learning mode:** A sentence will be input and converted into its MREP; then the understander phase will locate the proper place for the new information and add it to the KB.

Each of these modes will be considered in turn.

Paraphrase Mode

In paraphrase mode a sentence will be input, parsed, and stored in an internal meaning representation; then an output sentence will be immediately generated from the meaning representation. If the generator were for a different language from the parser, the process would be called *translation*. In other words, if the original sentence is in English, but the generator produces French, then we have an English-to-French translator program. The internal forms for the sentence and the knowledge base are language-independent—not related to one specific language, although the lexicon is language dependent. For now we will consider only English-to-English conversion.

Figure 10.5 illustrates the processing involved in paraphrasing a sentence. The input string is accepted by the parser, which first splits it into individual words. Each word is found in the lexicon, either directly or after morphological analysis, and the syntactic and semantic information from the lexical entry is attached to the word. This information facilitates parsing. Parsing involves both determining the structure of the sentence (syntax) and building the MREP (semantics). The structure of the sentence depends on the main verb of the sentence. As we saw in Chapter 8, the initial parts of the sentence will simply be saved until an acceptable candidate for the verb is located. The verb identifies the form of the sentence, as with case grammar and conceptual dependency. The basic structure then is obtained from the lexicon, and the parser proceeds to fill in the slots as directed by the condition-action modules (called *requests* in Chapter 8) identified by the lexical entry. The major problem which can arise at this stage is that the wrong word is selected as the verb; however if the vocabulary is restricted enough, that occurrence will be rare, if possible at all.

When all the words from the input sentence have been accounted for, the MREP is as complete as possible. Any slot not filled by specific input information will be given its default value, if any, or will be filled by inferencing, if requested. In paraphrase mode, control now goes to the generator module, which is responsible for producing the output string from the MREP passed

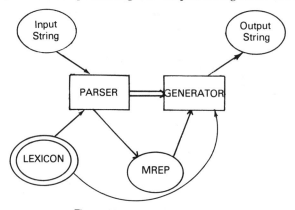

Figure 10.5   Paraphrase Mode

to it. The generator functions like the parser in reverse. It uses the MREP to determine the basic sentence pattern to be generated. Then each part of the sentence pattern is filled in by the word with its feature list attached. The features can be eliminated as they are used; thus when an item is classified as the subject part of the sentence, the feature identifying it as subject can be removed. The final features to be removed are the morphological ones, since the last phase of generation will be producing the surface version of the sentence. Thus until the last stage a noun phrase might include the following:

>block NP . . . and   John POSS . . .

then the last step would produce:

>John's blocks

Let us go through an example in detail to delineate the steps involved in paraphrasing a sentence. The input sentence is

>John left town because Mary was sick.

The first step is to access the lexicon to find all the words and attach features to each one. The result of that step might look like the following list with semantic information in parentheses. (Actually the parser would probably access the lexicon one word at a time as it attempted to build the structure to represent the sentence since there are often multiple senses for words. Knowing what the structure is as early as possible can help eliminate many of the choices.)

WORD	FEATURE LIST
John	N NS PERS (male human)
left	A [ROOT leave] TRANS PAST IREG (PTRANS form)
town	N NS (location; DEFAULT New Orleans)
because	BINDER (causation)
Mary	N NS PERS (female human)
was	A [ROOT be] BE PAST IREG (. . .)
sick	NM ADJ (State HEALTH −5)

As the parser analyzes each word, the pieces of the sentence are saved or stored into the MREP. The first word *John* is saved on a temporary list (called the **CLIST** in Chapter 8) as a possible subject for the verb. The word *left* is a good candidate for the main verb, and its feature list identifies it as a **PTRANS** verb. The **PTRANS** form is selected to structure the clause; it includes an animate actor so the noun *John* can fill that slot. The **PTRANS** structure also needs an object, a source, and a goal. The object is not immediately apparent, but can be filled in with the noun *John*, since the sentence

>John left town.

is equivalent to

> John **PTRANS**ed John *from* town *to* somewhere.

The source is the noun *town* which satisfies the location feature of the **FROM** slot of **PTRANS**. (The fact that the location is the **FROM** filler and John is the object as well as the actor is part of the requests attached to the verb *leave* in specifying how to fit a sentence with the verb *leave* into the **PTRANS** structure.) Thus the actor, object, and source slots can be filled, but the goal slot is still empty. Since the sentence does not state where John went after he left town, that slot will have to remain empty.

The binder *because* identifies the end of the clause and thus the first event of the sentence. It also indicates that another clause is expected which will be linked to the first through its causation section. The noun *Mary* is saved on the **CLIST** until a verb can be found. The verb *was* is identified as a *be* verb which can serve various purposes: as a verb linking the subject and predicate nominative, as a verb linking the subject and predicate adjective, or as an auxiliary verb as in the verb phrase *was singing*. Since the next word following *was* is the adjective *sick*, the second choice is taken and the structure to be filled in is determined to be an entity with attributes. Thus Mary is the entity and the primary attribute is the fact that her health was negative (**HEALTH −5**). Since that completes the list of words, the causation link is then established between the **PTRANS** structure and the entity structure to indicate that the state of Mary's health caused John's action. The parser is now finished with the sentence and passes the MREP on to the generator.

The generator starts by finding the two structures in the MREP and determines that the sentence can be one of several forms:

> clause1 *because* clause2
>
> state2 *caused* clause1

If the first choice is taken, then the **PTRANS** structure is identified with the first clause and is generated. The **PTRANS** structure establishes several possible sentence patterns, given that the actor and the object are the same:

actor **PTRANS** object *from* source *to* goal	(unacceptable English)
actor *go from* source *to* goal	(with either *from* or *to* part optional)
actor *leave* <*from*> source	(assuming source is a location, the word *from* would be omitted)

Thus the possible sentence patterns with the slots filled in, but not yet polished, are:

John go from town.	(somewhat awkward with *to* part missing)
John go from New Orleans.	(since New Orleans is the default value for town)

John leave town.

John leave New Orleans.

The second clause can produce several patterns as well:

state *of* entity *is* state-value

entity *is* (adjective describing state value)

The generated clauses without the final feature changes are:

The health of Mary is poor.

Mary is sick.

The two clauses are modified to include the past tense form of the verbs and to smooth out the phrasing. Combining some of the possible versions of the structures produces the following:

John went from New Orleans because the health of Mary was poor.

John left town because Mary was sick.

John left New Orleans because Mary's health was poor.

Mary's poor health caused John to leave town.

Thus paraphrasing the original sentence produced several possible versions with essentially the same meaning.

Exercise: Write the parser and generator modules to implement the paraphrase mode.

Inference Mode

There are three main types of inferencing possible in NLS: inferencing to fill slots in the MREP, inferencing from the structures in the KB, and inferencing from the assertions related to the subject. The first is fairly simple; the MREP of the input sentence is analyzed for possible empty slots and an attempt is made to fill the slots without accessing the KB. An example of this sort of inferencing was discussed in Chapter 8; in conceptual structures (and packets) the instrumental case can often be filled in just by knowing the action part. The instrumental case for INGEST is usually PTRANS, for GRASP is MOVE, and so on. Other possible inferences involve sentences which include pronouns. For example in the sentence

John watched his ball float down the stream.

the pronoun *his* can only refer to John, an inference which can be drawn because the pronoun requires a male antecedent and John is the only one. However if the sentence were

John told Tom about watching his ball float down the stream.

the inference would not be as certain (particularly since it is not clear even to a human understander whether the pronoun refers to John or Tom). Resolving pronominal references is one of the major difficulties in natural language processing.

The second type of inferencing requires access to the KB. First let us consider how to locate relevant information in the KB. Assume that a sentence has been input and its MREP generated by the parser. An example would be

Trout fishing is a popular sport in America.

This sentence would produce the MREP shown in Figure 10.6. Notice that the phrase *trout fishing* produces a situation packet, since it is an activity consisting of various steps. The KB representation for *sport* would include the fact that each sport involves activity. The adjective *popular* generates an attribute for the word *sport* in this case. The prepositional phrase *in America* is difficult because it could modify several words: trout fishing in America, sport in America, or popular in America. (Figure 10.6 shows *in America* modifying *trout fishing*, but intuitively it should perhaps modify *popular*.)

Locating relevant information in the KB involves scanning the various access lists: the list of entities for *trout*, the list of situations for *fishing* and *sports*, and possibly a list of attributes for *popular* things and *American* things. If a reference to other sports were found, then a search could be made for sports which are popular or American, producing sentences such as:

Popular sports include trout fishing, football, and cricket.

Popular American sports include trout fishing, football and basketball.

Connections with *fishing* might list various types of fishing (deep sea fishing, etc.), whereas links to *trout* might include recipes for cooking trout, biological classification of trout, and locations for finding trout streams. Any of these could be used to produce an MREP to pass to the generator for output.

The third type of inferencing accesses the assertion list rather than the packets in the KB. The access path could be either from the entities and situations to the assertions or directly to the assertion list. The various packets would be linked to the assertions about them; some sample assertions related to the previous sentence might be:

All trout recipes require a pan.

Some trout streams are in Colorado.

All popular sports require an audience.

If the last assertion were found, then inferencing might be somewhat complicated since there is no mention of an audience in the situation packet for trout fishing. Therefore either the assertion in the KB is wrong or the new sentence is wrong. Another possibility is that the packet is not complete, i.e., that trout fishing requires an audience, but that role was not included when the trout fishing packet was designed.

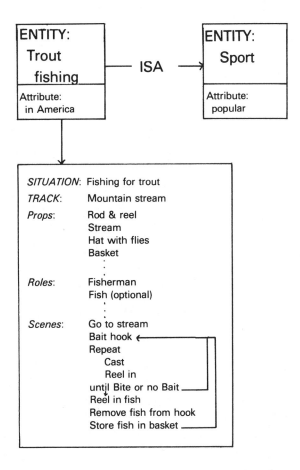

Figure 10.6   Trout fishing is a popular sport in America

Assume that the sentence input is,

Walter went fishing in Colorado.

From this sentence the inferencer would connect with the information in the KB that

Trout fishing is a popular sport in America.

and

Some trout streams are in Colorado.

and could therefore infer that Walter was fishing for trout. The probability is fairly strong that the conclusion is true, but it is not necessarily true based on the information available. Figure 10.7 shows the scheme for inferencing mode.

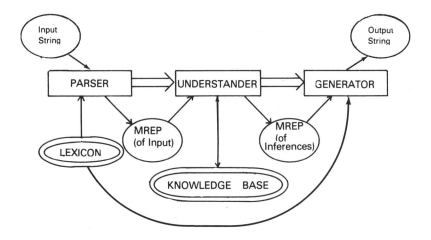

Figure 10.7   Inference Mode

Question Answering Mode

Questions to be answered are first converted into their MREP and then analyzed in order to determine what type of question is being asked before the KB is accessed to find an answer. Knowing the type of question enables the appropriate answer to be formulated. In her book, *The Process of Question Answering*, Wendy Lehnert classifies questions into thirteen conceptual categories [3]:

1. Causal Antecedent
2. Goal Orientation
3. Enablement
4. Causal Consequent
5. Verification
6. Disjunctive
7. Instrumental / Procedural
8. Concept Completion
9. Expectational
10. Judgmental
11. Quantification
12. Feature Specification
13. Request

Each category can be recognized by the features of the MREP into which the question has been stored. Let us consider each category in turn.

Causal antecedent questions ask about the event or situation that caused the situation in the question. The MREP for this type of question consists of two packets linked by a causal relation known as *leadto*. Not all the information in the first packet is available, and filling in that information will answer the question. Examples of this type of question are:

> Why did Tom quit his job?
>
> What caused the building to collapse?

Goal orientation questions seek the motivation behind a situation and may be why-questions. As with the previous type, these questions are recognized by having two packets in the MREP linked by a *reason* causation. Again not all the information in the first packet is known. Examples are:

> For what purpose did Mary dye her hair?
>
> Why did Mary dye her hair?

Enablement questions are similar to goal orientation questions except that the causal relation linking the two packets is an *enable* link. An example is:

> What did Walter need to do to join the Yacht Club?

Causal consequent questions are similar to causal antecedent questions except that the second packet in the chain does not include all the information needed. This type of question is asking about what is caused by the situation. For example:

> What happens if I leave?
>
> What happens if John buys the car?

Verification questions ask whether a situation is as described, whether the statement made by the question is true. These questions are stored as a statement in a single packet. The mode of the statement is identified as a question. These are essentially yes/no questions. For example:

> Did John know that Mary left town?
>
> Is Data Structures a required course?

Disjunctive questions are similar to verification questions, but they have multiple answers. They are represented by two packets combined by an *or* relation. One of the packets is true and is the answer. Examples are

> Was John or Mary here?
>
> Is John coming or going?

Instrumental/procedural questions are asking about the instrumentality of the statement. Questions with simple answers are instrumental; questions with lengthy multiple step answers are procedural. Questions of this type can be recognized by having an incomplete or empty instrument slot. Procedural questions are asking directions, such as:

> How do I get to Mississippi from here?
>
> How will John get the money?

Examples of instrumental questions are:

> How did John go to New York? (by plane?)
>
> What did Mary use to eat? (chopsticks?)

Concept completion questions are referred to as fill-in-the-blank questions in that one slot of the packet is empty and the question requests that the information be provided to fill it. Filling in the missing component answers the question. Examples of this type are:

> Who mowed the lawn? (Who was the actor?)
>
> What did John buy? (What was the object?)

Exceptational questions are like causal antecedent questions except that they ask about situations that did not occur. They ask about the cause for the event not happening. Examples include:

> Why isn't John smiling?
>
> Why didn't Mary take the job?

Judgmental questions ask for an opinion from the listener. They involve a top-level mental state of the actor who is the listener; in other words they ask what is in the mind of the listener. For example,

> What should John do now?
>
> Why do you think that Mary is wrong?

Quantification questions ask for a numeric value—an amount. They are frequently *how-many* questions, such as,

> How many angels can dance on the head of a pin?
>
> How many students enrolled for Data Structures?

Other quantification questions ask about state scales:

> How sick is John?

This type of question is recognized by having a missing numerical attribute value.

Feature specification questions ask about attribute values other than numerical, such as

> What color are John's eyes?
>
> What breed of cat do you have?

How old is Mary?

Notice that the last question would be answered with a number; it is considered a feature specification question rather than a quantification question because the quantity requested is not normally thought of as a scale value. Some feature specification questions must infer the attribute being asked about as well as the value for that attribute. For example,

What kind of cat do you have?

could be asking about breed or size or color or personality. These questions are recognized by an unknown attribute value.

Requests are questions which ask for an action to take place whereas the other types of questions, referred to as inquiries, involve a mental exchange of information. One difference between requests and inquiries is that although requests can be answered yes or no, that sort of answer is not appropriate.

Would you take out the garbage?

Will you get me my coat?

Answering yes or no, but not performing the action would undoubtedly annoy the person making the request.

Lehnert's method for determining the type of question being asked is shown in Figure 10.8. [4] This approach uses a discrimination net that tests various features of the MREP for the question in order to categorize it. The concept completion type of question is essentially a default type, in that it is assumed when no other type is found. It is usually difficult to recognize anyway since components of a packet are frequently missing.

After questions have been analyzed according to their category, the answer must be found by referring to the KB. As with inferencing, the particular part of the KB is located through the access lists. Then the information sought is located (if it is there), and an MREP for the answer is produced. This MREP is then passed to the generator for output.

Sometimes the question asked is not complete, but if considered in the context in which it occurs, is quite easily understood. For example, if the question were,

How much?

with no context, it would be impossible to develop an answer. However if the question occurred in the following conversation:

A: Does it rain much in New Orleans?

B: Yes.

A: How much?

then the listener knows that the question is actually:

How much does it rain in New Orleans?

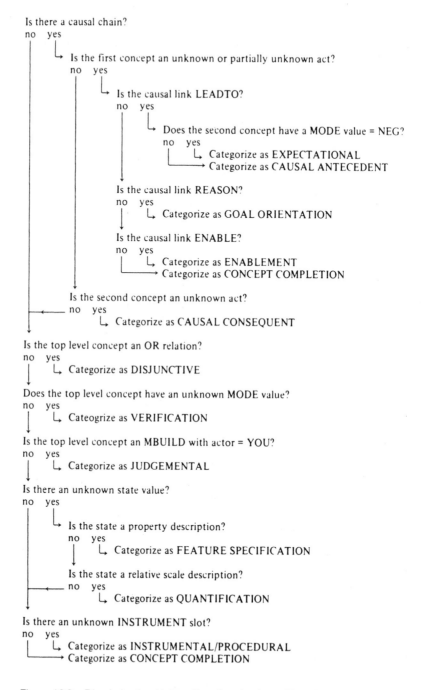

Is there a causal chain?
no   yes

  Is the first concept an unknown or partially unknown act?
  no   yes

    Is the causal link LEADTO?
    no   yes

      Does the second concept have a MODE value = NEG?
      no   yes
        Categorize as EXPECTATIONAL
        Categorize as CAUSAL ANTECEDENT

    Is the causal link REASON?
    no   yes
      Categorize as GOAL ORIENTATION

    Is the causal link ENABLE?
    no   yes
      Categorize as ENABLEMENT
      Categorize as CONCEPT COMPLETION

  Is the second concept an unknown act?
  no   yes
    Categorize as CAUSAL CONSEQUENT

Is the top level concept an OR relation?
no   yes
  Categorize as DISJUNCTIVE

Does the top level concept have an unknown MODE value?
no   yes
  Cateogrize as VERIFICATION

Is the top level concept an MBUILD with actor = YOU?
no   yes
  Categorize as JUDGEMENTAL

Is there an unknown state value?
no   yes

  Is the state a property description?
  no   yes
    Categorize as FEATURE SPECIFICATION

  Is the state a relative scale description?
  no   yes
    Categorize as QUANTIFICATION

Is there an unknown INSTRUMENT slot?
no   yes
  Categorize as INSTRUMENTAL/PROCEDURAL
  Categorize as CONCEPT COMPLETION

Figure 10.8   Discrimination Net for Question Analyzer (From Lehnert, p. 77)

Lehnert suggests a simple means for completing questions of this sort. [5] She creates a temporary storage buffer called Last MLOC Update (LMU) to hold the representation for the most recent complete statement (either question or answer). Thus in the previous example when the question, *How much?*, occurs LMU holds the MREP for the question, *Does it rain much in New Orleans?* The short answer, *Yes*, does not affect LMU. In a sequence like the following, the answer is stored when the incomplete question occurs:

A: Was John in class today?

B: I don't know.

A: Why not?

The question, *Why not?*, refers to why B doesn't know whether John was in class, not to why John wasn't in class. Compare that sequence with the following:

A: Was John in class today?

B: No.

A: Why not?

Using the LMU can also help with the problem of pronominal reference (sometimes). For example

A: Is Dr. Smith teaching Data Structures?

B: No, Dr. Jones is.

A: Who's he?

In this case the pronoun *he* refers to Dr. Jones. If we follow the sequence of statements, when the first question is asked, the LMU would start out empty and would be filled in with the MREP for the statement, *Dr. Smith is teaching Data Structures.* Then when the answer is made, the LMU would be changed to the MREP for *Dr. Jones is teaching Data Structures.* Thus when the question, *Who's he?* is considered, the pronoun would be assumed to refer to the last male human mentioned, in this case Dr. Jones. (If Dr. Jones were female, the LMU reference should still outweigh the sex discrepancy and answer Dr. Jones.)

Another example of question/answer sequences presented by Lehnert illustrates a more complex situation [6]:

A: Did Mary get the book from Susan?

B: No.

A: Who gave it to her?

In this case the pronoun *it* can be resolved easily to refer to *the book*, since the book is the only inanimate object mentioned, but *her* could refer to either Mary or Susan. Only by comparing the roles each plays in the statement can the reference be established. Mary is the recipient of the book in the first question, and Susan is the donor.

Susan *atrans* the book *from* Susan *to* Mary.

In the second question the pronoun *her* is in the recipient position:

? *atrans* the book *from* **?** *to* her

Since Mary was in the recipient position in the first sentence, the pronoun is assumed to refer to Mary.

There are many more issues involved in question answering which are beyond the scope of this book. The reader is directed to Lehnert's book, *The Process of Question Answering*, for a more complete analysis of the problems.

Learning Mode

The last stage of implementing the NLS is concerned with adding knowledge to the existing knowledge base. Knowledge is acquired and added to the KB whenever a statement is input. For example,

John left town.

Mary bought a house on the lake.

The Apple IIe is faster than the Apple II.

Each of these statements would require additions to the KB. The process would start by converting the statement into its MREP. The MREP would be passed to the understander module which would determine whether the information contained in the MREP is relevant to anything already in the KB. This step would be accomplished through the access lists, as was done for inferencing and question answering. If the information is related to pre-existing knowledge, then it would be added to that knowledge. For example if the statement

John left town.

was input, then the structures identifying John's location as being in town would be modified to indicate the change. The second sentence,

Mary bought a house on the lake.

would require an additional structure to indicate that Mary, who is presumably known to the system, now has the additional attribute of being a homeowner of a house with the attribute that it is located on the lake. The use of the definite article *the* indicates that the system has prior knowledge of which lake is being referred to. Use of the indefinite article *a* means that the house being referenced is not a specific one known to the system. The third sentence,

The Apple IIe is faster than the Apple II.

would add an assertion to the KB to the effect that all Apple IIe's have a speed attribute greater than that of all Apple II's. If the information is totally new to the system and all the entities mentioned are previously unknown, then more extensive additions must be made to the KB.

When additions or modifications are made to the structures in the KB, the access lists will have to be modified as well. Any new entities, such as the house on the lake, will be added to the list of entities, and new assertions will be added to the list of assertions. Modifications which are as simple as that involved with John leaving town will not require changes to the access lists. Thus the knowledge structures can grow as the system is used. The output from the system in learning mode is usually just an acknowledgment that the information has been processed. As mentioned earlier in the chapter, the response to a statement adding new information to the KB would be *Okay* or *I understand*.

CONTROL STRUCTURES FOR NLS

The earlier presentation of the major modules of NLS—the parser, the understander, and the generator—implied that a simple sequential control scheme would be used. In such a scheme first the parser handles all the input problems, then passes a completed structure to the understander which accesses the KB and completes the processing, passing any structures to be output to the generator, which in turn converts the MREP structures into natural language statements which are output. Only after the process is completed can more input be accepted, which starts the cycle again. In actual systems this simple scheme has not been adequate. As we have seen throughout the book, the parsing stage will often require world knowledge available in the knowledge base rather than the lexicon. This section will consider several control schemes used for natural language systems.

Sequential Control

Sequential control follows logically from the theories of the linguists who believed that the various stages of analysis of language had to be considered separately. Recall from Chapter 1 that Bloomfield insisted that the phonological aspects of language had to be described independently from any syntactic or semantic concerns. Similarly Chomsky retained the separation of interpretation into syntactic and semantic phases. This separation of phases led to a computational model known as the *hierarchical model*, shown in Figure 10.9. [7] This approach is entirely data-driven in that it starts at the bottom with the smallest linguistic units—phonetic data or input characters of a sentence, combines these into lexical units, and parses them into syntactic structures. Only after parsing is complete will semantic aspects of the data be considered. The control is one-directional, moving from analysis of the smallest units up through the modules to handle larger and larger units. Control in this model is simple; each module executes in sequence. However computationally the model is not sufficient; it is not always possible to complete all lexical analysis before any syntactic analysis is begun, and all syntactic analysis before semantic, and so on. Therefore this model is not especially useful although it has been tried for many parsers.

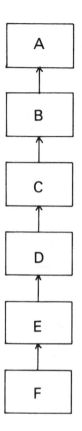

Figure 10.9   Hierarchical Model

Predictive Control

Another approach to organizing the control of the parsing phase of a NLS is considered a top-down or *predictive method*. In this scheme the system starts by assuming a particular sentence pattern which must be tested and confirmed by successively lower levels. For example we could assume that the input will be a sentence in a particular pattern, such as

S → NP + VP

The parser will then look for the NP by predicting that a NP is made up of a determiner and a noun:

NP → Det + N

Since a noun phrase can be many different patterns, this rule may not apply. If the input contradicts that pattern, as in

Aux + NP + V . . .

or

Det Adj Adj N

then processing cannot proceed as predicted. If the assumption is wrong, then the system must back up and try another approach. This method of parsing is commonly used with considerable success for compiling programming languages. [8] The difficulty with parsing natural language top down is that there are so many possible patterns that the method proves to be quite inefficient.

Heterarchical Model

The understander module of NLS described earlier falls into an organizational scheme known as the *heterarchical model,* in which each module interacts with nearly every other module. [9] See Figure 10.10. The modules function as co-routines which call each other back and forth. For example the question answering module may need information provided by inferencing, so it calls the inferencing module, which in turn must access the KB to find the structures related to the inferences to be made. Under other circumstances the access module may have to call the inferencing module to increase the information it knows about a particular subject—i.e., to fill in some of the blanks—in order to proceed with its access function.

With only a small number of modules as in our version of the understander, the heterarchical model is fairly workable. However with more modules the number of interconnections becomes quite large and control of processing becomes increasingly difficult. See Figure 10.11.

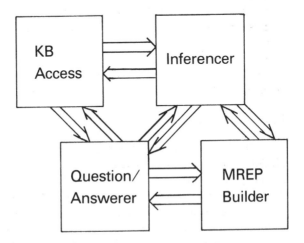

Figure 10.10   Co-Routines in Understander Module

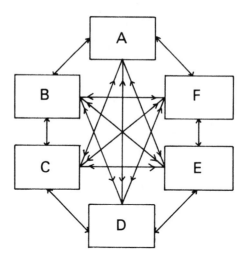

Figure 10.11   Heterarchical Model

Locus Model

Another approach to parsing which has been used more successfully under certain circumstances than the methods described above requires that all the lexical, syntactic, and semantic information be precompiled into a network, which might be similar to an ATN. This network is accessed during parsing to find the specific occurrence of the lexical items encountered in the sentence and then to build the internal representation. This method is quite efficient because much of the analysis is accomplished during the compilation of the network and need not be repeated. However it is quite restrictive in that no changes can be made to the grammar or lexicon without recompiling the network. The language structures which are recognizable by the network are limited to those precompiled into it. The method, known as the *locus model*, was used in the HARPY speech understanding system developed at Carnegie-Mellon University. [10]

Blackboard Model

The Hearsay II speech understanding system also developed at Carnegie-Mellon University used another control scheme worth considering. [11] The system is made up of a number of knowledge sources (KSs) which are independent condition-action modules which do not communicate directly. They communicate only through access to the *blackboard*, an internal working data structure that contains the original text and all the hypotheses made about it during processing. The blackboard does two things: 1) "It represents intermediate states of problem-solving activity, and 2) it communicates messages (hypotheses) from one KS that activate other KSs." [12] Let us consider the structure of the blackboard and the KSs.

In the Hearsay II system, the blackboard is a multilevel data structure which begins at the lowest level with only the input text. As analysis proceeds, additional levels representing various stages of interpretation are added to the blackboard. The KSs are also multilevel in the sense that each one operates on only one level of data, forming hypotheses from that level about the possible representations needed at the next level.

KSs are made up of two modules: the condition part and the action part, much like the structure of requests used for building conceptual structures in Chapter 8. The condition part of a KS specifies the environment in which the action part can contribute to problem-solving activity. For example a KS which disambiguates multiple word senses during lexical analysis would be needed if the word found had multiple senses. A KS which builds noun phrase structures would not be useful during analysis of the verb phrase. The action part of a KS can serve several purposes: it can create part of the MREP structure, it can specify what additional information is needed before it can continue processing, and it can request that it be reactivated when that additional information is found. The action part of some KSs provides statistical ratings for the probability that a particular hypothesis will apply. The ratings would be evaluated by other higher level KSs in developing the final hypothesis.

The Hearsay II blackboard model for handling knowledge has been incorporated into the NLS described in this chapter. The two parts of a KS are implemented with a function and a procedure, respectively. Using a function to define the condition allows the testing to be performed by a code segment and a value to be returned. The function value is then checked to determine whether the action part should proceed. For example the structure of a KS can be defined as follows:

```
procedure KSn;
var ...

    function condn : Boolean;
        .
        .
        .
    end;  (* function *)
    procedure actionn;
        .
        .
        .
    end;  (* procedure *)
begin
    if (condn)
        then actionn
end;  (* KSn *)
```

The sequence of control is determined by the requests for KS activations which appear on the blackboard. These requests are made by the actions of other KSs rather than by explicit calls from the KSs or by some central monitor. Thus the blackboard structures must include these requests as well as the input text and the knowledge structures being built. Process control is handled by a blackboard monitor and a process scheduler. The blackboard monitor keeps track of any changes to the requests for activation of KSs and sets the priorities of the requests in a scheduling queue. The scheduler evaluates the priorities set in the queue and activates the appropriate KS, as shown in Figure 10.12. Since changes to the requests in the blackboard can cause the scheduling queue to be modified, the process control is essentially determined by the KSs with the blackboard monitor and the scheduler simply acting on those requests.

Notice the flow of control (the double lines) in Figure 10.12. The scheduler would call the first KS to begin processing the input text. That KS would do whatever analysis was possible and set the request change flag and a pointer to the next KS which should be executed. Control would pass to the monitor which would test the request change flag; since it would be set, the monitor would add the KS pointer to the scheduling queue and pass control to the scheduler. The scheduler would analyze the queue to determine which KS had the highest priority at that point and pass control to the appropriate KS. The pointer to the next KS should be a list of KSs to be called, since sometimes one KS could determine that several others were needed. In addition a KS might not be able to proceed until after other KSs had performed their work, but it could request itself at a lower priority than the others to assure that control would eventually return to it.

One problem with the blackboard model is that process control can be difficult to manage since it is not predefined, but is essentially established during execution by the processes executing. So many possibilities exist at every point that deciding which way to go is quite complex.

KRL Model

KRL is an experimental knowledge representation language proposed by Daniel G. Bobrow and Terry Winograd to test several theories of natural language processing. [13] In KRL-0, the experimental implementation of KRL, these researchers attempt to "integrate procedural knowledge with a broad base of declarative forms" and to "integrate data-directed and goal-directed processing by using multiprocessing." [14] Many of the ideas proposed for the declarative and procedural representation of knowledge are similar to those described in various knowledge representation schemes presented in Chapter 9. The control structures have a somewhat different emphasis from those of other systems. In KRL,

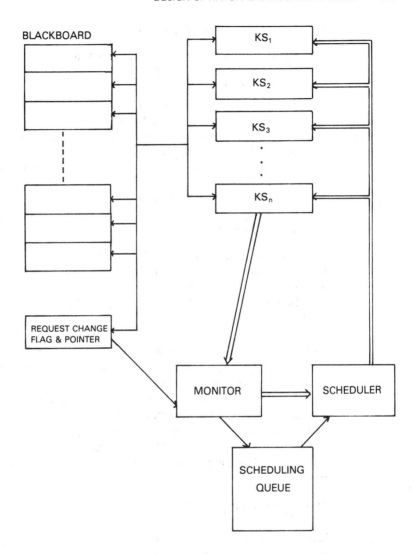

Figure 10.12   NLS (Blackboard Model)

the underlying control structure has been extended in several directions: object-oriented process specification (*procedural attachment*); a general *signal* mechanism for error handling, notification, and dynamic procedural parameterization; organization of the basic system functions around *process frameworks*; and a multiprocess executive, based on a *multilevel scheduling agenda* with resource and priority management facilities. [15]

The central executive of the multiprocessing system is based on

> an *agenda* of "runnable" processes, and a scheduler for running them in a systematic order. The agenda is a priority ordered list of queues, with all processes on a higher priority queue run before any on lower priority queues.
>
> All scheduling is done by cooperation, not preemption. A process runs until it explicitly returns control to the scheduler. It can add any number of other calls to the agenda before it gives up control, including a call to continue itself. Whenever the scheduler runs, it scans down a series of *priority levels* on the agenda, and runs the first process in the highest priority nonempty queue. It removes that process and starts it (if it is new) or resumes it (if it has been suspended). [16]

Procedural attachment in KRL places the emphasis on operations performed on a particular class of data object rather than grouping operations which apply to various types of data.

In many respects the organization of the executive seems similar to that of the blackboard model, in that a scheduler accesses a list of queues to determine the next process to start. The essential difference between the control structures of the blackboard model and the KRL model is the agenda used by the scheduler. Although individual processes can change the agenda in KRL, it is established before processing begins and is oriented to the data objects being processed. The agenda serves as the goal-directed aspect of the executive by predicting in advance the sequence of control which will be desired. The system is still extremely flexible because the processes can manipulate the queues. Although the KRL system has not been implemented beyond the experimental version, many of the ideas have influenced the design of other natural language systems.

CONCLUSION

Natural language systems which accept natural language input, answer questions about a knowledge base, make inferences, and generate natural language responses are complex, and the techniques for designing them are not adequately developed yet. Many researchers are working on various aspects of these systems to develop more complete grammars, lexicons, and knowledge representation schemes and to improve efficiency by finding better access techniques, search methods, and parsing techniques. This book is an attempt to provide a foundation for those interested in studying the design of natural language understanding systems. It has presented an overview of the major directions of natural language research over the last fifteen years as well as suggesting methods for implementing some of the more important theories. Hopefully, the ideas presented here will serve to inspire more research into the important and growing field of natural language processing.

Bibliography

Bach, Emmon, and R. T. Harms, ed. *Universals in Linguistic Theory*. New York: Holt, Rinehart, Winston, 1968.

Baron, Naomi. *Speech, Writing, and Sign: A Functional View of Linguistic Representation*. Bloomington, Indiana: Indiana University Press, 1980.

Beaugrande, Robert De. *Text, Discourse, and Process*. New Jersey: Ablex, 1980.

Berkeley, E. C., and D. G. Bobrow. *The Programming Language LISP: Its Operation and Applications*. Cambridge, Massachusetts: MIT Press, 1966.

Birnbaum, Lawrence, and Mallory Selfridge. "Conceptual Analysis of Natural Language." *Inside Computer Understanding*, Roger Schank and Christopher K. Riesbeck. Hillsdale, New Jersey: Lawrence Erlbaum Associates, 1981, 318–353.

Bloomfield, Leonard. *Language*. New York: Holt, Rinehart, Winston, 1933.

Bobrow, D. G. et al. "GUS: A Frame-Driven Dialog System." *Artificial Intelligence 8* (1977), 155–173.

Bobrow, D. G., and Terry Winograd. "An Overview of KRL: A Knowledge Representation Language." *Cognitive Science 1*, No. 1 (1977), 3–46.

——. "KRL: Another Perspective." *Cognitive Science 1*, No. 3 (1977), 29–42.

Boden, Margaret A. *Artificial Intelligence and Natural Man*, Basic Books, Inc., 1977.

Borko, H., ed. *Automated Language Processing*. New York: John Wiley, 1967.

Brachman, Ronald J. "On the Epistemological Status of Semantic Networks." In *Associative Networks: Representation and Use of Knowledge by Computers*. Ed. Nicholas V. Findler. New York: Academic Press, 1979, 3–46.

Bresnan, J. W. et al. *The Mental Representation of Grammatical Relations*. Cambridge, Massachusetts: MIT Press, 1981.

Bruce, Bertram. "A Model for Temporal References and its Application in a Question Answering Program." *Artificial Intelligence 3* (1973), 1–25.

——. "Case Systems for Natural Language." *Artificial Intelligence 6* (1975), 327–360.

Carnap, R. *The Logical Syntax of Language*. New York: Harcourt Brace, 1937.

Celce-Murcia, Marianne. "Paradigms for Sentence Recognition." Technical Report afhrl-tr-72-30. Air Force Human Resources Laboratory, Training Research Division, Lowry Air Force Base, Colorado 80230, 1972.

Cercone, Nicholas. "Morphological Analysis and Lexicon Design for Natural-Language Processing." *Computers and the Humanities 11*, No. 4, 1977, 235–258.

——. "The Representation and Use of Knowledge in an Associative Network for the Automatic Comprehension of Language." *Representation and Processing of Natural Language*. Ed. L. Bolc. Carl Hanser Verlag, Munchen, 1980, 121–205.

Cercone, Nicholas, and Robert Mercer. "Design of Lexicons in Some Natural Language Systems." *Association for Literary and Linguistic Computing Journal 1*, No. 2, 1980, 37–54.

Cercone, Nicholas et al. "Minimal and Almost Minimal Perfect Hash Function Search with Application to Natural Language Lexicon Design." *Computers and Mathematics 9*, No. 1, 1983, 215–231.

Chandrasearan, B. "Artificial Intelligence: The Past Decade." *Advances in Computers 13*, 1975, 170–232

Charniak, E. and Yorick Wilks, ed. *Computational Semantics*. New York: North-Holland, 1973.

Cherry, Colin. *On Human Communication*. 3rd Edition. Cambridge, Massachusetts: MIT Press, 1978.

Chomsky, Noam. *Aspects of the Theory of Syntax*. Cambridge, Massachusetts: MIT Press, 1965.

——. *Syntactic Structures*. The Hague: Mouton, 1957.

Cittadino, M. L. et al. "Three Computer-based Bibliographic Retrieval Systems for Scientific Literature: Agricola, Biosis, and Cab." *Bioscience 27*, No. 7, 1977, 739–742.

Colby, K. M., and R. C. Parkinson. "Pattern-Matching Rules for the Recognition of Natural Language Dialogue Expressions." *American Journal of Computational Linguistics 1*, 1974, 1–70.

Collins, Allan. "Why Cognitive Science?" *Cognitive Science 1*, No. 1, 1977, 1–2.

Davey, Anthony. *Discourse Production*. Cambridge: Cambridge University Press, 1979.

Dearing, Vinton, et al., ed. *Literary Data Processing*. IBM Publication No. GE20-0383. Yorktown Heights, New York: IBM, 1971.

Dineen, Francis P., S. J. *An Introduction to General Linguistics*. New York: Holt, Rinehart, and Winston, 1967.

Elithorn, Alick, and David Jones, ed. *Artificial and Human Thinking*. Amsterdam: Elsevier Scientific Publishing Company, 1973.

Erman, Lee D., et al. "The Hearsay II Speech-Understanding System: Integrating Knowledge to Resolve Uncertainty." *Computing Surveys 12*, No. 2 (1980), 213–253.

Fillmore, Charles. "The Case for Case." *Universals in Linguistic Theory*. Ed. Emmon Bach and R. T. Harms. New York: Holt, Rinehart, Winston, 1–88.

——. *Summer School Lectures*, University of Pisa, Italy, 1974.

Findler, Nicholas V., ed. *Associative Networks: Representation and Use of Knowledge by Computers*. New York: Academic Press, 1979.

Fodor, Janet Dean. *Semantics: Theories of Meaning in Generative Grammar*. Cambridge, Massachusetts: Harvard University Press, 1977.

Fredkin, E. "Trie Memory." *Communications of ACM 3* (1960), 490–500.

Galloway, Patricia. "Narrative Theories as Computational Models." Paper presented at Modern Language Association Conference, December, 1980, forthcoming in *Computers and the Humanities* (1984).

Goldstein, Ira, and Seymour Papert. "Artificial Intelligence, Language, and the Study of Knowledge." *Cognitive Science 1*, No. 1 (1977), 84–123.

Goldstein, Ira, and Bruce Roberts. "Using Frames in Scheduling." *Artificial Intelligence: An MIT Perspective*, Vol. 1. Cambridge, Massachusetts: MIT Press, 1979, 253–284.

Goodman, Gary, and Raj Reddy. "Alternative Control Structures for Speech Understanding Systems." *Trends in Speech Recognition*. Ed. Lea, W. A. Englewood Cliffs, New Jersey: Prentice-Hall, 1980, 237–246.

Grinder, John T., and Suzette Haden Elder. *Guide to Transformational Grammar: History, Theory, Practice*. New York: Holt, Rinehart, and Winston, 1973.

Griswold, Ralph. *The ICON Programming Language*. Englewood Cliffs, New Jersey: Prentice-Hall, 1983.

Griswold, R. E., et al. *The SNOBOL4 Programming Language*. Englewood Cliffs, New Jersey: Prentice-Hall, 1968.

Harris, Zellig. "From Morpheme to Utterance." *Language 22*, No. 3 (1946), 161–183.

Hawkinson, L. "The Representation of Concepts in OWL." Proceedings of the 4th International Joint Conference on Artificial Intelligence, 1975, 107–114.

Hayes, Phillip. "On Semantic Nets, Frames and Association." CSD Technical Report 5612, University of Rochester, 1977.

——. "Mapping Input into Schema." CSD Technical Report 6068, University of Rochester, 1978.

Hendrix, Gary. "Semantic Knowledge." *Understanding Spoken Language*. Ed. Donald E. Walker. New York: North-Holland, 1978, 121–226.

——. "Encoding Knowledge in Partitioned Networks." *Associative Networks: Representation and Use of Knowledge by Computers*. Ed. Nicholas V. Findler. New York: Academic Press, 1979, 51–92.

Hendrix, Gary, and Earl Sacerdoti. "Natural Language Processing: The Field in Perspective." *BYTE 6*, No. 9 (1981), 304–352.

Hiatikka, J. "Quantifiers in Logic and Quantifiers in Natural Languages." *Philosophy of Logic*. Ed. S. Korner. Berkeley, California: University of California Press, 1976.

Hiedorn, G. E. "Automatic Programming through Natural Language Dialogue: A Survey." *IBM Journal of Research and Development*, 20, No. 4 (1976), 302–313.

Hofland, Knut, and Stig Johansson. *Word Frequencies in British and American English*. Norwegian Computing Centre for the Humanities, P. O. Box 53, N-5014 Bergen-University, Norway, 1981.

Horn, Laurence. *On the Semantic Properties of Logical Operators in English*. Bloomington, Indiana: Indiana University Linguistics Club Publication, 1972.

Joshi, A. K., I. A. Sag, and B. L. Webber, ed. *Elements of Discourse Understanding*. Cambridge: Cambridge University Press, 1980.

Katz, J. J. "Interpretive Semantics vs. Generative Semantics." *Foundations of Language 6* (1970), 220–259.

Katz, J. J., and J. A. Fodor. "The Structure of a Semantic Theory." *The Structure of Language*. Ed. J. Fodor and J. Katz. Englewood Cliffs, New Jersey: Prentice-Hall, 1964, 479–518.

Kelly, Edward and Philip Stone. *Computer Recognition of English Word Senses.* Amsterdam: North-Holland, 1975.

Kent, Ernest. **The Brains of Men and Machines. New York:** McGraw-Hill, 1981.

Knuth, Donald. *The Art of Computer Programming.* Vol. 1, *Fundamental Algorithms,* Second Edition. Reading, Massachusetts: Addison-Wesley, 1975.

——. *The Art of Computer Programming.* Vol. 3, *Sorting and Searching.* Reading, Massachusetts: Addison-Wesley, 1973.

Kowalski, Robert. *A Logic for Problem Solving.* New York: North Holland, 1979.

Lea, W. A., ed. *Trends in Speech Recognition.* Englewood Cliffs, New Jersey: Prentice-Hall, 1980.

Lehnert, Wendy. *The Process of Question Answering.* Hillsdale, New Jersey: Lawrence Erlbaum Associates, Inc., 1978.

Levesque, Hector, and John Mylopoulos. "A Procedural Semantics for Semantic Networks." *Associative Networks.* Ed. Nicholas V. Findler. New York: Academic Press, 1979, 93–120.

Lowerre, B. T., and R. Reddy. "The HARPY Speech Understanding System." *Trends in Speech Recognition.* Ed. W. A. Lea. Englewood Cliffs, New Jersey: Prentice-Hall, 1980.

Marcus, Mitchell. *A Theory of Syntactic Recognition of Natural Language.* Cambridge, Massachusetts: MIT Press, 1980.

Minsky, Marvin. "A Framework for Representing Knowledge," *The Psychology of Computer Vision.* Ed. Patrick Henry Winston. New York; McGraw-Hill, 1975, 211-277.

Minsky, Marvin ed. *Semantic Information Processing.* Cambridge, Massachusetts: MIT Press, 1968.

Minsky, Marvin, and Seymour Papert. *Artificial Intelligence.* Condon Lectures. Eugene, Oregon: Oregon State System of Higher Education, 1974.

Montague, Richard. *Formal Philosophy.* Ed. R. Thomason. New Haven: Yale University Press, 1974.

Mott, Joe L., Abraham Kandel, and Theodore P. Baker. *Discrete Mathematics for Computer Scientists.* Reston, Virginia: Reston Publishing Company, 1983.

Naur, Peter. "Programming Languages, Natural Languages, & Mathematics." *Communications of ACM 18* (1975), 675–682.

Newell, Allen, and Herbert Simon. *Human Problem Solving.* Englewood Cliffs, New Jersey: Prentice-Hall, 1972.

Newmeyer, Frederick J. *Linguistic Theory in America.* New York: Academic Press, 1980.

Partee, Barbara. "Montague Grammar and Transformational Grammar." *Linguistic Inquiry 6* (1975), 203–300.

Partee, Barbara, ed. *Montague Grammar.* New York: Academic Press, 1976.

Peterson, James L. "Computer Programs for Detecting and Correcting Spelling Errors." *Communications of ACM 23* (1980), 676–687.

Petrick, S. R. "Transformation Analysis." *Natural Language Processing.* Ed. R. Rustin. New York: Algorithmic Press, New York, 1973.

Plath, W. J. "Request: A Natural Language Question-Answering System." *IBM Journal of Research and Development 14,* No. 4 (1976), 326–335.

Quillian, M. R. "Semantic Memory." *Semantic Information Processing*. Ed. Marvin Minsky. Cambridge, Massachusetts: MIT Press, 1968.

Raphael, B. "SIR: A Computer Program for Semantic Information Retrieval." *Semantic Information Processing*. Ed. Marvin Minsky. Cambridge, Massachusetts: MIT Press, 1968.

Reeker, Larry H. "The Computational Study of Language Acquisition." *Advances in Computers 15* (1976), 181–238.

Rubin, Frank. "Experiments in Text File Compression." *Communications of ACM 19* (1976), 617–623.

Rustin, R. *Natural Language Processing*. New York: Algorithmics Press, 1973.

Sadock, Jerrold. *Toward A Linguistic Theory of Speech Acts*. New York: Academic Press, 1974.

Sager, Naomi. *Natural Language Processing: A Computer Grammar of English and Its Applications*. Reading, Massachusetts: Addison-Wesley, 1981.

Sager, Naomi, and Ralph Grishman. "The Restriction Language for Computer Grammars of Natural Language." *Communications of ACM 18* (1975), 390–400.

Sandewall, E. J. "Representing Natural Language Information in Predicate Calculus." *Machine Intelligence 6* (1971), 255.

Schank, Roger C. "Conceptual Dependency: A Theory of Natural Language." *Computer Models of Thought and Language*. Ed. Roger Schank and Kenneth Colby. San Francisco: W. H. Freeman and Co., 1973.

——. *Conceptual Information Processing*. Amsterdam: North-Holland, 1975.

Schank, Roger C., and Robert Abelson. *Scripts, Plans, Goals and Understanding*. Hillsdale, New Jersey: Lawrence Erlbaum Associates, Inc., 1977.

Schank, Roger C., and Kenneth M. Colby, ed. *Computer Models of Thought and Language*. San Francisco: W. H. Freeman and Co., 1973.

Schank, Roger C., and Charles Rieger. "Inference and the Computer Understanding of Natural Language." *Artificial Intelligence 5* (1974), 373–412.

Schank, Roger C., and Christopher K. Riesbeck. *Inside Computer Understanding*. Hillsdale, New Jersey: Lawrence Erlbaum Associates, Inc., 1981.

Schank, Roger C. et al. "MARGIE: Memory, Analysis, Response, Generation and Inference on English." Proceedings of the 3rd International Joint Conference on Artificial Intelligence, 1973.

Schmolze, James G., and Ronald J. Brachman. *Proceedings of the 1981 KL-ONE Workshop*. Fairchild Technical Report No. 618, May, 1982.

——. "An Overview of the KL-ONE Knowledge Representation System." *Cognitive Science*. Forthcoming, 1984.

Schneider, Ben Ross, Jr., and Reid M. Watts. "SITAR: An Interactive Text Processing System for Small Computers." *Communications of ACM 20* (1977), 495–499.

Schubert, Lenhart K., Randolph G. Goebel, and Nicholas J. Cercone, "The Structure and Organization of a Semantic Net for Comprehension and Inference." *Associative Networks*. Ed. Nicholas V. Findler. New York: Academic Press, 1979.

Searle, J. *Speech Acts*. Cambridge: Cambridge University Press, 1969.

Sherman, Donald. "A New Computer Format for Webster's Seventh Collegiate Dictionary." *Computers and the Humanities 8*, No.1 (1974), 21-26

Simmons, Robert F. "Semantic Networks: Their Computation and Use for Understanding English Sentences." *Computer Models of Thought and Language.* Ed. Roger Schank and Kenneth Colby. San Francisco: W. H. Freeman and Co., 1973, 63–113.

Simmons, Robert F. and Bertram Bruce. "Some Relations Between Predicate Calculus and Semantic Net Representations of Discourse." Proceedings of the 2nd International Joint Conference on Artificial Intelligence, 1971.

Simmons, Robert F., and Jonathan Slocum. "Generating English Discourse from Semantic Nets." *Communications of ACM 15* (1972), 891–905.

Stockwell, R. P., P. Schachter, and B. H. Partee. *The Syntactic Structures of English.* New York: Holt, Rinehart, and Winston, 1973.

Tanenbaum, Andrew S. *Structured Computer Organization.* Englewood Cliffs, New Jersey: Prentice-Hall, 1976.

Tenenbaum, Aaron M., and Moshe J. Augenstein. *Data Structures Using Pascal.* Englewood Cliffs, New Jersey: Prentice-Hall, 1981.

Tennant, Harry. *Natural Language Processing.* New York: Petrocelli Press, 1981.

Thompson, Frederick B., and Bosena Henisz Thompson. "Practical Natural Language Processing: The REL System as Prototype." *Advances in Computers 13* (1975), 110–169.

Tucker, Allen B., Jr. *Text Processing: Algorithms, Languages, and Applications.* New York: Academic Press, 1979.

Walker, Donald E. *Understanding Spoken Language.* New York: North-Holland, 1978.

Waltz, David L. "An English Language Question Answering System for a Large Relational Database." *Communications of ACM 21* (1978), 526–539.

Weizenbaum, Joseph. "Contextual Understanding by Computers." *Communications of ACM 10* (1967), 474–480.

——. "ELIZA." *Communications of ACM 12* (1969), 476–80.

——. *Computer Power and Human Reason.* San Francisco: W. H. Freeman and Co., 1976.

Wilks, Yorick A. "Natural Language Understanding Systems within the AI Paradigm: A Survey and Comparisons." Stanford University AI Memo No. 237, 1974.

——. "An Intelligent Analyzer and Understander of English." *Communications of ACM 18* (1975), 264–274.

Winston, Patrick Henry. "Learning and Reasoning by Analogy." *Communications of ACM 23* (1980), 689–703.

Winston, Patrick Henry, ed. *The Psychology of Computer Vision.* New York: McGraw-Hill, 1975.

Winston, Patrick Henry and Richard Henry Brown, ed. *Artificial Intelligence: An MIT Perspective.* 2 vols. Cambridge, Massachusetts: MIT Press, 1979.

Winograd, Terry. *Understanding Natural Language.* New York: Academic Press, 1972.

——. "What Does It Mean to Understand Language?" *Cognitive Science 4,* (1980), 209–241.

——. *Language as Cognitive Process.* Vol. 1, *Syntax.* Reading, Massachusetts: Addison-Wesley, 1983.

Wolff, J. G. "Recoding of Natural Language for Economy of Transmission or Storage." *The Computer Journal,* 21 (1978), 42–44.

Woods, W. A. "Transition Network Grammars for Natural Language Analysis." *Communications of ACM 13* (1970), 591–606.

——. "Transition Network Grammars." *Natural Langauge Processing.* Ed. R. Rustin. New York: Algorithmics Press, 1973, 111–154.

Woods, W. A. et al. "The Lunar Science Natural Language Information System; Final Report." BBN Report 2378, Bolt, Beranek and Newman, Cambridge, Mass, 1972.

Zadeh, L. A. "PRUF: A Meaning Representation Language for Natural Language." Memo No. ERL-M77/61, Electronics Research Lab, College of Engineering, University of California, Berkeley, 1977.

Zampolli, A.. ed. *Linguistic Structures Processing.* New York: North Holland, 1973.

References

To the Reader

1. Donald Knuth, *The Art of Computer Programming,* Vol. 1 of *Fundamental Algorithms,* Second Edition (Reading, Massachusetts: Addison-Wesley, 1975), xvii.

Introduction

1. From Richard Montague, *Formal Philosophy,* ed., R. Thomason (New Haven: Yale University Press, 1974), 2. Copyright © 1974, Yale University Press. All rights reserved.

2. Alick Elithorn and David Jones, ed., *Artificial and Human Thinking* (Amsterdam: Elsevier Scientific Publishing Company, 1973), 2–3. (Elithorn, A. 1973 "Introduction" in *Artificial and Human Thinking.* Edited by Elithorn, A. and Jones, D. Elsevier, Amsterdam 1973.)

3. Elithorn and Jones, 6.

4. Allan Collins, "Why Cognitive Science?" *Cognitive Science,* Vol. 1, No. 1 (January, 1977), 1–2. Copyright © 1977 by Ablex Publishing Company, by permission.

5. Terry Winograd, "What Does It Mean to Understand Language?" *Cognitive Science,* Vol. 4, No. 3 (1980), 209–241. Copyright © 1980 by Ablex Publishing Company, by permission.

6. Ira Goldstein and Seymour Papert, "Artificial Intelligence, Language, and the Study of Knowledge," *Cognitive Science,* Vol. 1, No. 1 (1977), 84–123. Copyright © 1977 by Ablex Publishing Company, by permission.

7. Marvin Minsky and Seymour Papert, *Artificial Intelligence,* Condon Lectures, Eugene, Oregon: Oregon State System of Higher Education, 1974, 86.

8. Minsky and Papert, 86.

9. Minsky and Papert, 87.

10. Montague, *Formal Philosophy,* 95.

11. Lewis Carroll, *Through The Looking Glass.*

Chapter 1

1. John T. Grinder and Suzette Haden Elder, *Guide to Transformational Grammar: History, Theory, Practice* (New York: Holt, Rinehart, and Winston, 1973), 31. Copyright © 1973 by Holt, Rinehart and Winston, Inc. Reprinted by permission of Holt, Rinehart and Winston, CBS College Publishing.

2. From *Language* by Leonard Bloomfield. Copyright © 1933 by Henry Holt and Co., renewed © 1961 by Leonard Bloomfield. Reprinted by permission of Holt, Rinehart and Winston.

3. Zellig Harris, "From Morpheme to Utterance," *Language,* No. 22, No.3 (1946), 63.

4. Noam Chomsky, *Syntactic Structures* (The Hague: Mouton, 1957), 57.

5. Chomsky, *Syntactic Structures,* 47.

6. Grinder and Elder, 110.

7. J.J.Katz and J.A. Fodor, "The Structure of a Semantic Theory," *Language* Vol. 39, No. 2 (Part I), (1964) 170–210. (By permission of Linguistic Society of America. Copyright © 1964. All rights reserved.)

8. Katz and Fodor, 507.

9. Grinder and Elder, 125. *Aspects of the Theory of Syntax* by Noam Chomsky was published in 1965 (Cambridge: MIT Press).

10. Grinder and Elder, 124.

11. Charles Fillmore, "A Case for Case," *Universals in Linguistic Theory,* Copyright © 1968 by Holt, Rinehart and Winston, CBS College Publishing.

12. Fillmore, "A Case for Case," 21.

13. Fillmore, "A Case for Case," 23.

14. Fillmore, "A Case for Case," 24–25.

15. Fillmore, "A Case for Case," 25.

16. Fillmore, "A Case for Case," 32.

17. Fillmore, "A Case for Case," 33.

18. Janet Dean Fodor, *Semantics: Theories of Meaning In Generative Grammar* (Cambridge: Harvard University Press, 1977), 89.

Chapter 2

1. Andrew S. Tanenbaum, *Structured Computer Organization,* © 1976, 38. Adapted by permission of Prentice-Hall, Inc., Englewood Cliffs, N.J. 07632.

2. Knut Hofland and Stig Johansson, *Word Frequencies in British and American English* (Norwegian Computing Centre for the Humanities, P. O. Box 53, N-5014 Bergen-University, Norway, 1981). Copyright © 1981, Norwegian Computing Centre for the Humanities.

3. From Donald Sherman, "A New Computer Format for Webster's Seventh Collegiate Dictionary," *Computers and the Humanities,* Vol. 8, No. 1 (1974), 21–26. Copyright © 1974, Elsevier/North-Holland. All rights reserved.

4. Ralph Griswold et al., *The SNOBOL4 Programming Language* (Englewood Cliffs, New Jersey: Prentice-Hall, 1968); and Ralph Griswold *The ICON Programming Language* (Englewood Cliffs, New Jersey: Prentice-Hall, 1983).

Chapter 3

1. Edward Kelly and Philip Stone, *Computer Recognition of English Word Senses* (Amsterdam: North Holland. 1975), 9. Copyright © 1975, Elsevier/North Holland. All rights reserved.

2. Francis P. Dineen, S.J., *An Introduction to General Linguistics* (New York: Holt, Rinehart, Winston, 1967), 44–67.

3. E. Fredkin, "Trie Memory," *Communications of the ACM*, Vol. 3 (1960), 490–500.

4. Donald Knuth, *The Art of Computer Programming*, Vol. 3. © 1973, Addison-Wesley, Reading, Massachusetts. Pg. 482, Table I. Reprinted with permission.

5. Reprinted by permission from *Computers and Mathematics*, Vol. 9, Nicholas Cercone et al., "Minimal and Almost Minimal Perfect Hash Function Search." Copyright 1983, Pergamon Press, Ltd.

Chapter 4

1. Noam Chomsky, *Syntactic Structures* (The Hague: Mouton, 1957), 57.

2. The traditional reference for data structures is Donald Knuth, *The Art of Computer Programming*, Vol. 1, *Fundamental Algorithms*, Second Edition (Reading, Massachusetts: McGraw-Hill, 1975). Another good reference which is more elementary and Pascal-oriented is Aaron M. Tenenbaum and Moshe J. Augenstein, *Data Structures Using Pascal*, (Englewood Cliffs, New Jersey: Prentice-Hall, 1981). There are many other data structures books with adequate coverage of trees and the other data structures discussed throughout this book.

3. J.J. Katz and J.A. Fodor, "The Structure of a Semantic Theory," *Language*, Vol. 39, No. 2 (Part I), (1964), 170–210.

4. Katz and Fodor, 198.

Chapter 5

1. Much of the work on transition networks is derived from Chomsky's *Syntactic Structures*. Material based on William Woods, "Transition Network Grammars for Natural Language Analysis," *Communications of ACM*, Vol. 13 (1970), 591–606. Copyright © 1970, Association for Computing Machinery.

2. A good introduction to graph theory can be found in the chapter on Graphs in Joe L. Mott, Abraham Kandel, and Theodore P. Baker, *Discrete Mathematics for Computer Scientists* (Reston, Virginia: Reston Publishing Company, 1983). Graphs as data structures are described in Aaron M. Tenenbaum and Moshe J.Augenstein, *Data Structures Using Pascal*, (Englewood Cliffs, New Jersey: Prentice-Hall, 1981) and most other data structures books.

Chapter 6

1. Charles Fillmore first discussed case grammar in a paper, "A Case for Case," presented at a conference on Universals in Linguistic Theory in 1968; it was later published in *Universals in Linguistic Theory*, ed. Emmon Bach and R. T. Harms (New York: Holt, Rinehart, Winston, 1968). A useful reference for case grammar in general is Bertram Bruce, "Case Systems for Natural Language," *Artificial Intelligence*, No. 6 (1975), 327–360. Bruce's article describes several versions of case grammar.

2. Robert F. Simmons, "Semantic Networks: Their Computation and Use for Understanding English Sentences," *Computer Models of Thought and Language*, ed. Roger

Schank and Kenneth M. Colby (San Francisco: Freeman and Company, 1973), 63–113. Copyright © 1973 by W. H. Freeman.

3. Simmons in Schank and Colby, 68.

4. Fillmore, 24–25. Marianne Celce-Murcia, "Paradigms for Sentence Recognition," Technical Report afhrl-tr-72-30 (1972), Air Force Human Resources Laboratory, Training Research Division, Lowry Air Force Base, Colorado 80230. Mitchell Marcus, *A Theory of Syntactic Recognition of Natural Language* (Cambridge: MIT Press, 1980), which refers to R. P. Stockwell et al., *The Syntactic Structures of English* (New York: Holt, Rinehart, Winston, 1973).

5. PARSIFAL is the name of the system described by Marcus.

6. Celce-Murcia and Simmons in Schank and Colby.

Chapter 7

1. M. R. Quillian, "Semantic Memory," *Semantic Information Processing*, ed. Marvin Minsky (Cambridge, Massachusetts: MIT Press, 1975).

2. Robert F. Simmons, "Semantic Networks: Their Computation and Use for Understanding English Sentences," *Computer Models of Thought and Language*, ed. Roger Schank and Kenneth M. Colby (San Francisco: Freeman and Company, 1973).

3. Hendrix's work is described in Gary Hendrix, "Semantic Knowledge," *Understanding Spoken Language*, ed. Donald E. Walker (New York: North-Holland, 1978), 121–226; and Gary Hendrix, "Encoding Knowledge in Partitioned Networks," *Associative Networks: Representation and Use of Knowledge by Computers*, ed. Nicholas V. Findler (New York: Academic Press, 1979), 51–92.

4. Hendrix in Walker, 126. (Reprinted by permission of the author from Gary Hendrix, "Partitioned Semantic Networks," by Donald Walker, *Understanding Spoken Language*. Copyright © 1978 by Elsevier Science Publishing Co., Inc.

5. Hector Levesque and John Mylopoulos, "A Procedural Semantics for Semantic Networks," *Associative Networks*, 93–120. (From Levesque et al., in Findler, *Associative Networks*. Copyright © 1979, Academic Press. All rights reserved.)

6. Levesque and Mylopoulos, 99

7. Levesque and Mylopoulos, 103.

8. Levesque and Mylopoulos, 112–13.

9. Levesque and Mylopoulos, 113.

10. Lenhart K. Schubert, Randolph G. Goebel, and Nicholas J. Cercone, "The Structure and Organization of a Semantic Network for Comprehension and Inference," *Associative Networks*, 121–175. (From Schubert et al. in Findler, *Associative Networks*. Copyright © 1979. Academic Press. All rights reserved.)

11. For further discussion of the problems of representing time, see Bertram Bruce, "A Model for Temporal References and its Application in a Question-Answering Program," *Artificial Intelligence*, Vol. 2 (1972), 1–26, and James F. Allen, "Maintaining Knowledge about Temporal Intervals," *Communications of ACM*, Vol. 26, No. 11 (1983), 832–843.

12. L. A. Zadeh, "PRUF—A Meaning Representation Language for Natural Language," Memo No. ERL-M77/61, Electronics Research Lab, College of Engineering, University of California, Berkeley.

13. Schubert et al., 154.

14. Nicholas J. Cercone, "The Representation and Use of Knowledge in an Associative Network for the Automatic Comprehension of Language," *Representation and Processing*

of Natural Language, ed. L. Bolc (Munchen: Carl Hanser Verlag, 1980), 169. (From L. Bolc (ed.), *Representation and Processing of Natural Language.* Copyright, Carl Hanser Verlag. © 1980. All rights reserved.)

Chapter 8

1. Conceptual dependency theory has been presented in various articles and books, including Roger Schank, "Conceptual Dependency: A Theory of Natural Language," *Computer Models of Thought and Language*, ed. Roger Schank and Kenneth Colby (San Francisco: W. C. Freeman and Company, 1973); Roger C. Schank, *Conceptual Information Processing* (Amsterdam: North-Holland, 1975); Roger C. Schank and Robert Abelson, *Scripts, Plans, Goals and Understanding* (Hillsdale, New Jersey: Lawrence Erlbaum Associates, Inc., 1977); and Roger C. Schank and Christopher K. Riesbeck, *Inside Computer Understanding* (Hillsdale, New Jersey: Lawrence Erlbaum Associates, Inc., 1981). Material from *Inside Computer Understanding* and *Scripts, Plans, Goals, and Understanding* used by permission of the author. Copyright 1981, 1977 by Lawrence Erlbaum Associates, Inc. All rights reserved.)

2. Lawrence Birnbaum and Mallory Selfridge, "Conceptual Analysis of Natural Language", *Inside Computer Understanding*, 318–353.

Chapter 9

1. Ira Goldstein and Seymour Papert, "Artificial Intelligence, Language, and the Study of Knowledge," *Cognitive Science*, Vol. 1, No. 1 (1977), 87.

2. Williams Woods, "Transition Network Grammars," *Natural Language Processing*, ed. R. Rustin (New York: Algorithmics Press, 1973), 111–154.

3. Goldstein and Papert, 98.

4. From Marvin Minsky, "A Framework for Representing Knowledge," in Patrick Henry Winston, *Psychology of Computer Vision*. Copyright © 1975 McGraw Hill Book Company. All rights reserved.

5. Goldstein and Papert, 89.

6. Minsky, 246.

7. Minsky, 212.

8. Patricia Galloway, "Narrative Theories as Computational Models," paper presented at Modern Language Association Conference, December, 1980, forthcoming in *Computers and the Humanities* (1984).

9. Minsky, 245.

10. Minsky, 246.

11. Phillip Hayes, "Mapping Input into Schema," CSD Technical Report 6068, University of Rochester, Rochester, New York (1978).

12. Galloway, 12.

13. Ira P. Goldstein and Bruce Roberts, "Using Frames in Scheduling," *Artificial Intelligence: An MIT Perspective*, Vol.1 (Cambridge, Massachusetts: MIT Press, 1979), 253–284.

14. Goldstein and Roberts, 262.

15. Goldstein and Roberts, 269.

16. Minsky in Winston, 212.

17. Goldstein and Papert, 90–91.

18. Eugene Charniak and Yorick Wilkes, eds., *Computational Semantics* (New York: North-Holland, 1973).

19. Roger C. Schank and Robert Abelson, *Scripts, Plans, Goals and Understanding* (Hillsdale, New Jersey: Lawrence Erlbaum Associates, Inc., 1977)

20. Schank and Abelson, 18.

21. Schank and Abelson, 18.

22. Schank and Abelson, 19.

23. Schank and Abelson, 48.

24. Schank and Abelson, 52.

25. Schank and Abelson, 52.

26. Schank and Abelson, 53.

27. Roger C. Schank and Christopher K. Riesbeck, *Inside Computer Understanding* (Hillsdale, New Jersey: Lawrence Erlbaum Associates,Inc., 1981).

28. Ronald J. Brachman, "On the Epistemological Status of Semantic Networks," *Associative Networks: Representation and Use of Knowledge by Computers*, ed. Nicholas V. Findler (New York: Academic Press, 1979), 3–46.

29. Brachman, 31.

30. Brachman, 29.

31. L. Hawkinson, "The Representation of Concepts in OWL," Proceedings of the 4th International Joint Conference on Artificial Intelligence, 1975, 107–114.

32. The best source of information on KL-ONE has been James G. Schmolze and Ronald J. Brachman, *Proceedings of the 1981 KL-ONE Workshop*, Fairchild Technical Report No. 618, May, 1982. In addition, there is an article by Schmolze and Brachman, "An Overview of the KL-ONE Knowledge Representation System," forthcoming in *Cognitive Science* in 1984, and an article by William Woods on Knowledge Representation forthcoming in IEEE/COMPUTER. (This section is based on material from *Proceedings of KL-ONE Workshop*. Copyright 1981. Fairchild Camera & Instrument Corp. Laboratory for Artifical Intelligence Research. All rights reserved. Adapted with permission.)

33. Schmolze and Brachman, *Workshop*, 231.

34. Schmolze and Brachman, *Workshop*, 236.

35. Schmolze and Brachman, *Workshop*, 253.

36. Recent versions of KL-ONE have been developed with different names: CRYPTON at Fairchild Laboratory for Artificial Intelligence Research and NIKL (New Implementation of KL-ONE) at Bolt, Beranek, and Newman.

Chapter 10

1. Nicholas Cercone, "Morphological Analysis and Lexicon Design for Natural Language Processing," *Computers and the Humanities*, Vol. 11, No. 4 (1977), 235–258.

2. Terry Winograd's blocks world is described in his book, *Understanding Natural Language* (New York: Academic Press, 1972).

3. Wendy Lehnert, *The Process of Question Answering* (Hillsdale, New Jersey: Lawrence Erlbaum Associates, Inc., 1978), 51–77. (Material used by permission of the author. Copyright 1978 by Lawrence Erlbaum Associates, Inc. All rights reserved.)

4. Lehnert, 77.

5. Lehnert, 94–95.

6. Lehnert, 95.

7. Gary Goodman and Raj Reddy, "Alternative Control Structures for Speech Under-standing Systems," *Trends in Speech Recognition*, ed. Wayne Lea (Englewood Cliffs, New Jersey: Prentice-Hall, Inc., 1980), 235–238. Adapted by permission of Prentice-Hall, Inc., Englewood Cliffs, N.J. 07632.)

8. Goodman and Reddy, 237–38.

9. Goodman and Reddy, 237–238.

10. Goodman and Reddy, 238–241.

11. Goodman and Reddy, 238–239.

12. Lee D. Erman et al., "The Hearsay II Speech-Understanding System: Integrating Knowledge to Resolve Uncertainty," *Computing Surveys*, Vol. 12, No. 2, 213–253. Copyright © 1980, Association for Computing Machinery, Inc., by permission.

13. Daniel G. Bobrow and Terry Winograd, "An Overview of KRL: a Knowledge Representation Language," *Cognitive Science*, Vol. 3, 29–42.

14. Bobrow and Winograd, 3.

15. Bobrow and Winograd, 32.

16. Bobrow and Winograd, 35.

Index